GOD'S REDEEMING LOVE FOUND

BEN N. BENSON, M.D.

GOD'S REDEEMING LOVE FOUND

Devotional Meditations Dealing with Faith, Marriage, Hurting Marriages, Separation, Divorce, and Reconciliation

TATE PUBLISHING
AND ENTERPRISES, LLC

Published by Tate Publishing & Enterprises, LLC
127 E. Trade Center Terrace | Mustang, Oklahoma 73064 USA
1.888.361.9473 | www.tatepublishing.com

Tate Publishing is committed to excellence in the publishing industry. The company reflects the philosophy established by the founders, based on Psalm 68:11,

"The Lord gave the word and great was the company of those who published it."

Book design copyright © 2013 by Tate Publishing, LLC. All rights reserved.
Cover design by Rodrigo Adolfo
Interior design by Jomar Ouano

Published in the United States of America

ISBN: 978-1-62510-489-2
1. Religion / Christian Life / Love & Marriage
2. Body, Mind & Spirit / Healing / Prayer & Spiritual
13.05.15

About God's Redeeming Love Found:

In our current culture, when about half of all marriages end in divorce, including Christian marriages, Dr. Benson has written a devotional book that deals with the root and core of the problem, a lack of a personal relationship with Jesus Christ. In each devotional we are called to build that relationship through scripture, prayer, and obedience. This book fills a need for all, but especially for those who are married.

—Larry Osborne,
Associate Minister,
Durango Christian Church,
Durango, Colorado

* * * * *

Knowing Ben, I see his heart in these inspired words, full of grace and Spirit, and sound Biblical teaching. Through these heart experiences and the Lord's visible nearness, Ben helps me apply God's Word to my life and my heart to God's joy. Ben so clearly shows how the "better and worse" of our life-conditions and relationships both lead us to encounter and bonding with our Lord who knows us, and loves us with a love beyond our containment.

—Greg Ingram,
Group Leader,
Bible Study Fellowship International,
Fort Worth, Texas

* * * * *

God's Redeeming Love Found leads one through the dark valleys by stopping to rest beside the still waters of prayer and by feasting in the luscious meadows of God's Word. This book will empower you and embolden you to trust in God's loving grace as you scale life's mountains so that you may attain that breathtakingly beautiful view from the top.

—Duane Jenks,
Minister of Missions,
The Hills Church of Christ,
Fort Worth, Texas

DEDICATION

You are our epistle written in our hearts, known and read by all men; clearly you are an epistle of Christ, ministered by us, written not with ink but by the Spirit of the living God, not on tablets of stone but on tablets of flesh, *that is,* of the heart.

—2 Corinthians 3:2–3 (NKJV)

This collection of devotionals and meditations is dedicated to my Lord and Savior, Jesus Christ. It is through my walk with Jesus during the difficult months of separation and divorce and with the inspiration of the Holy Spirit that I have penned these studies of God's Word. In addition, I wish to dedicate this collection to Jeannette who was on my heart and mind as I wrote these devotionals. I also wish to dedicate this collection to those courageous men and women who, like myself, being obedient to God's call and will for their lives, are standing for the covenant marriage vows they made before God and their spouse. Ours is a difficult Christian walk not often understood and/or accepted by our families, our friends, our church family, or our clergy. However, we press onward, putting our total trust in God and not ourselves, in the realization that our future will be so much better than the life and dysfunctional marriages we left behind. To God be the glory forever!

These writings were penned over five and a half years and document the growth of my personal walk with Jesus Christ. Each devotional is signed with that part of my covenant marriage vows that I hold so dear and firmly believe in. It speaks to the permanence in God's eyes of those vows: Standing firm until parted by death.

ACKNOWLEDGMENTS

The devotionals written here are my own personal thoughts (except as noted reflecting the writings of other authors) guided by my closest mentor, the ever-present Holy Spirit. I wish to acknowledge the following men for I have studied at their feet and learned much. First is Rick Atchley, Minister of the Word, the Hills Church of Christ, Fort Worth, Texas. Next is Larry Osborne, Associate Minister and Elder of the Durango Christian Church, Durango, Colorado. These two ministers have honed my knowledge of the Scriptures and who I am in Christ. Finally, William Cothron, Minister of Reconciliation in Alvord, Texas, has taught me so much about marriage and covenant as found in God's Word. I also want to thank the many leaders and participants of Bible Study Fellowship International as I am in my eleventh year of study with them.

Who could forget the Steinkamps, Bob (deceased) and Charlyne of Rejoice Marriage Ministries in Pompano Beach, Florida. Their inspiration and recognition of my writings inspired me to compile this manuscript. I also want to thank Amy Allen of Pompano Beach, Florida, a Baptist minister's wife who spent many hours as the first person to review and edit my completed manuscript.

CONTENTS

FOREWORD

The first time I met Dr. Ben Benson was in the Marriage Reconciliation Support Group when he was having marriage problems in 2004. Sadly, he is not alone! Many marriages are struggling, not just in America, but around the world. I believe we are in a war—a spiritual war. In John 10:10 Jesus said; "the thief (Satan) comes only to steal and kill and destroy; but Jesus came, so that we might have life and might have it abundantly." Satan wants to destroy marriages and families. Nothing is more important to the stability of our society than strong marriages and families. Many Christians are struggling with the challenge of building healthier marriages and families.

Dr. Ben Benson's first marriage ended with the death of his wife after thirty-nine years. She was ill for 25 years. He took care of her and was faithful to his wife and marriage covenant. When he said "until death do us part," he meant it!

Ben married again. His second marriage was a struggle, but he did everything in his power to make it work, but to no avail. He and his wife separated, and she filed for divorce. Ben believes that the vows he spoke at their wedding matter to God, so Ben is praying and trusting God for the healing, reconciliation, and restoration of his marriage. In the Marriage Reconciliation Ministry, many marriages are restored, even after years of divorce. We believe these are modern day miracles.

Because of Ben's experience with separation and divorce, he understands the pain and suffering that goes with such a loss. I believe Ben is uniquely qualified to write this book. I also believe you will be blessed by reading it. You will learn about faith, marriage, covenant, reconciliation, and restoration.

—William F. Cothron,
Minister of Reconciliation
658 School Oaks Rd.
Alvord, Texas 76225

PREFACE

Death reigns in the world. It reigns in the form of *divorce.* Statistics suggest that approximately 50 percent of all marriages in Western society (Christian, non-Christian, atheist, and agnostic) end up in divorce court. Today, most marriages are not held in high esteem; they are disposable! An *epidemic* of divorce exists. Yet we know that divorce existed in ancient times as revealed in the earliest writings of the Old Testament.

Yes, when a marriage breaks down resulting in divorce, a death occurs. It is a death of the fellowship that exists between a man and a woman and, yes, often with God. If that breakdown is taken to extremes, relationships are severed between the man and woman, but never with God.

God ordained marriage in the Garden of Eden and intended the man and woman to be in continual fellowship and relationship with him. But sin entered the picture, and death reigned. Jesus Christ, God's one and only Son, defeated sin and death by his work on the cross. Through him, our lives, our marriages, our fellowships, and our relationships can be redeemed. Divorce is a scourge that our enemy, Satan, uses to imprison so many of us. Through Jesus Christ, Satan has lost the battle and the war. Thanks be to God, we have been set free!

Written herein are meditations and statements of faith written by myself over a period of five and a half years as I walked through the shadow of death of my marriage ending in an unwanted divorce (a true death of a fellowship and a relationship that existed between my wife and I). Along this journey, Jesus Christ entered my life, and I experienced freedom in him. Most of the meditations herein are therefore rich in Scripture as I feel that God's Holy Word needs to be read and studied to understand his wisdom and feel his comfort. My commentary in each is just that—*my own, personal thoughts*. It is God's Word that is important, and many of these meditations are directed studies of his Holy Word. It is my hope that as you read through these meditations, you too will find freedom and healing that comes from a personal fellowship and relationship with Jesus Christ.

I have lost two wives through death. My first marriage of thirty-nine years ended with the physical death of my wife. My second marriage ended through the death of a fellowship and a relationship in a secular court (divorce) after three years of marriage. Yet in my heart, she is still my wife for I believe a marriage ends only when we are parted by physical death. She is my wife, *not* my ex-wife.

The commentaries herein are the product of my own personal study, conversations with believers and nonbelievers, teachings from various church and religious leaders, and through personal revelations from the Holy Spirit. It has been a truly remarkable journey through and past an unwanted divorce that has revealed to me God's redeeming love for all mankind. There is a freedom in Jesus Christ, and I hope that you may find it also.

May God, through the Holy Spirit, open your heart and mind as you read these meditations, and may you be blessed. Please do not take my words as final authority on any subject for they are the meditations and thoughts of a sinner, saved by grace, who has walked this road before you. My writings are guided by inspiration from the ever-present Holy Spirit. Seek first God's Word for clarity and understanding; study his Word for yourself. You will never be disappointed. Always remember what God has said: "Never will I leave you; never will I forsake you" (Hebrews 13:5b, NIV 1984).

PROLOGUE

The devotionals herein are organized under several subheadings that reflect the main thrust of that particular devotional. However, most devotionals will fall into several subheadings in the subject matter discussed. For help, I refer the reader to the Subject Matter Index at the end of this book. I will start with a poem, "Through the Valley," that sets the framework and mood needed as one reads and receives "God's Redeeming Love Found."

THROUGH THE VALLEY

*N**ote:* This poem was written shortly after the death of my first wife in late 2001. I am including it in this collection of devotionals as it represents grieving over the loss (death) of a loved one. When we are separated or divorced from the spouse for whom we are standing, we go through a similar grieving process for that loved one, one of similar intensity as with the physical death of a spouse.

"Yea, though I walk through the valley of the shadow of death..."
How familiar are these words from the twenty-third Psalm.
But to one who is in the darkness of the valley,
Grief, heartache, and loneliness for my loved one departed
Appear like steep, forbidding, almost vertical walls,
Encircling, trapping, preventing escape, leading to despair.

The valley...walls of grief, heartache, and loneliness.
Here I find myself, confused, in shock, in disbelief!
Why did my loved one have to die?
Why am I caught in this place, unable to pass through?
Oh, how will I escape? How will I survive?
Why, Oh Lord, must I suffer with this heartache?

So many questions, yet they are not unlike questions
Asked by people down through the ages.
But for me, the answer is simple...
I need only to turn to my faith and the Holy Bible!
For the Lord *is* my Shepherd,
He and He alone will see me through the valley!

Through the valley to the other side, beyond despair, that is my goal.
For now, while in the valley, I need only to look up...
Up to my Father in heaven, my Creator, my Maker,
For it is He who gives me strength,
Strength to move forward through the valley
Confronting my heartache, my loneliness, my grief!

The Lord *is* my Shepherd, and His promise is...
He will guide my footsteps through the valley and past my despair.
He will vanquish my grief, my heartache, my loneliness, until finally...
I break out into the sunlight, and the valley is far behind.
There I will find peace, hope, the dawning of a new day, and I will have
Beautiful memories of my loved one departed.

Faith

Faith

Now faith is the assurance of *things* hoped for, the conviction of things not seen.

—Hebrews 11:1 (NASB)

But the righteous will live by his faith.

—Habakkuk 2:4b (NASB)

The Good News shows how God makes people right with himself. God's way of making people right begins and ends with faith. As the Scriptures say, "The one who is right with God by faith will live forever."

—Romans 1:17 (ERV)

And Abram believed the Lord, and the Lord counted him as righteous because of his faith.

—Genesis 15:6 (NLT)

In this New Year, a year of many uncertainties, yet a year with so many possibilities, faith asks this question: *can God be trusted?* In a time of suffering that so many of us are going through, trusting God gets put to the test. Political unrest both here in the USA and in other countries, nations at war, corporations failing, layoffs, banking industry in turmoil, retirement funds and savings evaporating, bills piling up, health problems, pollution, global warming, marriages falling apart, and the end is nowhere in sight. Many may feel that God has abandoned mankind and feel that our prayers are going unheeded and unanswered. Storm clouds are overhead, and the future looks bleak. It is at these times that our faith in God and his plans for mankind become so important to our survival.

We need to remember that God has not abandoned us, that he can be trusted. He tells us to lean on him and that he will provide. Man first exhibited his lack of trust of God in the garden as told in Genesis 3:1–7. That lack of trust in God was, in essence, mankind's first sin. Faith and trust go hand in hand. An entry by D. Mark Parks in *Holman Illustrated Bible Dictionary* on faith states that since the fall of mankind, God nurtures and inspires us to trust him through what he says and does for us, thus making himself known to mankind. Thus, biblical faith is man's limited personal knowledge of God. Faith is our response to do obediently (obey) what God asks of us.

> So faith comes from hearing the Good News. And people hear the Good News when someone tells them about Christ.
>
> Romans 10:17 (ERV)

Reading the Word of God and pondering the stories and teachings from the Old Testament and the New Testament brings a new sense of hope into our lives. Hebrews 11:1 defines *faith* as how Christians should view the world. For many, that is a giant step, truly a step of faith. Remember that the Word of God is dynamic, it is alive, and it is as much applicable today as it was in the days when the Bible was written. The Word is the inspired and infallible writings of God's message to his children. Study God's Word each and every day.

> For the word of God is living and powerful, and sharper than any two-edged sword, piercing even to the division of soul and spirit, and of joints and marrow, and is a discerner of the thoughts and intents of the heart. And there is no creature hidden from His sight, but all things are naked and open to the eyes of Him to whom we must give account.
>
> Hebrews 4:12–13 (NKJV)

When you and I are unaware of it, God is behind the scenes, working hard to protect and defend his children. That's you and me; we are his children! He will not let us down. Trust him. Have faith in his promises. In the Old Testament, the consistent theme of salvation by faith can be traced in God's acts and deeds. Faith is the proper response to God's self-revelation. So have faith that your needs will be met. Thus, you and I may ask, "How?" By trusting in God's promises and in the Creator of the universe who created everything, including you and me. Read what Jesus said in the Sermon on the Mount.

> That is why I tell you not to worry about everyday life—whether you have enough food and drink or enough clothes to wear. Isn't life more than food, and your body more than clothing? Look at the birds. They don't plant or harvest or store food in barns, for your heavenly Father feeds them. And aren't you far more valuable to him than they are? Can all your worries add a single moment to your life? And why worry about your clothing? Look at the lilies of the field and how they grow. They don't work

or make their clothing, yet Solomon in all his glory was not dressed as beautifully as they are. And if God cares so wonderfully for wildflowers that are here today and thrown into the fire tomorrow, he will certainly care for you. Why do you have so little faith? So don't worry about these things, saying, "What will we eat? What will we drink? What will we wear?" These things dominate the thoughts of unbelievers, but your heavenly Father already knows all your needs. Seek the Kingdom of God above all else, and live righteously, and he will give you everything you need. So don't worry about tomorrow, for tomorrow will bring its own worries. Today's trouble is enough for today.

Matthew 6:25–34 (NLT)

In the Old Testament, the message was *the fear of the Lord*. This was more fear than respect or reverence. This was to underscore the importance and the need to submit to God. From the Genesis and Habakkuk scriptures listed above, we see the principle that God saves those people who both sincerely trust him and how he says they are to relate to him. In the New Testament, the message of faith conveys the idea of trust, a trust in a God of love. We see a personal trust develop as a result of God's self-revelation of who he is in the life, ministry, death, and resurrection of Jesus Christ. In the New Testament, faith takes on a sense of sincere trust and warmth, a closeness that one would expect from a loving father. Yet throughout the whole Bible, God has always required faith as the expected response to his self-revelation. This faith is linked to the reliability of the promise maker: God. God can be trusted because of who he is. He doesn't forget his promises to his children. He is not indifferent to our pain and suffering for he knows the trials we face. In the person of Jesus, he was fully man; his compassion is genuine.

The God of the Bible has consistently related to people via trust in what He says and does. Biblical faith is a complex idea. God, His Word, His actions, the whole human being, and the physical world all play critical roles. When saving faith occurs, God has enabled someone to know Him through His revelation of Himself in the words and actions of Christ. God Himself activates faith in the hearer of His word, enabling that hearer to become faithful in Christ, just as He is faithful (Revelation 19:11).

D. Mark Parks, Adjunct Professor of Religion, Dallas Baptist University, Dallas, Texas.[1]

* * * * *

I have some additional thoughts to finish out this devotional. The Gospel (the Word) must be heard or read and understood before faith can happen. Faith develops when a person moves through the words and the biblical evidence and calls upon Christ to save them. This is expressed best by Paul.

> That if you confess with your mouth, "Jesus is Lord," and believe in your heart that God raised him from the dead, you will be saved. For it is with your heart that you believe and are justified, and it is with your mouth that you confess and are saved. As the Scripture says, "Anyone who trusts in him will never be put to shame." For there is no difference between Jew and Gentile—the same Lord is Lord of all and richly blesses all who call on him, for, "Everyone who calls on the name of the Lord will be saved."

Romans 10:9–13 (NIV 1984)

God is faithful, always faithful. We are his children, and his loyalty to us is priceless. We in like manner need to call upon the Lord, professing faith in him and trusting in him. It is through

God's words (his Word) that mankind is led to him; his words mediate faith in him. Without faith, one cannot please God. The object of our faith is God in Christ Jesus. Faith is a spiritual gift.

> Because of the privilege and authority God has given me, I give each of you this warning: Don't think you are better than you really are. Be honest in your evaluation of yourselves, measuring yourselves by the faith God has given us.
>
> Romans 12:3 (NLT)

> Test yourselves to see if you are in the faith; examine yourselves! Or do you not recognize this about yourselves, that Jesus Christ is in you—unless indeed you fail the test?
>
> 2 Corinthians 13:5 (NASB)

Standing firm until parted by death.

Put Your Trust In The Lord

> Trust in the LORD and do good...Delight yourself in the LORD and he will give you the desires of your heart. Commit your way to the LORD; trust in him and he will do this: He will make your righteousness shine like the dawn, the justice of your cause like the noonday sun.
>
> Psalm 37:3a, 4–6 (NIV 1984)

As each of us struggle with our troubled marriages, we continue to hear the following words from those who have successfully navigated these waters before us: "Put your total trust in the Lord! He will see you through these tough times. Trust!" In the passage above, King David encourages us to put our trust in the Lord, following his ways, and the Lord will give us the desires of our heart—more specifically, a restored marriage. Is this not "the justice of your cause," a restored marriage? Let's look at what David says next: "Be still before the LORD and wait patiently for him" (Psalm 37:7a, NIV 1984).

As we stand for our covenant marriage vows during times of marital dysfunction, during separation, or even following divorce, we need to be still. We need to listen to our Lord and wait patiently for him to work both in our own life and the life of our spouse. The question we should be asking is, "Am I willing to focus on my own relationship with God and leave my spouse in God's able hands?" Isn't this what marriage reconciliation is really all about? Are we reconciling ourselves to God? We need to put our total trust in him, trust him to comfort us, to guide us, to teach us, and to forgive us. After all, our troubled marriages are the result of two people's failure to follow God's tenants in marriage. That's right, two people, you (me) and your (my) spouse. With God's help, you and I can become reconciled to God while leaving our spouses in God's capable hands as we pray for them. God knows what our spouses need better than we do, so trust him!

> Trust in the LORD with all your heart and lean not on your own understanding; in all your ways acknowledge him, and he will make your paths straight.
>
> Proverbs 3:5–6 (NIV 1984)

When we trust in the Lord, we commit our way to the Lord. Lean not on our own understanding of our own needs or those of our spouse; this is in God's realm. Trust him! When we acknowledge him, we are being ever mindful of the God we serve with a willing and faithful heart. In the passage below, King David is speaking.

> And you, my son Solomon, acknowledge the God of your father and serve him with wholehearted devotion and with a willing mind, for the LORD searches every heart and understands every motive behind the thoughts. If you seek him, he will be found by you; but if you forsake him, he will reject you forever.
>
> 1 Chronicles 28:9 (NIV 1984)

A person with a willing and faithful heart serves God "with wholehearted devotion and with a willing mind." God knows our every thought and those of our spouses. So seek his face as you look for answers in your troubled marriage.

As we take a final look at the passage in Proverbs 3:6, we see that God makes our paths straight. He removes obstacles from our path and brings us to our appointed goal: that of a reconciled and restored marriage built on the solid rock of Jesus Christ.

As we continue to look at our troubled marriages, we see another reason to put our trust in God. Psalm 91:2 (NIV 1984) states: "I will say of the LORD, 'He is my refuge and my fortress, my God, in whom I trust.'"

God is our comforter in our times of trial. He walks along beside us as we go through the valley of despair and grief over marital dysfunction, separation, or divorce. As we love God with all of our heart, mind, and strength, we find he responds with this reassurance:

> "Because he loves me," says the LORD, "I will rescue him; I will protect him, for he acknowledges my name. He will call upon me, and I will answer him; I will be with him in trouble, I will deliver him and honor him. With long life will I satisfy him and show him my salvation."
>
> Psalm 91:14–16 (NIV 1984)

God is our comforter, our refuge, our shelter in times of trouble. When confronted by a hostile spouse or similar situation, turn to God. He feels our pain and our suffering, and he will comfort us.

> But I will rescue you on that day, declares the LORD; you will not be handed over to those you fear. I will save you; you will not fall by the sword but will escape with your life, because you trust in me, declares the LORD.
>
> Jeremiah 39:17–18 (NIV 1984)

Here again, God states very plainly that when we put our trust in him, he is there to protect us from those who seek to do us harm in our troubled marriage.

> Trust in the LORD forever, for the LORD, the LORD, is the Rock eternal. He humbles those who dwell on high, he lays the lofty city low; he levels it to the ground and casts it down to the dust. Feet trample it down—the feet of the oppressed, the footsteps of the poor. The path of the righteous is level; O upright One, you make the way of the righteous smooth. Yes, LORD, walking in the way of your laws, we wait for you; your name and renown are the desire of our hearts.
>
> Isaiah 26:4–8 (NIV 1984)

Yes, put your total trust in our awesome God, and he will see you through your marital problems to a reconciled and restored marriage. "In God we trust" should not be just the motto on our money; it should be the motto of our lives! Let me close with a psalm about trust in God.

> A psalm of David. The LORD is my shepherd, I shall not be in want. He makes me lie down in green pastures, he

leads me beside quiet waters, he restores my soul. He guides me in paths of righteousness for his name's sake. Even though I walk through the valley of the shadow of death, I will fear no evil, for you are with me; your rod and your staff, they comfort me. You prepare a table before me in the presence of my enemies. You anoint my head with oil; my cup overflows. Surely goodness and love will follow me all the days of my life, and I will dwell in the house of the LORD forever.

Psalm 23 (NIV 1984)

May your stand for your covenant marriage be blessed, trusting in the one true God.

Standing firm until parted by death.

The Battle Is Not Yours But God's

Note to reader: This devotional was written early in my separation, while I was searching to understand standing with God for the healing of my marriage relationship.

This is what the LORD says to you: "Do not be afraid or discouraged because of this vast army. For the battle is not yours, but God's."

2 Chronicles 20:15b (NIV 1984)

With the beginning of a new year, most of us review the year just completed and look forward to the year ahead with greater hopes and expectations. I start the new year standing for our marriage, and I find myself alone as my one flesh wife is not by my side. I cry out to God for comfort for I find myself in a battle for the very survival of our marriage relationship. I am in a spiritual battle, a battle against the evil one (Satan) who tore down and destroyed what was our marriage. As I search the Bible for God's will and direction for our dead marriage, I find the Old Testament story of King Jehoshaphat of Judah. One day, he looked out from Jerusalem to see the armies of the Moabites, the Ammonites, and the Meunites gathered together to make war against Judah. They were coming toward Judah from Edom. Alarmed, King Jehoshaphat proclaimed a fast in the whole land of Judah. He then called upon (prayed to) the Lord for his help. Then the Spirit of the Lord came to Jahaziel, a Levite, and he came and proclaimed before Judah:

> Listen, King Jehoshaphat and all who live in Judah and Jerusalem! This is what the LORD says to you: "Do not be afraid or discouraged because of this vast army. For the battle is not yours, but God's.... You will not have to fight this battle. Take up your positions; stand firm and see the deliverance the LORD will give you, O Judah and Jerusalem. Do not be afraid; do not be discouraged. Go out to face them tomorrow, and the LORD will be with you."

> 2 Chronicles 20:15, 17 (NIV 1984)

Hear and read out loud these comforting words of our Lord! Do not be afraid. Do not be discouraged. The battle is not yours. The battle is God's. You do not have to fight this battle. Stand firm. See the deliverance the Lord will give you. Again, do not be afraid. Again, do not be discouraged. Go face your enemy. The Lord will be with you. Each of these statements brings such comfort and relief to my heart as I realize what I have known all along: if I put my trust, my total trust in God, he will do that which I cannot do—resurrect our dead marriage. Matthew's Gospel states, "Jesus looked at them and said, 'With man this is impossible, but with God all things are possible'" (Matthew 19:26, NIV 1984).

I cannot change my wife. Only God through the Holy Spirit can change her as he reconciles her to himself. The only person I can change is me. I am *not alone* in this battle for my heavenly Father is by my side, standing with me in my stand. He ordained marriage, he loves marriage, and he wants our marriage to be all that it can be. So I stand firm, being patient and still, waiting upon the Lord to see his deliverance. As Moses told the Israelites at the Red Sea:

> Moses answered the people, "Do not be afraid. Stand firm and you will see the deliverance the LORD will bring you today. The Egyptians you see today you will never see again. The LORD will fight for you; you need only to be still."

Exodus 14:13–14 (NIV 1984)

May God bless each of you as you stand for your marriage. Stand firm for the battle is not ours to fight, but the Lord's!

Standing firm until parted by death.

Invite God's Help

Have you ever noticed how often we have heard that when we are in troubled waters, we need to pray? We hear stories of persons crying out to God for deliverance during times of personal crisis. We ourselves have had that experience of crying out to God in times of our own need. We often forget about praising God during the good times and only seek his face when we find ourselves in troubled waters. That is just human nature, our lack of understanding of our awesome God and of his boundless love for us. What we need to do is to invite God to walk along with us, both in the good times and in the bad times, not just through the valley of our troubles, our crumbling marriages, and our broken relationships. When we invite God to wipe away our tears of anguish, we invite him to point us in the direction of healing and to share in the glory of victory over our problems. "For the battle is not ours, but God's" (2 Chronicles 20:15b, NIV 1984). We need to invite God's intervention, his help. Let us look at several familiar scriptures that reaffirm God's love for us when we invite his help.

> A psalm of David. The LORD is my shepherd, I shall not be in want. He makes me lie down in green pastures, he leads me beside quiet waters, he restores my soul. He guides me in paths of righteousness for his name's sake. Even though I walk through the valley of the shadow of death, I will fear no evil, for you are with me; your rod and your staff, they comfort me. You prepare a table before me in the presence of my enemies. You anoint my head with oil; my cup overflows. Surely goodness and love will follow me all the days of my life, and I will dwell in the house of the LORD forever.
>
> Psalm 23 (NIV 1984)

This is probably the one scripture most quoted in times of need, in times of sorrow, in times of anguish. Here David invites God to walk with him during troubled times. I know personally that when my first wife was ill and later died, this was one of the scriptures I looked to for comfort. For it says "The *Lord* is my shepherd," which means that he looks after me and cares about me. He has my personal well-being uppermost on his mind. He loves me! Notice that next statement: "I shall not be in want." God fills my needs, my every need, at the time of my trials, at all times.

What does he do next? "He makes me lie down in green pastures, he leads me beside quiet waters, he restores my soul. He guides me in paths of righteousness for his name's sake." When I invite God into my situation, he brings comfort and revives me; he calms my restless spirit. He directs my footsteps in ways that conform to his moral will, thus bringing honor to his name. Then with God walking with me, he will lead me through the dark times of my life. "Even though I walk through the valley of the shadow of death, I will fear no evil, for you are with me; your rod and your staff, they comfort me." Oh, how comforting it is to know that God is there with me, fighting my battles, protecting me, binding up my wounds!

As he triumphs over my adversaries, he brings me to that place of quiet rest. "You prepare a table before me in the presence of my enemies. You anoint my head with oil; my cup overflows." When I realize how much God loves and cares for me, he directs my thoughts to "surely goodness and love will follow me all the days of my life, and I will dwell in the house of the *Lord* forever." God offers me peace, a perfect peace, a place of quiet rest. I need only to invite God's help.

In Matthew, we find another reassurance: "And looking at them Jesus said to them, 'With people this is impossible, but with God all things are possible'" (Matthew 19:26, NASB).

Here we just need to realize that God is God. He is all-powerful and all knowing; he is pure love. He is in control. He can do things (modern-day miracles) in our lives and in our spouses' lives that you and I cannot even begin to do. He can also work miracles in our other relationships as well. We just need to invite God's help.

So how do we invite God's help? We need only to seek his face through prayer. In the Message, we read, "Prayer is essential in this ongoing warfare. Pray long and hard" (Ephesians 6:18, MSG).

Brothers and sisters, we are in a war! A war for our souls and the souls of our loved ones. Satan is our enemy, not our spouse, kids, or family. His schemes and methods are simple: he comes to kill, steal, or destroy. So we need help. When we invite God's help through prayer, he becomes our defender, and the battle becomes his, not ours. We by ourselves cannot win the battle because Satan is more powerful than we are. We, however, have a trump card—the cross. We have prayer and we invite our Holy Father, his Son Jesus, and the Holy Spirit to take our side. Satan was defeated at Calvary, and we as professing Christians are covered by the blood of Jesus. Through prayer, we reaffirm that faith relationship and seek God's intervention in our lives. We need only to put our total trust in him and his promises.

> [God] will keep in perfect peace all who trust in [God], whose thoughts are fixed on [God].
>
> Isaiah 26:3 (NLT)

Max Lucado, in his book *Facing Your Giants*, states,

> God promises not just peace but perfect peace. Undiluted, unspotted, unhindered peace. To whom? To those whose minds are fixed on God. Forget occasional glances. Dismiss random ponderings. Peace is promised to the one who fixes thoughts and desires on the king.[2]

How do we get this peace in the midst of our troubled waters? It is through prayer that we invite God's help.

> Do not let your heart be troubled; believe in God, believe also in Me…. Peace I leave with you; My peace I give you; not as the world gives do I give to you. Do not let your heart be troubled, nor let it be fearful.
>
> John 14:1, 27 (NASB)

So, dear brothers and sisters, when we trust in God and invite his help, we will have peace in our hearts and victory over our adversary, Satan. The battle for our marriages and our relationships is not ours, but God's.

May God bless each of you in your stand.

Standing firm until parted by death.

God's Perfect Timing!

As persons standing for the restoration/reconciliation of our marriages or other relationships that Satan has destroyed or damaged, we have often been told that these things take time and to be patient and allow things to fall in place. We so often try to manipulate the process by interfering, sending notes or letters, making phone calls, sending others, etc., to communicate with the other person (our prodigal spouse or loved one). So often, this just slows the reconciliation process down or even sidelines it for a while. When we finally get ourselves oriented like we should be by the study of God's Word and by prayer, we realize that we need only to turn these things over to God for *only* he knows just what needs to be done. We need to *Let go and let God!* We need to get out of God's way!

Once our problems have been turned over to God, we get impatient, and we wonder why it is taking so long. This is our humanness showing through; we are so impatient! Here again, the answer is right there in front of us: it is in *God's perfect timing*. At first that sounds great that God has it all taken care of (and he has), but then a new problem or question arises. What does it mean this *perfect timing*? In a recent devotional by a stander from Nebraska about the story of Lazarus and his resurrection from the dead, the writer pointed to Jesus's answer. "This sickness will not end in death. No, it is for God's glory so that God's Son may be glorified through it" (John 11:4, NIV 1984). He further states, "Did I not tell you that if you believed, you would see the glory of God?" (John 11:40, NIV 1984).

Read the story of Lazarus in John 11:1–44 (NIV 1984). In this story, Jesus was several days' journey from Lazarus's house when he heard about his illness. He could have just prayed that

Lazarus be healed without ever going to his bedside. He had done this before, so why not now? Jesus waited for four days after Lazarus's death to raise him from the dead; there was no question in anyone's mind that Lazarus was dead. When Jesus appeared on the scene calling Lazarus forth from the tomb, this action, in front of Mary, Martha, and many other local people, was to bring *glory* to our awesome God and his Son Jesus through this spectacular miracle!

In our situations as standers, Jesus wishes us to believe in his mighty power and recognize that he can resurrect our dead or dying marriages or relationships. Then we will give him all the praise and glory. This is God's work, not ours, a true modern-day miracle. The only part we as standers play in this miracle is to become reconciled to our Father God, to pray for our prodigal, and to prepare ourselves for the homecoming of our prodigal spouse or loved one. God's timing, *his perfect timing*, occurs when we least expect it, so be prepared.

Our Father God has our situations (yours and mine) in his sights and on his heart, and his timing is *perfect!*

> "For I know the plans I have for you," declares the LORD, "plans to prosper you and not to harm you, plans to give you hope and a future. Then you will call upon me and come and pray to me, and I will listen to you. You will seek me and find me when you seek me with all your heart."
>
> Jeremiah 29: 11–13 (NIV 1984)

May God bless each of you as you go on this spiritual journey, this spiritual walk with our Lord and Savior Jesus Christ called *standing* for our covenant marriages. The world doesn't understand our walk, nor do many of our Christian brothers and sisters. So educate them when the occasion arises. Paul states:

Therefore put on the full armor of God, so that when the day of evil comes, you may stand your ground, and after you have done everything, to stand. Stand firm then.

Ephesians 6: 13–14a (NIV 1984)

So stand firm for your covenant marriage, your covenant vows taken before God and your spouse.

Standing firm until parted by death.

Be Still, O My Soul!

Be still, and know that I am God.

—Psalm 46:10a (NIV 1984)

The LORD will fight for you; you need only to be still.

—Exodus 14:14 (NIV 1984)

As we begin our stand for our troubled marriages, we quickly realize how restless is our soul and our heart. We are deeply wounded. Our heart is bleeding from the separation from our loved one, our spouse with whom we are *one flesh*. In our desperation, we cry out to our Lord for help, for solace, and for understanding. We want our marriage fixed now, if not sooner! However, as we find out, our situation (our separation, pending divorce, or even a completed divorce) is, in reality, a wake-up call from the Lord. He is telling us that our relationship with him is not in order, that he is not on the throne in our hearts. Thus, we seek answers to our situation. Who is at fault? What must I do? How can I fix my marriage? How can I get my spouse back? So many questions, yet so few answers as we look to our Father

God. We pray, but our prayers are shallow, frequently just a want list. We are seeking answers, but we are not listening. Have you been there? I have. Our Father God loves us and wants us to become reconciled to him. He wants to communicate with us, so he begins to speak to us through his Word. Our first scripture from Psalm 46:10a states, "Be still, and know that I am God."

We are so impatient, so restless, so hurt, yet God wants so much to minister to our wounded heart. But we will not be still; we will not be quiet. We must be still, putting everything out of our mind but him. We need to focus on God and listen. If we seek him with all of our heart, he will come to us and make himself known to us. Jeremiah speaks of that: "You will seek me and find me when you seek me with all your heart" (Jeremiah 29:13, NIV 1984).

We may not realize that God is all-powerful, all knowing, and full of love for his children. After all, he created us in his own image. He wants an intimate relationship with each of us. However, here again we fail, for not only are our prayers shallow, our faith is often shallow. Jesus tells us, "I tell you the truth, if you have faith as small as a mustard seed, you can say to this mountain, 'Move from here to there' and it will move. Nothing will be impossible for you" (Matthew 17:20, NIV 1984).

Looking at our situations and our failure to repair them by our own efforts, Jesus teaches us to look to him. "With man this is impossible, but with God all things are possible" (Matthew 19:26b, NIV 1984).

Yes, *all* things are possible with God, even the resurrection of our dead or dying marriages. We must put our total trust (faith) in our Lord Jesus Christ. Until we reach this place of total trust (faith), this place of quiet rest, our souls will remain troubled, and our prayers may be unanswered (or so it seems). Even when we don't meet God where he wants to meet us, he is still working behind the scenes. It is only when we are still, listening for his voice, that we realize he has been there with us all the time. His answers take many forms, and they may be hidden from us by our anxiety, our impatience, and our lack of trust in him. We just need faith and, through faith, turn our marriages, ourselves, and our spouse over to him. For he knows just what is needed to restore and heal our marriages in his perfect timing. Regular prayer is essential in our stand.

One of the ways to reach our place of quiet rest is to establish a regular devotional time, a quiet time with the Lord. This is often very difficult in our modern rush-rush world to find such a time. However, it is extremely important that we spend some quality time with God. God is not hung up on form or on a certain length of time for our devotionals. He just wishes to commune with us, one-on-one, and is desirous that we approach him with a humble heart, a heart that is open and that he can instruct. He is available 24-7. He wants more than anything an intimate relationship with each of us. I repeat, we just need to be still and listen for his quiet voice. We are not obligated to seek a quiet time with God, but he really wants one. However, it is an incredible privilege that the Creator, the one True God, wants more than anything to meet with us, one-on-one.

> Show me your ways, O LORD, teach me your paths; guide me in your truth and teach me, for you are God my Savior, and my hope is in you all day long.
>
> Psalm 25:4–5 (NIV 1984)

Now for some thoughts and suggestions about quiet times and how to establish them:

1. For many of us, selecting a quiet time with the Lord at the beginning of the day will help us get our focus on God for the day ahead and allow him to feed our heart and show us his ways. It is our morning briefing with our boss (God), the CEO of our lives.

2. Pick a place where you can be alone with God.

3. Start your quiet time with a prayer, asking God to reveal himself to you.

4. As you begin your Bible reading, start with prayer, seeking insight, understanding, and direction as you study the Word.

5. Like the manna that the Israelites received in the wilderness on a daily basis for their physical needs, so it is with our daily meeting with God for our spiritual needs.

6. This time is not just something you or I need; it also fulfills a longing in God's heart. God wants to see our face and hear our voice.

7. Be sure to tell God that you love him and need him.

8. When we neglect to seek his face in the morning to get his daily provisions for us, we are saying that we can make it through the day on our own.

9. Get to bed early enough the night before to allow sufficient, unhurried time the next morning.

10. Finally, realize that this is the most important meeting of the day with the most important person in your life: God.

As we become still, listening for his soft voice and communicating with our awesome God, we come to the realization that the battle for the restoration of our marriage is not ours but the Lord's. He knows our needs and knows just what is needed for the battle. In Exodus, we read, "The LORD will fight for you; you need only to be still" (Exodus 14:14, NIV 1984).

How reassuring it is to know we are not alone in our struggle for the rebuilding of our troubled marriages. The Lord God grieves with us over our broken marriage covenant for it was he who ordained marriage at the time of Adam and Eve. He made us one flesh with our spouse. So who is our enemy? Is it our spouse? *No!* It is the evil one, the prince of this world, Satan. While the war with Satan has already been won at Calvary, he is still winning small battles in our marriages as he kills our relationship with our spouse, steals our marital joy, and destroys our family. We need only to put our hope and trust in our Lord Jesus Christ. We just need to be still and wait upon the Lord. "Wait for the LORD; be strong and take heart and wait for the LORD" (Psalm 27:14, NIV 1984).

> The LORD is my shepherd, I shall not be in want. He makes me lie down in green pastures, he leads me beside quiet waters, he restores my soul. He guides me in paths of righteousness for his name's sake. Even though I walk through the valley of the shadow of death, I will fear no evil, for you are with me; your rod and your staff, they comfort me. You prepare a table before me in the presence of my enemies. You anoint my head with oil; my cup overflows. Surely goodness and love will follow me all the days of my life, and I will dwell in the house of the LORD forever.
>
> Psalm 23 (NIV 1984)

The Lord comforts us, he shields us from the evil one, and his love for us endures *forever*.

May our awesome God bless and keep you and your prodigal spouse safe and secure while you are apart, and may you have the faith of a mustard seed in his resurrection powers for your marriage.

Standing firm until parted by death.

Do Not Forget The Lord

As each of us look at our present circumstances with our marriage problems and look ahead at what we think the future holds for us, we as Christians need to remember one thing, one extremely important thing: our Lord is with us. Never forget that! Never forget that our Lord is with us 24-7! In our trials and tribulations, we need to seek humbly our God's help and his will for our lives and our marriages. We need to be still and listen for him speak to us. Let us take a moment and look in the Old Testament at the Israelites. In the book of Deuteronomy, Moses is in the process of handing over the reins to Joshua and reminding the people of Israel of God's promises and his commandments. In chapter 8, he reminds the people about specific things. Looking at this chapter, I see many parallels in the story of the Israelites to our stand for our covenant marriages as we fight for our marriages through our trials of separation, divorce, and then reconciliation and rebuilding.

> You must obey all the commands that I give you today, because then you will live and grow to become a great nation. You will get the land that the LORD promised to your ancestors. And you must remember the entire trip that the LORD your God has led you through these 40 years in the desert. He was testing you. He wanted to make you humble. He wanted to know what is in your heart. He wanted to know if you would obey his commands. He humbled you and let you be hungry. Then he fed you with manna—something you did not know about before. It was something your ancestors had never seen. Why did the Lord do this? Because he wanted you to know that it is not just bread that keeps people alive. People's lives depend on what the LORD says.

> Deuteronomy 8:1–3 (ERV)

Moses reminds the people of many things, most very obvious to them. God led them for forty years through the desert to humble them, to test them, and to examine what was in their hearts. In like manner, God is taking us through the desert of separation and, in many cases, the desert of divorce to humble us. He is testing our resolve to lean on him always, but especially in our time of need. He looks at our hearts—are we seeking his face in true humility, or in blatant arrogance are we trying to fix our mess the world's way? If we seek the Lord's face, he will humble us, causing us to hunger for manna (the Bread of Life, the Word, the Bible). In the Bible, we do truly find the Bread of Life that sustains us in our trials with our troubled marriages, just as the Israelites found manna in the desert to sustain themselves.

> You must remember that the LORD your God teaches and corrects you as a father teaches and corrects his son. "You must obey the commands of the LORD your God. Follow him and respect him. The LORD your God is bringing you into a good land."
>
> Deuteronomy 8:5–7a (ERV)

As we stand and fight for our covenant marriages, God teaches us, refines us, and disciplines us to make us more like his son, Jesus Christ. For if we seek to be more like Jesus, then our spouse will notice the changes occurring in us, that we are becoming a more humble and gentle person. Following God's *rules and regulations* for our lives, he will bring us into a good land, the land of marriage reconciliation and rebuilding. Isn't that what we have been praying for? Isn't that why we are standing? Hasn't he called us to stand in the gap for the restoration of our marriages?

> You will have all you want to eat. Then you will praise the LORD your God for the good land he has given you.
>
> Deuteronomy 8:10 (ERV)

When we have eaten of the fruits of his grace (the reconciliation of our marriage), we must remember who is responsible for our reconciliation. It is God and only God, and we need to come before him with praise and thanksgiving. We are to put him at the center of our marriage, as "number 1" in our personal lives and in our marriage.

When we do this, we are honoring God and pleasing him. What better way to worship him and thank him than to acknowledge him 24-7! Then Moses gives the people a stern warning.

> Be careful. Don't forget the LORD your God! Be careful to obey the commands, laws, and rules that I give you today. Then you will have plenty to eat, and you will build good houses and live in them. Your cattle, sheep, and goats will grow large. You will get plenty of gold and silver. You will have plenty of everything. When that happens, you must be careful not to become proud. You must not forget the LORD your God. You were slaves in Egypt, but he made you free and brought you out of that land. He led you through that great and terrible desert where there were poisonous snakes and scorpions. The ground was dry, and there was no water anywhere. But he gave you water out of a solid rock. In the desert he fed you manna—something your ancestors had never seen. He tested you to make you humble so that everything would go well for you in the end. Don't ever say to yourself, "I got all this wealth by my own power and ability." Remember the LORD your God is the one who gives you power to do these things. He does this because he wants to keep the agreement that he made with your ancestors, as he is doing today! Don't ever forget the LORD your God. Don't ever follow other gods or worship and serve them. If you do that, I warn you today: You will surely be destroyed! The LORD is destroying other nations for you. But if you stop listening to the LORD your God, you will be destroyed just like them!

> Deuteronomy 8:11–20 (ERV)

As we stand and fight for the reconciliation and rebuilding of our marriages upon the Solid Rock of Jesus Christ, we must acknowledge that all this is impossible without God's intervention. God warns us not to become disobedient or arrogant. We need to continually seek his face, trust him, and follow his commands (his will for our lives and our marriages). If we forget that it was God who healed our marriages and start following the ways of the world, then our marriages will again fall apart. Remember that our God loves us and cares about us, but we must follow his will for our lives. Remember that our God is the Alpha and Omega, the Beginning and the End, and he is *everything in between.* So look to him for strength, for nourishment, for hope, for peace. He will see you through your stand if you will just stand firm and trust him.

> But Moses answered, "Don't be afraid! Don't run away! Stand where you are and watch the LORD save you today. You will never see these Egyptians again. You will not have to do anything but stay calm. The LORD will do the fighting for you."
>
> Exodus 14:13–14 (ERV)

To paraphrase Moses, he tells us to stand firm, and the Lord will deliver us from our trials of separation and/or divorce. The Egyptians (our prodigal spouse's worldly ways) we will see no more. Our awesome God will do battle with the enemy (Satan), restoring our marriages, and we need only to be still (turn our prodigal spouses over to the Lord) and allow him time to reconcile our spouses to himself. So put your trust in the one sure thing in this life, your Lord and Savior, Jesus Christ. He will see you through your trials (your desert), guiding you ever homeward to your promised land (your restored marriage). Just trust him, and do not ever forget him. We do serve an awesome God.

> Trust in the LORD with all your heart and lean not on your own understanding; in all your ways acknowledge him, and he will make your paths straight.
>
> Proverbs 3:5–6 (NIV 1984)

Standing firm until parted by death.

Come To Jesus Just As You Are

Just as I am, without one plea,
But that Thy blood was shed for me,
And that Thou bidst me come to Thee,
O Lamb of God, I come, I come.

Just as I am, and waiting not,
To rid my soul of one dark blot,
To Thee whose blood can cleanse each spot,
O Lamb of God, I come, I come.

Just as I am, though tossed about,
With many a conflict, many a doubt,
Fightings and fears within, without,
O Lamb of God, I come, I come.[3]

This beautiful old classic hymn (the first three verses listed above) were born in the heart of a young lady in London, England, in 1835. Ms. Charlotte Elliott was visiting some friends in the West End of London, and there she met a prominent minister of that day, Dr. César Malan. During the visit, he told her he hoped she was a Christian. She took offense at this and replied that she would rather not discuss that question. Dr. Malan said he was sorry he had offended her, and he hoped that she would someday become a worker for Christ. When they met again some three weeks later, Ms. Elliott told him that ever since he had spoken to her, she had been trying to find her Savior and that she now wished him to tell her how to find Christ. "Just come to him as you are," Dr. Malan said. This she did and went away rejoicing. Shortly thereafter, she wrote this hymn.

Many of us have come to know this hymn as the Invitation Hymn at the end of a church service. It is an invitation to come to Jesus confessing our sins, seeking forgiveness, and accepting Jesus Christ as our Lord and Savior. The hymn describes our sinful selves as we seek our Lord and Savior, Jesus Christ. It describes the situations so many of us find ourselves in as we struggle with our marriages. When we respond, we come to Jesus just as we are, with all our sins, our fears, our hopes, our tears. We bring all the baggage of our prior sinful life, and we lay it at the foot of the cross. There we find Jesus, smiling with his arms outstretched, saying, "Come to me, and you will find rest and peace for your soul." For when we come seeking Jesus, we take the first of many steps in the reconciliation of our troubled marriages.

> For I know the thoughts that I think toward you, says the LORD, thoughts of peace and not of evil, to give you a future and a hope. Then you will call upon Me and go and pray to Me, and I will listen to you. And you will seek Me and find *Me,* when you search for Me with all your heart.

> Jeremiah 29:11–13 (NKJV)

Marriage reconciliation is a misnomer. In reality, what we are seeking is reconciliation to God and his Son, Jesus Christ. In seeking marriage reconciliation, we must first and foremost be reconciled to God, our Heavenly Father. Reconciliation to God begins when we accept Jesus Christ into our life and receive the indwelling of the Holy Spirit in our heart. We can only change ourselves; we cannot change our spouses. Only God can change our spouses as he reconciles them to himself. Then when God feels the timing is appropriate (in his perfect timing), he and he alone will orchestrate the reconciliation of our marriages. Remember, true marriage reconciliation can never be lasting unless it is built on the Solid Rock of Jesus Christ.

Jesus said to him, "I am the way, the truth, and the life. No one comes to the Father except through Me."

John 14:6 (NKJV)

But seek first the kingdom of God and His righteousness, and all these things shall be added to you.

Matthew 6:33 (NKJV)

God makes people right through their faith in Jesus Christ. He does this for all who believe in Christ. Everyone is the same. All have sinned and are not good enough to share God's divine greatness. They are made right with God by his grace. This is a free gift. They are made right with God by being made free from sin through Jesus Christ.

Romans 3:22–24 (ERV)

From these scriptures, we see that the hope for our personal life and that of our spouse and our marriage is found in only one place: in our Lord and Savior, Jesus Christ. We need only to humble ourselves and seek Jesus, and he will see us through the darkest days of our troubled marriages, our separations, our unwanted divorces.

Come to Me, all *you* who labor and are heavy laden, and I will give you rest. Take My yoke upon you and learn from Me, for I am gentle and lowly in heart, and you will find rest for your souls. For My yoke *is* easy and My burden is light.

Matthew 11:28–30 (NKJV)

Dear brothers and sisters in Christ, our destiny is found in only one person and one relationship: it is in our personal relationship with Jesus Christ. He and he alone will see us through our hardships and our troubled marriages. Trust him, he will never fail you!

> Trust in the LORD with all your heart and lean not on your own understanding; in all your ways acknowledge him, and he will make your paths straight.
>
> Proverbs 3:5–6 (NIV 1984)

> Trust ye in the LORD for ever: for in the LORD JEHOVAH is everlasting strength.
>
> Isaiah 26:4 (KJV)

May our awesome God and his Son, Christ Jesus, bless each of you as you stand in covenant for your marriage.

Standing firm until parted by death.

Don't Be Unbelieving! Believe!

> But Thomas, sometimes called the Twin, one of the Twelve, was not with them when Jesus came. The other disciples told him, "We saw the Master." But he said, "Unless I see the nail holes in his hands, put my finger in the nail holes, and stick my hand in his side, I won't believe it." Eight days later, his disciples were again in the room. This time Thomas was with them. Jesus came through the locked doors, stood among them, and said, "Peace to you." Then he focused his attention on Thomas. "Take your finger and

examine my hands. Take your hand and stick it in my side. Don't be unbelieving. Believe." Thomas said, "My Master! My God!" Jesus said, "So, you believe because you've seen with your own eyes. Even better blessings are in store for those who believe without seeing."

John 20:24–29 (MSG)

At this Easter season, we come back to the roots of our Christian faith. We are all familiar with the events that occurred during the week leading up to the crucifixion of our Lord and Savior Jesus Christ. In like manner, we are familiar with the events of the Crucifixion and then the marvelous events of Easter morning and the resurrection of Jesus Christ. But the story does not end there. There were many witnesses to his resurrected body over the next few days. But none are more poignant than the story of Doubting Thomas. Thomas needed to see for himself the physical evidence that this person claiming to be Jesus had the marks of his Lord's crucified body. When he saw and felt the marks, he believed. Then Jesus said to Thomas, "Because you have seen me, you have believed; blessed are those who have not seen and yet have believed" (John 20:29, NIV 1984).

Jesus's message to us is this: we are blessed because we believe even though we have not seen the physical evidence of crucifixion on our Lord's resurrected body. This is called *faith*. In the book of Hebrews, the Apostle Paul gives us a most profound definition of faith: "Now faith is the assurance of *things* hoped for, the conviction of things not seen. For by it the men of old gained approval" (Hebrews 11:1–2, NASB).

This chapter in Hebrews is sometimes known as the faith chapter or the *Faith Hall of Fame* of the Bible. I like how this passage reads in the Message.

The fundamental fact of existence is that this trust in God, this faith, is the firm foundation under everything that makes life worth living. It's our handle on what we can't see. The act of faith is what distinguished our ancestors, set them above the crowd.

Hebrews 11:1–2 (MSG)

Faith is our handle on what we today cannot see or touch. Faith that there is one God over all the universe, and that he is the God of the Bible. Faith that his Son, Jesus, came and lived among us in human form. Faith that this Jesus, who was fully God and fully man, died upon a cross for the atonement for our sins, and faith that Jesus experienced physical resurrection from the dead and offers the same to us spiritually that we might have eternal life with him and our Father God. In like manner, it is faith in God's resurrection power for our dead or dying marriages. It is the faith for a healed marriage that you and I need to have each and every day as we stand in the gap for our marriages.

So are you a Doubting Thomas? Thomas needed to see physical evidence of the crucifixion on his Lord's resurrected body. Is your stand wavering because of the lack of evidence before your eyes of the restoration and reconciliation of your marriage? Haven't you been called by God to *stand firm* for your marriage and those covenant marriage vows you took before God and your spouse? Are your current trials of marital discord, separation, or possibly divorce derailing you in your quest for a healed marriage? Don't be unbelieving! Believe! Have faith that your stand and your path are straight, true, and righteous. Don't be like Thomas, but believe through faith in what our Lord has promised you and I. Our God is unchanging: he is the same yesterday, today, and tomorrow.

Have faith in his promises to you. You need only to be still and listen for his soft voice to speak to you. God can speak to you through a *rhema* word or verse in the Bible, through a thought that comes into your mind that is in line with his Word, through the feeling of a gentle nudge on your shoulder to go a certain way, through a spoken word from another person, through the sighting of a Covenant Transport truck (a physical sign many standers trust as a message from our Lord), or through a special spiritual event whose meaning is known only to you. God speaks to us in so many ways if you will just *listen* and be aware of his presence. Moses told the Israelites when they reached the Red Sea to have faith and believe. "Moses answered the people, 'Do not be afraid. Stand firm and you will see the deliverance the Lord will bring you today'" (Exodus 14:13a, NIV 1984).

So God's message to each of you is that you need to have faith, unwavering faith. Faith in God's many promises. Believe in them. Believe that if you will confess your sins, asking for forgiveness from God's one and only Son, Jesus Christ, you will be saved. Believe that when you become reconciled to our Father God, your life will be changed forever. Believe that God wants your marriage restored; he wants you to be reconciled with your spouse and family. Have faith and believe!

> Jesus answered, "The truth is, if you have faith and no doubts, you will be able to do the same as I did to this tree. And you will be able to do more. You will be able to say to this mountain, 'Go, mountain, fall into the sea.' And if you have faith, it will happen. If you believe, you will get anything you ask for in prayer."
>
> Matthew 21:21–22 (ERV)

So, brothers and sisters, stand firm, have faith, and believe that God will restore your relationship of marriage with your beloved spouse. Don't be like Thomas! Don't be unbelieving! Believe! May God bless each of you in your stand.

Standing firm until parted by death.

We Be Free!

It is for freedom that Christ has set us free. Stand firm, then, and do not let yourselves be burdened again by a yoke of slavery.

—Galatians 5:1 (NIV 1984)

So Christ has truly set us free. Now make sure you stay free, and don't get tied up again in slavery to the law.

—Galatians 5:1 (NLT)

In Paul's Epistle to the churches in southern Galatia, he expresses his concern that the Galatians were being influenced by the false teachings of the Judaizers, an extremist Jewish group. They believed that Gentiles had to follow the Jewish law and traditions in order to become a Christian. This included such items as the covenant of circumcision and the Jewish dietary laws. Paul's message is that we cannot be saved by the keeping of the Old Testament law, including the Ten Commandments. All the law (the Old Covenant) can do is point out our sin. The *law* cannot save us. It is in Christ that we have a new freedom (the New Covenant), a freedom from sin, for our sins were nailed to the cross at Calvary. We have a salvation received by faith in Jesus Christ through belief in him as our Lord and Savior. I repeat, we have a new freedom through Jesus Christ. We are now no longer being held in bondage under the old Jewish law and traditions and our own futile attempt to keep the law. But the story doesn't end there. This new freedom comes with a price and a special privilege. The price: we are not to disobey Christ or live immorally. The privilege: we are now free under the New Covenant to serve a risen Christ. We find our freedom in service and love for others. For it is in Christ, through his forgiveness of our sins, that we can now come before a Holy God, clothed in the gift of Christ's righteousness. Christ took our sins upon his body at Calvary and exchanged them for his robe of righteousness.

So where do we go from here? Paul continues in his Epistle to the Galatians.

> For you have been called to live in freedom, my brothers and sisters. But don't use your freedom to satisfy your sinful nature. Instead, use your freedom to serve one another in love. For the whole law can be summed up in this one command: "Love your neighbor as yourself." But if you are always biting and devouring one another, watch out! Beware of destroying one another. So I say, let the Holy Spirit guide your lives. Then you won't be doing what your sinful nature craves. The sinful nature wants to do evil, which is just the opposite of what the Spirit wants. And the Spirit gives us desires that are the opposite of what the sinful nature desires. These two forces are constantly fighting each other, so you are not free to carry out your good intentions. But when you are directed by the Spirit, you are not under obligation to the law of Moses. When you follow the desires of your sinful nature, the results are very clear: sexual immorality, impurity, lustful pleasures, idolatry, sorcery, hostility, quarreling, jealousy, outbursts of anger, selfish ambition, dissension, division, envy, drunkenness, wild parties, and other sins like these. Let me tell you again, as I have before, that anyone living that sort of life will not inherit the Kingdom of God.

> Galatians 5:13–21 (NLT)

All of us have wandered from our faith in Jesus Christ as our Lord and Savior. We have all, at one time or another, disobeyed Christ's teachings to a greater or lesser degree. No matter how you say it, we are sinners. Or perhaps, you are not a Christian.

Paul entreats us to find the freedom that exists by following Christ and his teachings. When we accept Jesus into our lives and ask for forgiveness of our sins, our lives are changed forever, and he lives in us and through us daily. Jesus Christ is our example for he lived a perfect life, free from sin.

In marriage reconciliation, we learn that before we can truly become reconciled to our spouse, we must first become reconciled to God. This means living as best we can with our lives modeled after our Lord and Savior, Jesus Christ. It is not easy, but by continually seeking the help of the Holy Spirit, we can live a life of freedom. For when we accept Christ into our lives, we receive the gift of the Holy Spirit who dwells in our heart. It is through the leading of the Holy Spirit that the Fruits of the Spirit come into our lives.

> But the Holy Spirit produces this kind of fruit in our lives: love, joy, peace, patience, kindness, goodness, faithfulness, gentleness, and self-control. There is no law against these things! Those who belong to Christ Jesus have nailed the passions and desires of their sinful nature to his cross and crucified them there. Since we are living by the Spirit, let us follow the Spirit's leading in every part of our lives.
>
> Galatians 5:22–25 (NLT)

So as we seek reconciliation to God, we live by faith, not by deeds. However, when Christ comes into our lives, we have a new freedom to love our neighbor, to help him, and to bring him to Christ. With this new freedom we have in Christ, we find a hope, a joy, a love, a happiness, and a peace that all the sinful living of this world could never bring. Paul goes on to say in Ephesians, "In Christ we come before God with freedom and without fear. We can do this because of our faith in Christ" (Ephesians 3:12, ERV).

Paul's message is this: *be free in Christ!* In Him, we can find the answers to all our fears, anxieties, and sorrows of our troubled marriages and lives. So *be free in Christ!* May God bless your stand for your marriage covenant taken before him and your spouse.

Note to reader: The title of this devotional comes from a sermon series by Rick Atchley.[4]

Standing firm until parted by death.

Yes, Lord, I Believe

Now to Him who is able to do exceedingly abundantly above all that we ask or think...

—Ephesians 3:20a (NKJV)

Are you looking for a miracle? A modern-day miracle? Yes, miracles still do occur every day; yes, even today! I know I am waiting for a miracle of resurrection, not of my Lord and Savior Jesus Christ (that already happened two thousand years ago), but the resurrection of my marriage relationship. Yes, God is in the business of resurrecting the dead: Lazarus after four days in the grave, Jesus Christ after three days on Easter morning, and even today, dead or dying marriages. You say, "Yes, that may happen to other people, but you do not know my situation. My situation is hopeless. You don't know my spouse. He (she) will never change! There is just no reason in my situation to believe that reconciliation is at all possible."

But Jesus looked at *them* and said to them, "With men this is impossible, but with God all things are possible."

Matthew 19:26 (NKJV)

This verse is a fundamental statement of belief of a Marriage Reconciliation Support Group I attend. We state that if we believe in Easter, then we can believe that all things are possible with God. That includes the resurrection of your marriage and mine. Are you a Doubting Thomas? Must you see the nail prints in the hands of your spouse to believe that the resurrection of your marriage can happen? It has been stated that *impossible* is one of God's favorite words. I wonder why? Surely that doesn't apply to dead or dying marriages. Maybe it is because God honors marriage and ordained it from the time of Adam and Eve. Or maybe it is because when God sees a good marriage, he gets a big smile on his face. Or perhaps it is when God sees an *impossible* marriage reconciled and healed, it brings glory to his name!

Last evening at our Marriage Reconciliation Support Group meeting, four couples (besides our facilitators) that have reconciled marriages were introduced to the group. While each of these couples had their own story and path to their reconciliation, each of these reconciled marriages represented modern-day miracles from God. What many called impossible, God called possible and said, "*Try my way this time.*"

All of us who are seeking reconciliation of our marriages must first put our hope and faith in God, reconciling ourselves to him. We must also believe and trust God with the job of changing our spouses as only he can. If we try to change our spouses, we just mess things up, delay reconciliation, or even worse, kill all chances of healing our marriage relationship. It is only through our belief in the resurrection powers of God that true and lasting reconciliation can occur with our spouses. We can only change ourselves with God's help; we must leave our spouses totally in God's hands.

So when you are faced with the impossible, be bold and imagine the unimaginable. *Yes, Lord, I believe!*

Standing firm until parted by death.

Never Will I Leave You

Today, I want to address the issue of *hope*. All of us who are standing for the restoration of our covenant marriages have some idea of what hope is. "I hope my husband [wife] will return to our marriage and family both in body and in spirit." "I hope I can find a job that will sustain our family." "I hope I can raise our kids without the help of their father [mother]." "I hope my spouse's addiction to alcohol, pornography, anger, rage, or another person has run its course, and he [she] seeks healing." "I hope ______ [you fill in the blank]." Hope is defined by Webster as "trust that what is wanted will happen." The Apostle Paul speaks often of hope, such as these words in Romans:

> And we exult in hope of the glory of God. And not only this, but we also exult in our tribulations, knowing that tribulation brings about perseverance; and perseverance, proven character; and proven character, hope; and hope does not disappoint, because the love of God has been poured out within our hearts through the Holy Spirit who was given to us. For while we were still helpless, at the right time Christ died for the ungodly.... But God demonstrates His own love toward us, in that while we were yet sinners, Christ died for us.
>
> Romans 5:2b–6, 8 (NASB)

Yes, Jesus Christ, our Lord and Savior, died for us while we were still sinners. He gives those who put their faith in him hope both for today and for eternity. Hebrews states, "Now faith is the assurance of *things* hoped for, the conviction of things not seen" (Hebrews 11:1, NASB). Faith and hope are interrelated, as you can see in that verse. Hebrews goes on to say, "For He Himself has said, 'I WILL NEVER DESERT YOU, NOR WILL I EVER FORSAKE YOU,' so that we confidently say, 'THE LORD IS MY HELPER, I WILL NOT BE AFRAID. WHAT WILL MAN DO TO ME?'" (Hebrews 13:5b–6, NASB).

What a comforting thought to know that God is with us and will never forsake us. He gives us hope! He is right here with us, walking with us and feeling our hopes, our joys, our pain and despair, and even our grief. Yes, we can call on him. And how do we call on God? It is called prayer. Prayer is how we talk (share) with God our praises, our hopes, our fears, and even our hurts. Even though he knows our thoughts before we utter them, he desires that we share them with him through prayer. Prayer is a two-way conversation with God in which we share our thoughts with him, and he responds to us in many ways. He speaks to us through our thoughts, through our dreams, through the Bible, and through the actions of others. He speaks to us in the peace that comes over us when we have bared our soul to him in prayers coming from the depths of our heart. So with advocates like Jesus and the Holy Spirit by our side, what can man do to us for which they do not have a solution or an answer?

So I leave you with these comforting thoughts from the inspired writings of the Apostle Paul.

> For in hope we have been saved, but hope that is seen is not hope; for who hopes for what he *already* sees? But if we hope for what we do not see, with perseverance we wait eagerly for it.

> Romans 8:24–25 (NASB)

> What then shall we say to these things? If God *is* for us, who *is* against us?

> Romans 8:31 (NASB)

> Yet in all these things we are more than conquerors through Him who loved us. For I am persuaded that neither death nor life, nor angels nor principalities nor powers, nor

things present nor things to come, nor height nor depth, nor any other created thing, shall be able to separate us from the love of God which is in Christ Jesus our Lord.

Romans 8:37–39 (NKJV)

Stand firm in your faith and hope for a healed marriage and family knowing that God's promise is "Never will I leave you; never will I forsake you" (Hebrews 13:5b, NIV 1984).

Standing firm until parted by death.

Do Not Grow Weary And Lose Heart

We have all these great people around us as examples. Their lives tell us what faith means. So we, too, should run the race that is before us and never quit. We should remove from our lives anything that would slow us down and the sin that so often makes us fall. We must never stop looking to Jesus. He is the leader of our faith, and he is the one who makes our faith complete. He suffered death on a cross. But he accepted the shame of the cross as if it were nothing because of the joy he could see waiting for him. And now he is sitting at the right side of God's throne. Think about Jesus. He patiently endured the angry insults that sinful people were shouting at him. Think about him so that you won't get discouraged and stop trying.

Hebrews 12:1–3 (ERV)

As I look around the room every week at the Marriage Reconciliation Support Group meeting at my church, I look into the eyes of those who have gotten the message that God heals hurting marriages. There is happiness and joy on their faces and in the message they tell as they share with others their stand for their marriage and their Christian walk. Yet I also see faces here that are filled with pain and sorrow as they realize that their dream of a wonderful marriage and family lies shattered at their feet. In desperation and without hope, they have ended up in our support group's meeting, seeking answers to ease and heal their pain and anguish. They, like each of us, are among the lucky few of the thousands upon thousands of individuals around the world with marital problems who have found help and are seeking a better solution than divorce. Each of us is not here by accident; rather, we are here by divine appointment. We are called by one who cares, our Heavenly Father and Jesus Christ.

In the above scripture, our Lord and Savior, Jesus Christ, has set a high standard for each of us. The world tells you and me to move on and divorce him (or her) as you can always find someone better. I heard this from my own family, my friends, and even one of my pastors (which pained me very much). Brothers and sisters in Christ, Jesus has set a high standard, a *gold standard*. It is not the world's standard. While God's standard is a lofty one, it is an attainable one. That standard is set forth in our marriage vows that we took before God and our spouse. God was and is the principal witness to our marriage vows, and it pains him whenever a marriage relationship breaks down. Remember these phrases that you and your spouse exchanged at your wedding: *in sickness and in health, for better or for worse*, and the one so many ignore, *until parted by death*?

The writer of Hebrews calls us to persevere though the bad times as well as the good times. He goes on to say that Jesus Christ's life and his ministry set the standard for our lives. The NIV 1984 translation uses the metaphor of a race marked out before us. That race includes our Christian walk of honoring our covenant marriage vows. Tim Coody writes in *Meaningless Words and Broken Covenants* that the words we say today have come to mean little or nothing. Our words have become empty. When we ignore our covenant vows, we are, in essence, telling Jesus Christ that he went to the cross for nothing, that he did not need to suffer his crucifixion and his separation from his Father. Yet through his love for each of us, he did die on a Roman cross for our sins, including the sin of covenant breaking. So we need to set our sights upon Jesus, our perfect example, who set the standard by which we must live. That standard includes honoring our covenant marriage vows. There is nothing that God loves more than a marriage built upon the Solid Rock of Jesus Christ. A God-honoring marriage relationship reflects the relationship of Jesus Christ and his bride, the Church (the Body of Christ). Satan hates it. Whenever Satan can destroy a Christ-honoring marriage, he feels that he is getting back at God. The author of Hebrews reminds us that Jesus endured the rejection of men and the physical pain associated with his arrest and crucifixion, yet he persevered because of his love for you and me. So he calls us to persevere and look to him for strength.[5]

The Apostle Paul shows us his own personal perseverance in his letter to Timothy as he spoke about his own Christian walk.

> I have fought the good fight. I have finished the race. I have served the Lord faithfully. Now, a prize is waiting for me—the crown that will show I am right with God. The Lord, the judge who judges rightly, will give it to me on that Day. Yes, he will give it to me and to everyone else who is eagerly looking forward to his coming.
>
> 2 Timothy 4:7–8 (ERV)

Paul calls us to follow his example of finishing the race and serving the Lord faithfully. When we stay the course and honor our covenant vows, a *crown* of being right with our Lord and Savior, Jesus Christ, awaits us in eternity. (Other versions have a *crown of righteousness* awaiting in eternity.) Yet even on this side of heaven, a crown awaits those who stand strong in the faith as we can experience a modern-day miracle of a resurrected and restored marriage with our spouse.

So take heart, and don't grow weary! The Lord is on your side in this battle with Satan. Persevere! God is in control!

Standing firm until parted by death.

Take The Word Impossible Out Of Your Vocabulary

Jesus looked at them and said, "With man this is impossible, but with God all things are possible."

—Matthew 19:26 (NIV 1984)

Jesus looked at them and said, "With man this is impossible, but not with God; all things are possible with God."

—Mark 10:27 (NIV 1984)

Jesus replied, "What is impossible with men is possible with God."

—Luke 18:27 (NIV 1984)

I cannot remember how many times I have sat in a room filled with fellow Christians seeking the healing of their respective marriages and listened to a newcomer in our midst state, "But my marriage situation is impossible. It cannot be healed!" I know that as I began to stand for my own marriage, similar thoughts would frequently go through my head, taking my focus off God's clear and true message about marriage restoration. Something was trying to derail my desire to seek healing for my marriage. The impossible dream scenario came front and center, and it was straight from the pits of hell. It is Satan's tool to convince us to abandon our marriage and its restoration. *Wrong, wrong, wrong*! The above scriptures testify that God is in the possible business, not the impossible business. We often quote Matthew 19:26 as our theme verse, but as you can see, Jesus continually reminds us in the Gospels that God has powers and resources that he brings into play that we humans cannot even begin to fathom.

> Jesus said to the father, "Why did you say 'if you can'? All things are possible for the one who believes."
>
> Mark 9:23 (ERV)

There are several keys, however, that we need to understand and grasp if we are to have lasting success in our desire for healing of our marriages. Those keys are *faith* and *belief* that healing, divine healing, is possible. Jesus refers to this in Mark 9:23 when he speaks to the father of a demon-possessed child seeking healing. He told him that if one believes, all things are possible. A person who truly believes will set *no limits* on what God can do. Look again at the message the writer of Hebrews tells us in chapter 11.

> The fundamental fact of existence is that this trust in God, this faith, is the firm foundation under everything that makes life worth living. It's our handle on what we can't see. The act of faith is what distinguished our ancestors, set them above the crowd.
>
> Hebrews 11:1–2 (MSG)

The words *believe* and *belief* are linked to the word *faith* as they express the same basic idea, the possibilities of something happening. As we stand for the healing of our respective marriages, we often cannot see our healed marriages. We, however, through faith and unwavering belief, know that God can do the impossible, and he does not have the word *impossible* in his vocabulary. When we get past all our hang-ups, our fears, and our unbelief, we understand that God loves us with a love that is unquenchable. His track record is this: *with God, all things are possible.* Our job is to believe and to have mustard seed–sized faith in him.

Standing firm until parted by death.

Worth Everything

Have you ever given a thought to the worth or value of your stand, your stand for and with Jesus Christ and for your covenant marriage? I think each of us, as we stand with Jesus for the healing of our marriages, have had thoughts about the worth of all this pain, this time alone, this time of struggling to survive. No matter where we may be in our walk, these thoughts from Satan creep into each of our minds. Most of you who have been standing with God for the healing of their respective marriages are familiar with Rejoice Marriage Ministries and Charlyne Cares daily devotionals. If you haven't read it yet, read her devotional for July 18, 2008, titled "Take My Pain Away!" In it she asks, "Was it worth the pain that I went through? A million times over again, yes!"[6]

This same message is seen in the Bible as the Apostle Paul in his writings to the Philippians.

> But whatever things were gain to me, those things I have counted as loss for the sake of Christ. More than that, I count all things to be loss in view of the surpassing value of knowing Christ Jesus my Lord, for whom I have suffered the loss of all things, and count them but rubbish so that I may gain Christ, and may be found in Him, not having a righteousness of my own derived from *the* Law, but that which is through faith in Christ, the righteousness which *comes* from God on the basis of faith, that I may know

Him and the power of His resurrection and the fellowship of His sufferings.

Philippians 3:7–10a (NASB)

We are standing with Jesus Christ for the resurrection of our dead or dying marriages. All other things are irrelevant when we consider our own salvation and praying for the salvation of our spouse. We can lose our job, our home, our friends, everything, but what is most important is our own personal relationship with our Lord and Savior, Jesus Christ. Paul was trying to make a point to the Philippians and to each of us that nothing in this world is more vital to our eternal souls than our relationship with Jesus. All else is *rubbish*. He talks about Christ's righteousness and our need to run from self-righteousness, to cast it off. Our true righteousness has its source in God with Jesus as the object of that righteousness and faith as its means. Source, object, means—all are reflected in the person of Jesus Christ, who was fully man yet fully God.

So as Paul states, *I count all things to be lost in view of the surpassing value of knowing Christ Jesus my Lord.* It is with this in mind that we should seek reconciliation first with God, then with ourselves, and finally with our spouse. It is through Christ's righteousness that we receive life that has eternal value and is *worth everything.* I know personally that it was through my personal stand that I found Jesus Christ as my Lord and Savior. And yes, I would go through it all again because it is *worth everything* to me, my wife, and my family...but especially to me! This has been a wonderful time of discovery for me of who I am in Christ Jesus.[7]

May each of you likewise find this time in your life equally rewarding as you contemplate where you will spend eternity. This time can be a time of discovery for each of you, so use it wisely.

Standing firm until parted by death.

The Peace Of God

The *peace of God*. Do you have it? Have you ever experienced the balm of God's peace? I am here to tell you that it really exists, that it is real! Two and half years ago (this devotional was written in July 2008), I was at the lowest point in my life, a broken man. In that very moment, a small group of Christian friends circled around me, laid hands on me, and prayed for God's peace to fill my heart and soothe my soul. A few minutes later, as I drove to a church prayer meeting, a most wonderful feeling of peace, God's peace, came over me. It was at that moment that I began to realize that Jesus and the Holy Spirit were with me, lifting me up, sustaining me, and that things were going to be okay. I realized that over the next several months, whatever might occur in my life was in God's hands and that I should just trust and obey him. While these two items, trust and obey, are often difficult to do consistently, I know that is what my Lord and Savior, Jesus Christ, expects. Brothers and sisters, I am here to tell you that God's peace is real, it is tangible, it is alive and active. (As I compile these devotionals into a manuscript some six years after my friends prayed over me, this peace of God is still alive and well in my heart, and I wouldn't trade it for anything.)

> And because you belong to Christ Jesus, God's peace will
> stand guard over all your thoughts and feelings. His peace
> can do this far better than our human minds.
>
> Philippians 4:7 (ERV)

> And the peace of God, which surpasses all understanding,
> will guard your hearts and minds through Christ Jesus.
>
> Philippians 4:7 (NKJV)

God's peace truly *surpasses all understanding*. Once you have experienced it, you never want it to leave. (I am now seventy-four years old and have never experienced a feeling quite like it.) And if I continue to follow Jesus, I will retain this peace for the rest of my life. One of the most comforting passages in the Gospels is found in the Gospel of John, chapter 14. John's Gospel is different from the other three Gospels. The first three Gospels are called the Synoptic Gospels as they basically tell Jesus's story, the record of his earthly ministry. John, on the other hand, tells the story of the *personal* Jesus, as seen through the eyes of the apostle he loved. In the latter part of this chapter, Jesus comforts his disciples by telling them about the Comforter, the Holy Spirit whom they would receive.

> But the Helper, the Holy Spirit, whom the Father will send in My name, He will teach you all things, and bring to your remembrance all that I said to you. Peace I leave with you; My peace I give to you; not as the world gives do I give to you. Do not let your heart be troubled, nor let it be fearful.

> John 14:26–27 (NASB)

It is the presence of the Holy Spirit in our hearts that becomes the source of the living peace of God. His presence in our hearts instructs us on how to keep that peace alive and vibrant and how to extend that peace to our spouse, our family, our friends, and all those we meet. God's peace is real. It is alive, and you can have it too if you will seek God's face.

> I have told you these things, so that in me you may have peace. In this world you will have trouble. But take heart! I have overcome the world.

> John 16:33 (NIV 1984)

Finally, all *of you be* of one mind, having compassion for one another; love as brothers, *be* tenderhearted, *be* courteous; not returning evil for evil or reviling for reviling, but on the contrary blessing, knowing that you were called to this, that you may inherit a blessing. For "He who would love life And see good days, Let him refrain his tongue from evil, And his lips from speaking deceit. Let him turn away from evil and do good; Let him seek peace and pursue it. For the eyes of the Lord *are* on the righteous, And His ears *are open* to their prayers; But the face of the Lord *is* against those who do evil."

1 Peter 3:8–12 (NKJV)

But seek first His kingdom and His righteousness, and all these things will be added to you. So do not worry about tomorrow; for tomorrow will care for itself. Each day has enough trouble of its own.

Matthew 6:33–34 (NASB)

When we approach God with a willing and contrite heart, he will grant us his peace—God's peace. Once you have experienced it, you will never want to let it go. Trust God! Obey God! Trust and obey! Then you can and will experience God's peace.

Standing firm until parted by death.

The North Star

As is my usual custom during the warmer part of the year, I go out late at night and sit on my patio and think. I live in the county where houses are not packed close together. Few trees block my view, and I can see for miles as the land is flat. It is very peaceful, especially late at night shortly before I go to bed. During this time, I think about God, about life, about the marriage I am standing for, and about my beautiful wife. God and I will have a conversation. This evening was no different except in one aspect. The Holy Spirit led my eyes to a rather faint star straight in front of me. As the night sky was sort of hazy, I thought it interesting that the star even caught my attention. As I stepped off my patio and out from under the overhanging roof, my eyes caught a familiar sight overhead in the night sky. It was the Big Dipper, a group of stars that I remember from my days as a Boy Scout. Any of you familiar with the Big Dipper know that it is made up of seven stars, three in the handle and four in the cup. The two stars forming the side of the cup away from the handle point to a very significant single star in the night sky, the North Star. Taking the *distance* between the two stars on the side of the cup and moving your eyes in a straight line approximately four *distances* from the top edge of the cup brings one to the region of a single star, the North Star. While the Big Dipper is very bright, the North Star is not as bright. Thus, it was very significant to me tonight that my eyes fixed upon that dimmer star.

As I thought about this experience, I realized that God was speaking to me in a new way he had never used before with me. You see, God was telling me to hitch my life, my stand, my all to that star for it would lead me home, to his (my) heavenly home. That star, the North Star, represents Jesus Christ in this scenario. What a powerful message God was speaking to me and to you. Mariners of old would navigate their ships using the constellations, but the one star in the ancient world that was always present and unchanging in location was the North Star. Know the position of that star, and you could find your way home. In like manner, Jesus Christ is our North Star, our gateway to that narrow path that leads to salvation and life eternal with him and Father God. The North Star concept represents a constant, never-changing idea or principle that can guide us heavenward each and every day.

Jesus answered, "I am the way, the truth, and the life. The only way to the Father is through me."

John 14:6 (ERV)

As you think about those constants in your life, many things come to mind. Such is the concept of a North Star as an anchor for so many things. Looking at the Bible and the Old Testament, the law was at the center of life for the Israelites. At the center of the law were the Ten Commandments, the North Star for the Jewish nation. Prior to Moses receiving the Ten Commandments, there was no absolute universal law. Everyone did what was right in their own eyes. Thus, each group of people made up their own rules to govern their people, but none proved to be an absolute set of rules that would fit all peoples until the advent of the Ten Commandments. These set down the basics for our relationship with our Creator and also our relationships with each other. Thus, the commandments became their North Star, an anchor for their lives.

If you have done much reading about our modern legal system, you know that it is based upon that North Star concept found in the Ten Commandments. Western-civilized countries' legal systems can trace their laws back to those key concepts found in the Ten Commandments. Without this North Star concept found in God's law, our societies would eventually fail. Christian nations look to this North Star concept. Our founding fathers recognized this North Star concept and incorporated it into the Declaration of Independence.

We hold these truths to be self-evident, that all men are created equal, that they are endowed by their Creator with certain unalienable Rights, that among these are Life, Liberty and the pursuit of Happiness.

Declaration of Independence (July 4, 1776)

These rights are from our Creator. As they are from him, man cannot truly take these rights away. Remember our faith (North Star) can be found only in Jesus Christ, our Lord and Savior. Jesus is the founder and perfecter of our faith. He introduced us to the New Covenant through his work on the cross, putting aside the need for the law. He is now our North Star!

> Therefore, since we have so great a cloud of witnesses surrounding us, let us also lay aside every encumbrance and the sin which so easily entangles us, and let us run with endurance the race that is set before us, fixing our eyes on Jesus, the author and perfecter of faith, who for the joy set before Him endured the cross, despising the shame, and has sat down at the right hand of the throne of God.

> Hebrews 12:1–2 (NASB)

So, friends and fellow standers, when life is bearing down on you and your marriage situation seems hopeless, fix your eyes on Jesus, our North Star. He will never let you down, and you will never be disappointed.

Standing firm until parted by death.

I Am The Way

> Jesus answered, "I am the way, the truth, and the life. The only way to the Father is through me."

> —John 14:6 (ERV)

At this Christmas season, the events that surround the birthday of our Lord and Savior focus our attention on the birth of the baby Jesus. Few realized that those events some two thousand years ago in a small village in Judea would change the face of the world forever. Jesus, born to a virgin teenage woman but fathered by the Holy Spirit, was both fully man and fully God. Into this sinful world, Jesus was born as an innocent baby who, in time, grew into manhood. As a sinless man, he died a sinner's death on a Roman cross at the age of thirty-three. During his three-year ministry, Jesus told his followers and us today how he has planned a future for all those who believe in him. Look again at these comforting words of Jesus from John's Gospel.

> Jesus said, "Don't be troubled. Trust in God, and trust in me. There are many rooms in my Father's house. I would not tell you this if it were not true. I am going there to prepare a place for you. After I go and prepare a place for you, I will come back. Then I will take you with me, so that you can be where I am. You know the way to the place where I am going." Thomas said, "Lord, we don't know where you are going, so how can we know the way?" Jesus answered, "I am the way, the truth, and the life. The only way to the Father is through me. If you really knew me, you would know my Father too. But now you know the Father. You have seen him."

> John 14:1–7 (ERV)

Today, we face unpredictable times with our economy, political changes, war on two fronts, and a world that is in so much turmoil. The Bible tells us of a hope of a better today and also a better tomorrow. That hope has been with us for some two thousand years, yet in many ways, we are just rediscovering it anew. That hope is in our Lord and Savior, Jesus Christ. In the passage above, Jesus lays it out very plainly that the pathway to the Father is through Jesus himself and *no one else*. He states, "I am the way, the truth, and the life. The only way to the Father is through me." In today's world, it is reassuring to know that Jesus has charted a simple pathway of hope and security for us all. *I am the way.* I like how the New Living Translation states part of this passage: "When everything is ready, I will come and get you" (John 14:3a, NLT). How comforting it is that the God of heaven and earth is making ready our lodging place where we will spend eternity in the presence of God, our Creator. How awesome are these promises!

In the early first-century church, Christ's followers were not known as Christians but became known as *the Way*. One of the earliest references to those followers is found in the book of Acts.

> Then Saul [Paul], still breathing threats and murder against the disciples of the Lord, went to the high priest and asked letters from him to the synagogues of Damascus, so that if he found any who were of the Way, whether men or women, he might bring them bound to Jerusalem.
>
> Acts 9:1–2 (NKJV)

This term, *the Way*, is interesting, but it is truly self-explanatory. In John 14:6, Jesus clearly points out to us that he is the only pathway to our Father God. Thus, the name the Way. No other religions offer such a pathway to their god. The Way is also selective.

> [Jesus speaking] "You can enter true life only through the narrow gate. The gate to hell is very wide, and there is plenty of room on the road that leads there. Many people go that way. But the gate that opens the way to true life is narrow. And the road that leads there is hard to follow. Only a few people find it."
>
> Matthew 7:13–14 (ERV)

Yes, only a few find it. There are only two roads or pathways in this life, two possible roads of travel for mankind, and only Jesus is the Way to Life Eternal. The other way leads to eternal damnation or destruction, and many will follow it for wide is its pathway. There is no third option!

So at this season of the year, as we celebrate the birthday of our Lord and Savior, Jesus Christ, those who are straddling the fence about becoming a Christian need to make a most important decision. Will it be the way of the cross, or will it be the way of eternal damnation? Start the new year with your life solidly anchored in Jesus Christ. You cannot enjoy eternal life with Jesus Christ if you have one foot in the world and one foot in the church. With Jesus Christ, relationships will heal, and reconciliation of families can occur. For those of you who have already accepted Jesus Christ as your Lord and Savior, then this is a good time for recommitment to him. For Christ has said in no uncertain terms that he is the only way to the Father. He says, "I am the way" (John 14:6a, ERV).

May our God bless each of you in this, your most important decision. Your eternal destination depends on it.

Standing firm until parted by death.

Simon Says

How many of you remember this game that many of us played as kids or perhaps even as adults? As you may remember, once you mess up, you are out of the game, period. This game came to mind as I was thinking about our relationship with Almighty God and his Son, Jesus Christ. The Bible is full of stories of the wayward Israelites of the Old Testament and the wayward Jews and Gentiles of the New Testament. Yet through his great mercy, we are saved and forgiven through his grace. Our God is a God of second chances as seen in the Old and New Testament stories. How many times did God's chosen people wander away from him? Yes, they incurred his wrath for their sins, but through his mercy and his Covenant with Abraham, the Israelites found redemption. They were all given a second chance. In New

Testament times, Jesus Christ's work on the cross became their second chance. Each of us today are sinners, and we continuously mess up. But by his grace, we are given a second chance through Christ's work on the cross some two thousand years ago. Our God believes in second chances. We are not out of the game as in Simon Says.

> But Christ died for us while we were still sinners, and by this God showed how much he loves us. We have been made right with God by the blood sacrifice of Christ. So through Christ we will surely be saved from God's anger. I mean that while we were God's enemies, he made friends with us through his Son's death. And the fact that we are now God's friends makes it even more certain that he will save us through his Son's life. And not only will we be saved, but we also rejoice right now in what God has done for us through our Lord Jesus Christ. It is because of Jesus that we are now God's friends.
>
> Romans 5:8–11 (ERV)

> Come to me all of you who are tired from the heavy burden you have been forced to carry. I will give you rest. Accept my teaching. Learn from me. I am gentle and humble in spirit. And you will be able to get some rest. Yes, the teaching that I ask you to accept is easy. The load I give you to carry is light.
>
> Matthew 11:28–30 (ERV)

I look at my own life, of the mess I made in my now-dead marriage, and I now know that as I seek reconciliation with my Heavenly Father, I am forgiven. I have been given a second chance. I am not out of the game of life; I am not in a game of Simon Says. And as I lean upon Jesus, I find comfort and reassurance in his forgiveness as I become reconciled first to Jesus Christ and then to myself. Then and only then can healing begin in the relationship with my wife. Second chances exist in this world, and when they occur in a dead marriage, God has worked one of his many modern-day miracles. Yes, miracles do happen in the healing of marriages as Jesus Christ gives each of us second chances. So stand firm for your marriage. Thank God for the promise of a second chance to make your marriage what God intended it to be—a marriage based upon the Solid Rock of Jesus Christ. Jesus Christ promises each of you a second chance in your own marriage if you will just ask in his name.

> And if you ask for anything in my name, I will do it for you. Then the Father's glory will be shown through the Son. If you ask me for anything in my name, I will do it.

> John 14:13–14 (ERV)

> "Haven't you read the Scriptures?" Jesus replied. "They record that from the beginning 'God made them male and female.'" And he said, "'This explains why a man leaves his father and mother and is joined to his wife, and the two are united into one.' Since they are no longer two but one, let no one split apart what God has joined together."

> Matthew 19:4–6 (NLT)

May God bless each of you as you seek healing of your marriage, knowing that our God is a God of second chances, and we are not out of the game as in Simon Says.

Standing firm until parted by death.

Pessimist or Optimist?

We have all been there. You are married and wake up one morning, and your spouse states point-blank that they want a divorce. Or perhaps they want you to leave, just get out! Or perhaps you are the breadwinner for your family, and you come home from work to find your house empty, devoid of furniture, and a note from your spouse stating the obvious. Your marriage is over. Or perhaps it is the pink slip from a company you have worked at for twenty-plus years. Or perhaps it is getting the results of medical tests that reveal the big C word: cancer. Or perhaps you are huddled in the emergency room waiting room with family and friends when the doctor comes out with the news that your loved one didn't make it. It is moments like these that become defining moments in our lives. We have all been there!

Yet these are truly moments in the time line of our lives. They become defining moments because it is how we react to them, how we view our lives from that moment forward that really matters.

> Praise be to the God and Father of our Lord Jesus Christ. He is the Father who is full of mercy, the God of all comfort. He comforts us every time we have trouble so that when others have trouble, we can comfort them with the same comfort God gives us. We share in the many sufferings of Christ. In the same way, much comfort comes to us through Christ. If we have troubles, it is for your comfort and salvation. If we are comforted, it is so that we can comfort you. And this helps you patiently accept the same sufferings we have. Our hope for you is strong. We know that you share in our sufferings. So we know that you also share in our comfort.
>
> 2 Corinthians 1:3–7 (ERV)

Defining moments in our lives. We see an eight-ounce glass that has four ounces of water in it. Is it half-empty or half-full? Defining moments. Those of us who have Jesus Christ in our lives look at our situations differently than nonbelievers. With the help of the ever-present Holy Spirit, we can see beyond the moment. We can see the *silver lining*. Jesus Christ and the Holy Spirit provide us with an optimistic view. For those whose faith is weak or nonexistent, they can only see the worst outcome. Defining moments.

In a Bible study that I attend, one of the participants made the comment that as Christians, rather than looking at a situation and seeing only the very obvious, we can look *through* the situation, look past it, and see the blessings that lie down the road. I have been down this road before. When my wife and I separated, divorce hung heavy in the air. I was a Christian, having accepted Jesus Christ as my Lord and Savior, baptized into his death, burial, and resurrection, but my faith was wavering. I could only see the obvious: divorce. My life and future was over, at least in my mind. It was at that time that through the prayers and the laying of hands from a core group of believers that I received a newfound peace, God's peace that passes all understanding. From that moment on, I knew that everything was going to be okay. I was then looking beyond the moment, seeing that there was a silver lining in this whole situation. A defining moment in my life.

For me, that defining moment became weeks then months of walking with Jesus, receiving his comfort, his wisdom, his encouragement. I cannot begin to tell you the wonderful feelings, the comfort, and experiences I have had as Jesus and the Holy Spirit directed my footsteps. Divorced, yes, but precious time spent with Jesus! Those of you who have walked this path know what I am talking about. They are eternal moments, defining moments about my personal future and my personal eternity. Sure, there is faith (as mentioned in Hebrews 11:1), a confident faith that God will heal my fellowship and relationship with my wife in his own special timing. Yet I see these precious moments with my Savior that could have been lost if I had allowed myself to only look at the obvious and not look through and beyond the situation. Defining moments in my life.

Satan gloats when a marriage breaks down; he wins when we just give up. Yet out of the ashes of our situation, hope springs eternal. Satan does not win when we turn to Jesus and lean on him. After all, did Jesus not say as he was leaving his disciples that he would send them another part of himself, the Holy Spirit, the Comforter, to be with them? This Comforter dwells in my heart; he has guided and directed my feet from that defining moment forward. What an awesome gift from God!

A new relationship with our Creator can exist when we can see beyond our immediate problems. Jesus Christ waits with open arms to turn your situation (and mine) into victory. Yes, at times it is hard to believe, but through faith, it is real.

Defining moments in your life and mine. Jesus Christ is the answer. He will see you through. Lean on him. I did, and I have never been sorry. Neither will you. It is never too late to take that first step of faith.

> Let not your heart be troubled; you believe in God, believe also in Me.… I am the way, the truth, and the life. No one comes to the Father except through Me.
>
> John 14:1, 6 (NKJV)

Standing firm until parted by death.

If You Don't Change Your Direction

A very wise person once shared with me the following: "If you don't change your direction, you will end up where you are heading!"[8] What a profound statement! And the amazing thing about this statement is that it applies to just about everything we do in this life. Stop and ponder this statement for a moment. Do you like the direction your life is going right now, or do you need to change direction? Would your family benefit by a change in direction from the way you are taking them? In what direction are you taking your life partner, your spouse? Let us look at what God has to say about the direction we are heading.

As people who are seeking God's will for our lives, the first and greatest change of direction we need to make is to *repent* of our personal sins. The dictionary defines repent as a turning away from sin, a changing of direction, a change toward righteousness, a feeling of remorse or sorrow. As descendants of Adam, we have all inherited a sin nature and are therefore not sin-free.

> Now it's time to change your ways! Turn to face God so he can wipe away your sins, pour out showers of blessing to refresh you, and send you the Messiah he prepared for you, namely, Jesus.

Acts 3:19 (MSG)

> This is how much God loved the world: He gave his Son, his one and only Son. And this is why: so that no one need be destroyed; by believing in him, anyone can have a whole and lasting life. God didn't go to all the trouble of sending his Son merely to point an accusing finger, telling the world how bad it was. He came to help, to put the world right again. Anyone who trusts in him is acquitted; anyone who refuses to trust him has long since been under the death sentence without knowing it. And why? Because of that person's failure to believe in the one-of-a-kind Son of God when introduced to him.

John 3:16–18 (MSG)

> But God showed his great love for us by sending Christ to die for us while we were still sinners.
>
> Romans 5:8 (NLT)

From these three passages, God shows us his remarkable love. He has the answer for our sin nature: profess faith in his Son, Jesus Christ. He seeks us out, wanting us to make a change in direction of our lives. Families are falling apart, and separation and divorce are rampant. But you say, "It is just too hard to change. He [she] will never change! What's the use!" Yet God is asking you to change. But you keep saying, "Jesus doesn't know what I have been through. He is up in heaven, living the good life. He has not experienced what I am going through!"

> So then, since we have a great High Priest who has entered heaven, Jesus the Son of God, let us hold firmly to what we believe. This High Priest of ours understands our weaknesses, for he faced all of the same testings we do, yet he did not sin. So let us come boldly to the throne of our gracious God. There we will receive his mercy, and we will find grace to help us when we need it most.
>
> Hebrews 4:14–16 (NLT)

God, through Jesus Christ, is here to help us through these rough waters of the breakdown of our family relationships. He knows our sin nature for he has witnessed it firsthand. Yet being God in human form, he is without sin. As we strive to hold on to our family relationships and the ones we love, look to Jesus as it says in Hebrews, *we will find grace to help us when we need it most.* It is through God's mercy and grace that our family relationships can be healed. But we must take that first step. We must turn back, turn around, and repent of our evil ways. Repenting, asking Jesus Christ for his forgiveness, we should ask for forgiveness from those we have hurt. In like manner, offer forgiveness to those who have hurt us.

A change in direction can be as simple as a sincere statement of apology. Another simple change in direction is not returning equally hurtful remarks or actions to our spouse or family when our old self would have lashed out and done so. Jesus Christ is our example. The Bible is our instruction manual, our life-application guidebook.

Each of us who are suffering the pains of family discord, separation, or divorce wish that things could have been different. When we got married, our goal was not divorce. We had no plans to fight with our spouse, to fracture our family unit, to distance ourselves from our children, etc. You get the picture. Our marriage was not to be a means to destroy ourselves or those we love. Yet we find ourselves going down a road fraught with numerous land mines that lead to family destruction. If we don't change direction, we will get to that place of destruction where we are headed.

Take heart! Jesus Christ is the answer. Let him be the center of your marriage and your family life. Let our families worship God together and pray together each and every day. Then your road will lead to life eternal with God, and no change in direction or course correction will be necessary.

Standing firm until parted by death.

Radical Faith, Radical Savior

When my marriage began to tank, I was desperate. Despite my feeble attempts to rescue it, I found that my faith and my Christian walk were too shaky to save my marriage. I (we) tried seeking help in the secular world, yet nothing seemed to work for very long. Even so-called *Christian* counselors were consulted, but their counsel fell short of the much-needed guidance and changes I (we) needed in our lives. Only one began to point me along the path I needed to walk—a walk with Jesus Christ. It was later during the turmoil of separation and the subsequent divorce that God got my attention, and recovery of my sanity and spiritual life began. Healing can only begin when we are willing to give up everything, turning our total dependency over to him who can heal—Jesus Christ. Notice that I said "give up everything." Despite my marriage problems, giving up everything sounds radical. Check out what Jesus said to the rich young man.

> Jesus started to leave, but a man ran to him and bowed down on his knees before him. The man asked, "Good Teacher, what must I do to get the life that never ends?" Jesus answered, "Why do you call me good? Only God is good. And you know his commands: 'You must not murder anyone, you must not commit adultery, you must not steal, you must not lie, you must not cheat, you must respect your father and mother….'" The man said, "Teacher, I have obeyed all these commands since I was a boy." Jesus looked at the man in a way that showed how much he cared for him. He said, "There is still one thing you need to do. Go and sell everything you have. Give the money to those who are poor, and you will have riches in heaven. Then come and follow me." The man was upset when Jesus told him to give away his money. He didn't want to do this, because he was very rich. So he went away sad.
>
> Mark 10:17–22 (ERV)

Jesus Christ calls us to give up everything! In the healing of our marriage relationships, Christ calls on us to turn over everything: our marriage relationship, our spouse, and our very lives to him. The story above describes many of us. Christ calls us to be totally dependent upon him. We must be willing to give up our selfishness, our control, our anger, our unforgiveness, our material belongings, etc., and humble ourselves before God. We also need to humble ourselves before our spouses.

What so many of us ask as God calls each of us to stand for the healing of our marriage relationship is "How long do I stand?" This Christian walk is not an easy walk. It is not something we do today and abandon tomorrow when the going gets tough. A Christian who is standing with God for the healing of their marriage is required to stand until they are parted by death (physical death) from their spouse. So many of us forget (or don't believe) those words in our marriage vows that state *until parted by death*. These vows are radical vows, covenant vows taken before God and our spouse. They are not negated by separation or by a secular divorce decree. Jesus Christ expects much from each of us who wish to follow him.

> If you come to me but will not leave your family, you cannot be my follower. You must love me more than your father, mother, wife, children, brothers, and sisters—even more than your own life! Whoever will not carry the cross that is given to them when they follow me cannot be my follower.

> Luke 14:26–27 (ERV)

Jesus Christ is stating here that to be his disciple, we must be willing to give up *everything* to follow him. That includes material wealth, relationships, even our very lives. That includes the giving up of our *right* to step down from our stand for our marriage and *move on with our lives*. Being a Christian is not just saying the words. It is how we live day to day and what our values are. It is a *radical faith* that recognizes that we own nothing, that it all belongs to God. Our actions, our thoughts, and our promises are his. Yet through this radical faith in Christ, there is an eternal reward of eternal life with God and his Son, Jesus. Yes, Jesus Christ is our *radical Savior*. The path toward salvation is not easy and not for the fainthearted. Study the passage above. The statement and the message is about a radical faith and was (and is) spoken by our radical Savior, Jesus Christ.

Do you have a *radical faith*? Do you follow a *radical Savior*? Standing firm until parted by death.[9]

On Wings Like Eagles

But those who trust in the LORD will find new strength. They will soar high on wings like eagles. They will run and not grow weary. They will walk and not faint.

—Isaiah 40:31 (NLT)

What wonderful words of encouragement come to us from the prophet Isaiah. Each of us who are seeking God's help to reconcile our marriage problems can find comfort in these words. What the enemy has stolen from us has left us wounded. Each of us needs to ponder these words from Isaiah as he speaks to God's people in chapter 40. I strongly suggest that each of you pull out your Bibles and read several times chapter 40. Meditate upon God's Word. Let God's Word penetrate your soul and soothe your wounded heart. The NIV 1984 translation uses the word *hope* for *trust*: "*those who hope in the LORD*" (Isaiah 40:31a, NIV 1984). Whichever way it is stated, the message is clear. We are to put our hope or trust in the only one who can make any sense of our marriage mess, the one and only Living God. He is our Creator, our Sustainer, our Comforter, our All in All.

Isaiah's message to God's people tells us that when we put our hope and trust in the Lord, we are strengthened. That means when our personal circumstances, our separation, finances, family, possibly divorce, etc., begin to fall into place, we can see them in their proper perspective. God gives us comfort for he directs us down the path toward spiritual and emotional healing. We are now able to look at our family relationships and situation as if we are soaring high above them, like on wings like eagles. Through this metaphor, God leads us to a place where we can see our situation more clearly. The NASB translation uses another term for *trust*: "*wait for the LORD*" (Isaiah 40:31a, NASB). When we wait for (or on) the Lord, he will speak to us if we will just be still, be quiet, and listen. As God strengthens us, we will run (go) down the narrow pathway that he has directed us to, yet we will not grow weary. To me that means that the length of my personal stand is not a factor for me to be concerned about. Sure, each one of us wishes that our marriage problems could be fixed right now, even today. But remember this: our marriages didn't get to where they are today overnight! In like manner, God will take whatever time is necessary to change (heal) your heart and the heart of your spouse. Sure, the time seems too long. However, God knows what he is doing. So don't grow weary in worrying about the time you and your spouse are apart. God has the proper perspective in mind for your marriage reconciliation, and he has the end in sight. Trust him daily, turning everything about your marriage relationship over to him. He will never fail you.

Finally, this passage suggests that we should slow down. We need to spend some quiet time with our Lord and Savior, Jesus Christ. We are to walk, not run around frantically as I suspect everyone has done at times as our marriages broke down. When we slow down, being quiet and listening, God can and will speak his wisdom for us to hear. When we are frantic and running about, God's still small voice is drowned out by our inattention to what really matters—our relationship with our Lord and Savior, Jesus Christ. He and he alone is the answer to all of our problems.

The scripture above states that those who look to the Lord *will walk and not faint*. The NASB translation states, "*Will walk and not become weary*" (Isaiah 40:31b, NASB). What this tells me is that when I slow down by letting my Lord take the lead, letting him take the driver's seat, he can fix my marriage mess. Then I will not grow weary or tired due to the length of my stand.

God knows and understands each of our situations. He knows when the healing time has been sufficient for reconciliation to take place. Waiting on his okay means that when we are reunited with our spouse, God is there to see us through the reconciliation process with our spouse. When we try to do it on our own, the road is very difficult, and most frequently, reconciliation does not work out in the long run.

So my prayer for each of you is this. Put your hope and trust in the one who is sure, lasting, and eternal; put your trust in our Lord Jesus Christ. You will never be disappointed.

Standing firm until parted by death.

Have You Accepted Jesus Christ, Or Are You A Follower Of Jesus Christ?

Last Sunday, our teaching minister challenged each of us. We have just completed the largest one-year special ministry campaign (that exceeds our annual budget) in the over-fifty-year history of our congregation. Following the lead of our elders and ministers who subscribed to 22 percent of the Greater Things Campaign, our congregation pledged or gave in cash in one week's time the balance needed to fund 100 percent of the campaign, plus a small surplus. These pledges are over and above our regular tithes and offerings. More significant was that greater than 95 percent of the membership participated, including hundreds of our small children and older youth. The challenge was and is, have you accepted Jesus Christ, or are you a follower of Jesus Christ?

Let me explain the difference in those two terms. When one accepts Jesus Christ as their Lord and Savior, baptism is the next step in their Christian walk. Many Christians, however, stop here. They became one of God's adopted children, baptized into his family, but their participation in the Body of Christ became stagnant. They became casual in their church attendance (Christmas and Easter), rarely tithe, seldom support special offerings, and are Bible illiterate. Sadly, that describes most people who identify themselves as Christians. They seldom share the story of Jesus with the unsaved masses. Yes, they are saved, but still, our Messiah, Jesus Christ, expects more.

> Jesus came and told his disciples, "I have been given all authority in heaven and on earth. Therefore, go and make disciples of all the nations, baptizing them in the name of the Father and the Son and the Holy Spirit. Teach these new disciples to obey all the commands I have given you. And be sure of this: I am with you always, even to the end of the age."
>
> Matthew 28:18–20 (NLT)

Christ's Great Commission contains our marching orders. This is not for the sedentary Christians but for dynamic Christians who are willing to step out, getting their hands and feet dirty, making new disciples daily. Jesus wants us to accept him as our personal Lord and Savior, but we are not to stop there. He also wants us to follow him, to emulate him.

> And Jesus, walking by the Sea of Galilee, saw two brothers, Simon called Peter, and Andrew his brother, casting a net into the sea; for they were fishermen. Then He said to them, "Follow Me, and I will make you fishers of men." They immediately left their nets and followed Him.
>
> Matthew 4:18–20 (NKJV)

Jesus expects more than just acceptance. Like Simon Peter and Andrew, he calls each of us to be his followers. When you became a follower of Jesus Christ, in essence, you put on Jesus Christ, and you wear him 24-7. You emulate him, and when others (nonbelievers and nominal Christians) interact with you, they see Jesus in you.

My church family stepped out in faith, challenged by the Great Commission, to be followers of Jesus Christ. For many of us, that meant moving out of our comfort zone. It meant going the extra mile, digging a little deeper into our pockets to fund a campaign that will have eternal benefits for hundreds even thousands of nonbelievers who will become followers of Jesus Christ.

> Then he said to the crowd, "If any of you wants to be my follower, you must turn from your selfish ways, take up your cross daily, and follow me. If you try to hang on to your life, you will lose it. But if you give up your life for my sake, you will save it. And what do you benefit if you gain the whole world but are yourself lost or destroyed?"
>
> Luke 9:23–25 (NLT)

God is recruiting followers. He does not need bystanders. He wants workers for the Kingdom. That is the call of the Great Commission.

Being a follower of Jesus facilitates the healing of our troubled marriages. When faced with separation and/or divorce, God steps in to heal our marriages if we actively seek him. In the reconciliation process, God grooms us to be followers of Jesus rather than being casual Christians. By standing for our marriages, we are followers, not that casual Christian sitting on the sideline watching life pass by. Jesus called his twelve disciples to emulate him as they won souls for him. In like manner, he calls each of us out of our comfort zone to stand for our marriages. In doing so, we are being followers of Jesus Christ.

How do you identify yourself today? Are you a follower of Jesus Christ? I sure hope so. It is *never* too late to take that next step. Jesus Christ is waiting with open arms. *Do it today!*

Standing firm until parted by death.

Take A Risk For God

And He answered and said to them, "Have you not read that He who made *them* at the beginning 'made them male and female,' and said, 'For this reason a man shall leave his father and mother and be joined to his wife, and the two shall become one flesh'? So then, they are no longer two but one flesh. Therefore what God has joined together, let not man separate."

—Matthew 19:4–6 (NKJV)

Each of us finds ourselves in an unpleasant yet unique position. We see our marriages crumbling right before our eyes and our family units splitting up in such ungodly ways. Our personal situations, while unique to each of us, are commonplace today, a fact of life in today's world. Families and marriages are breaking up so frequently that it is hard to find a family that has not been touched by divorce. In the tidal wave that follows broken marriages, there are shattered lives and broken promises (broken covenant). Who is at fault? Who is to blame? Take a good look in the mirror. The truth hurts, but it must be reckoned with. Acknowledge your sin and your part in the breakdown of your marriage. Seek God's counsel, love, and grace, and you will start on the road toward marriage reconciliation. Stand strong for your marriage. Take a risk for God.

Standing (with God) for one's marriage is a difficult road to walk. Family, friends, your associates at work, the world, and even your own church leaders don't understand this Christian walk. It can be lonely if you don't take Jesus along. Yet for those of us who have been called by God to walk with him in salvaging our marriages, it is one of life's greatest blessings. Each of us have been handpicked by our Creator to suffer for him as we witness to the world about the truth and the value of the marriage covenant. I am fortunate to belong to a marriage reconciliation support group through my church. Such groups are few and far between. Only yesterday I drove by a large modern-looking church that had a big sign out front stating Divorce Care. What about marriage care? It was nowhere to be seen at that church or most other churches. In the support group I attend, we acknowledge that each of us is not there by accident but called by divine appointment. Take a risk for God. Stand for your marriage.

I cannot even begin to count the number of times well-meaning people have suggested to me that I should move on with my life. Sound familiar? In response, I proudly state that I am moving on with my life by standing with God as he works in my life and in my wife's life, using his healing powers in reconciling our marriage. At times, this takes people aback; they are lost for words. You see, I am taking a risk for God.

When we witness to the world (including our church leaders and fellow Christians) about the sanctity of marriage and our covenant marriage vows, we are taking a risk for God. God recognizes that life at times is difficult, yet perseverance in our walk brings great rewards. It was through the turmoil of the breakdown of my own marriage that I found my Lord and Savior, Jesus Christ. Frequently, I tell people that I am thankful that God led me down this path of the breakdown of my marriage and subsequent divorce for now I know where I am going to spend eternity. I took a risk for God.

I am standing with God as he heals me and my wife. My marriage failed because God was placed on a sidetrack; he was not on the main track of my life or our marriage. But even here, God must be the engine that pulls the Christian family along that track of life. God is in control of the universe, and he wants to be in control of your life and mine. Take a risk for God.

Notice that I have been saying take a risk *for* God, not *with* God. While God is with you as you stand and take a risk *for* God, you are on the front line of the battle against Satan. You see, God has given us everything we need to defeat Satan as you take a risk for God.

Jesus has the power of God. And his power has given us everything we need to live a life devoted to God. We have these things because we know him. Jesus chose us by his glory and goodness, through which he also gave us the very great and rich gifts that he promised us. With these gifts you can share in being like God. And so you will escape the ruin that comes to people in the world because of the evil things they want. Because you have these blessings, do all you can to add to your life these things: to your faith add goodness; to your goodness add knowledge; to your knowledge add self-control; to your self-control add patience; to your patience add devotion to God; to your devotion add kindness toward your brothers and sisters in Christ, and to this kindness add love. If all these things are in you and growing, you will never fail to be useful to God. You will produce the kind of fruit that should come from your knowledge of our Lord Jesus Christ.

2 Peter 1:3–8 (ERV)

One final note, and you have already read it over and over again: take a risk for God.

Standing firm until parted by death.

Legacy

Legacy. The Oxford University Press defines it as (1) "an amount of money or property left to someone in a will," and (2) "something handed down by a predecessor." For the Christian, the second definition fits best as we look at what is lasting from changed lives.

Yesterday, I attended the funeral of a single mom whose life was cut short by the ravages of diabetes. What material wealth she left behind was in a small storage locker. Yet her legacy was her unyielding faith in Jesus Christ as it flowed out into the two young ladies she raised while working three different jobs. Her lasting legacy was in the hundreds of lives she touched as she faced the challenges and ravages of diabetes since her teen years. Legacy was seeing her two daughters graduate from a Christian university and the marriage of the oldest. Material wealth, no. But wealth beyond compare in the lives touched by her unrelenting fervor for her Lord and Savior, Jesus Christ, despite her ongoing battle with diabetes.

Legacy. For a Christian, it is in the lives we touch as we witness for Christ. I think of my youngest grandson. At the tender age of four, he placed a picture of his recently deceased grandmother in his room so he would not forget her face. It was the memory of love she poured into him during their short time together. Christian values, Christian love. Legacy. It was not toys but love and faith in Jesus Christ that my deceased wife left him. Those memories and values will be with him and his older brother for a lifetime.

Legacy. I think back to the time during my separation from my second wife as the divorce action she initiated was nearing completion. The Lord spoke to me through a sermon by my pastor about legacy. The legacy he spoke about was the family and friends that we leave behind with all the experiences, values, love, etc. (both positive and negative), that linger through the years in their lives and memories long after we are gone. I thought about the legacy of divorce being generated now in our family with all its negative effects on our kids and grandkids. The Lord also brought to my mind the reconciliation and restoration of our marriage that he has planned for us. This positive legacy will be that of God's healing of a dead marriage and the message that divorce is not the answer to marital problems. That legacy is the Son of God, Jesus Christ. The Lord spoke to me of his plans for my family's legacy, what part I played in it, and what we (my wife and I) would be passing on to our families.

Legacy. I think back some two thousand years to a bloodstained cross on a windswept hill and the events of that day.

I think of events surrounding the empty tomb three days later. Legacy. Jesus Christ, fully God and fully man, left us a legacy of love and a legacy of forgiveness of our many sins and the promise of life eternal with him and Father God for all who believe in him as God's only Son. Yes, the legacy of the cross and the empty tomb changed the world like no other event since time began.

> But God demonstrates His own love toward us, in that while we were still sinners, Christ died for us.
>
> Romans 5:8 (NKJV)

Legacy. A life well-lived and lives touched despite overwhelming physical hardships. Legacy. Memories and values experienced by a young boy of four and his desire to carry that legacy forward. Legacy. The negative legacy that comes with the breakup of a family through divorce that flows down through generations. Yet the possibilities of a positive legacy through Christ's healing of that dead marriage that can likewise flow down through generations. Legacy. The cross and the empty tomb say it all. The faith and values demonstrated by Christians down through the centuries give meaning and purpose to your life and mine, to our families, to our friends, to our country, and to our world. Legacy.

> For God so loved the world that He gave His only begotten Son, that whoever believes in Him should not perish but have everlasting life. For God did not send His Son into the world to condemn the world, but that the world through Him might be saved. He who believes in Him is not condemned; but he who does not believe is condemned already, because he has not believed in the name of the only begotten Son of God.
>
> John 3:16–18 (NKJV)

Legacy. What are you leaving behind?
Standing firm until parted by death.

Belief and Unbelief

Life is a series of events, some good and some not so good. These events paint a picture of what God has in store for each of us. As these events impact each of us, God has put into man a system of checks and balances, a system of beliefs to help us evaluate these events and their impact upon us. Our personal faith in a Supreme Being (our God and our Heavenly Father) and his Son Jesus is central to Christian beliefs. We believe that the man Jesus is the Christ (the Messiah), the one and only Son of God. By belief in Christ, our sins (past, present, and future) are forgiven; thus, God promises eternal fellowship with him (Father, Son, and Holy Spirit) in heaven. What a promise! What a future!

> For God so loved the world, that He gave His only begotten Son, that whoever believes in Him shall not perish, but have eternal life. For God did not send the Son into the world to judge the world, but that the world might be saved through Him. He who believes in Him is not judged; he who does not believe has been judged already, because he has not believed in the name of the only begotten Son of God.
>
> John 3:16–18 (NASB)

The Apostle John, in this most quoted verse of the Bible (John 3:16), lays out what mankind (those who have been exposed to the Word) can expect through belief or unbelief. It is cut and dried. There is no middle ground, no gray area. Yet so many of us suffer from a flaw in our character called *unbelief*.

Remember the story in Mark's Gospel of the young demon-possessed boy whose father came to Jesus seeking help.

It has often thrown him both into the fire and into the water to destroy him. But if You can do anything, take pity on us and help us!" And Jesus said to him, "'If You can?' All things are possible to him who believes." Immediately the boy's father cried out and said, "I do believe; help my unbelief."

Mark 9:22–24 (NASB)

Is this not the cry of so many of us when we are faced with problems such as marital discord, separation, and/or divorce? We cry out to God, hoping for relief from our pain. Yet in the back of our minds, there is unbelief that even God cannot make this situation right. I know that in my own life, even with a promise from God that he will heal my marriage relationship, I still periodically cry out and seek reassurance through prayer that this promise of marital restoration is still in his plans (will) for my life.

Today, as I was doing my Bible study, it included the passage where the Jews were seeking signs to authenticate Jesus's authority. "Some Jews said to Jesus, 'Show us a miracle as a sign from God. Prove that you have the right to do these things'" (John 2:18, ERV). My study guide went on to ask, *Does asking for a sign reflect our unbelief and thus rebellion against Jesus Christ?* Wow! Did that set me back upon my heels! Am I in unbelief or in rebellion of God's awesome power? Below I have listed several scriptures that should put our hearts and minds at ease. Meditate upon them and understand the deeper messages that are here in God's Word.

In the beginning was the Word, and the Word was with God, and the Word was God. He was in the beginning with God. All things came into being through Him, and apart from Him nothing came into being that has come into being.

John 1:1–3 (NASB)

And the Word became flesh, and dwelt among us, and we saw His glory, glory as of the only begotten from the Father, full of grace and truth.

John 1:14 (NASB)

And looking at *them* Jesus said to them, "With people this is impossible, but with God all things are possible."

Matthew 19:26 (NASB)

One simple conclusion should come out of this. Jesus (God) is omnipresent for he is the Creator. He is in control of everything, thus, in control of whatever goes on in our lives 24-7; we need only to believe and to trust. When Jesus lived among us some two thousand years ago, he was fully man, yet fully God. He knows and understands our doubts, our sorrows, and the everyday situations that trouble us because he experienced them both as man and as God. Therefore, unbelief should no longer be a factor in our lives. For those who believe, there is hope, and out of that hope comes a new beginning in him. "Therefore if anyone is in Christ, *he is* a new creature; the old things passed away; behold, new things have come" (2 Corinthians 5:17, NASB).

"I do believe. Help my unbelief!"

Standing firm until parted by death.

Standing: A Special Christian Walk

Why Do I Stand?

Have you ever had a thought like this? This is the question that many of us (standers) ask as we begin our stand for our marriage. We come to this critical juncture in our lives, seeking understanding and seeking God's will and his direction in our marriage. Many of us are just learning what it means to stand, to be a *stander*. We learn from talking with those in marriage reconciliation ministry that standing is a special Christian walk, a walk of which many Christians have very little understanding, including family, friends, and most clergy, elders, and other leaders in the Body of Christ. One is indeed fortunate when he/she finds a church or other Christian organization that runs an educational forum and/or support group. For it is only when God and his teachings are at the center of these support groups that real lasting success in marriage reconciliation can occur. The thoughts below are both an affirmation of my faith and a testimony of my personal walk with our Lord. So looking for God's help as written in Matthew's Gospel: "Jesus looked at them and said, 'With man this is impossible, but with God all things are possible'" (Matthew 19:26, NIV 1984).

I stand because I still love my wife, despite our troubled marriage and our divorce. I love my wife because even when I didn't deserve being loved, Christ first loved me. I can do no less for her. So I stand.

> Love is patient, love is kind. It does not envy, it does not boast, it is not proud. It is not rude, it is not self-seeking, it is not easily angered, it keeps no record of wrongs. Love does not delight in evil but rejoices with the truth. It always protects, always trusts, always hopes, always perseveres. Love never fails.

> 1 Corinthians 13:4–8a (NIV 1984)

I stand because of a marriage relationship I have lost, yet one that I treasure. By the time I got to this point in my separation and later divorce, I realized that both parties were at fault, that each of us had made significant mistakes leading to the breakdown of our relationship. I realized that my marriage was flawed, but the relationship is a treasure I do not wish to lose. So I stand.

I stand because God called me to stand. As I became reconciled to my Father, I realized that I wished to reconcile with my wife. My Father was speaking to me via the Holy Spirit to stand firm. When my wife and I were married, we took vows before the Lord and each other. We made a covenant before God, and the rings we exchanged were symbols of that covenant. While my wife has chosen at the present time to break covenant, I am still in covenant with my Lord and my wife. I want to and will honor that covenant. The Lord honors covenant! Our marriage vows are a covenant! So I stand.

> He said: "O LORD, God of Israel, there is no God like you in heaven or on earth—you who keep your covenant of love with your servants who continue wholeheartedly in your way."

> 2 Chronicles 6:14 (NIV 1984)

> Have we not all one Father? Did not one God create us? Why do we profane the covenant of our fathers by breaking faith with one another.... You ask, "Why?" It is because the LORD is acting as the witness between you and the wife [husband] of your youth, because you have broken faith with her [him], though she [he] is your partner, the wife [husband] of your marriage covenant.
>
> Malachi 2:10, 14 (NIV 1984)

I stand because of God's promise to me of a restored marriage. This will occur in his own special timing when he reconciles both of us back into a new marriage, one built upon the Solid Rock of Jesus Christ. The Holy Spirit spoke words of encouragement to me early in my separation, and following a prayer of supplication, he led me to a scripture, Luke 21:19, which told me to stand firm in my faith and my walk with Christ (as I stand for my marriage). In doing so, I will receive eternal rewards. So I stand.

Finally, the most important reason that I stand is that *I must stand*. I have no other option. First, I took vows, covenant vows before the Lord and my wife, vows that in God's eyes end only with the death of myself or my wife. Next, my stand for my marriage is a test of my obedience to God's will to honor that covenant. Just as Christ said in the garden of Gethsemane: "Father, if you are willing, take this cup from me; yet not my will, but yours be done" (Luke 22:42, NIV 1984).

So as a Christian, it is an honor and a privilege for me to have the opportunity to obey God's will. I can do nothing less. My stand is a gift of witness for my Lord Jesus Christ, a witness to all believers as well as nonbelievers. So I stand.

So, fellow standers, take heart for the Lord God is on our side. He will never fail you! He will never fail me! Give thanks to him always, and praise his holy name.

A Psalm of Thanksgiving. Make a joyful shout to the Lord, all you lands! Serve the Lord with gladness; Come before His presence with singing. Know that the Lord, He *is* God; *It is* He *who* has made us, and not we ourselves; *We are* His people and the sheep of His pasture. Enter into His gates with thanksgiving, *And* into His courts with praise. Be thankful to Him, *and* bless His name. For the Lord *is* good; His mercy *is* everlasting, And His truth *endures* to all generations.

Psalm 100 (NKJV)

Standing firm until parted by death.

A Road Less Traveled By

Have you ever wondered about the rationale of your stand for your covenant marriage vows? Do you find yourself trying to justify your stand not only in your own mind but also in the minds of family, friends, and even at times the clergy? Think back to your wedding day. You and your spouse promised before God and each other some very powerful statements of togetherness that included such things as (1) in good times and bad, (2) for richer and poorer, (3) in sickness and in health, and let us not forget that most far-reaching promise (4) until parted by death. These promises made and this covenant spoken, once entered into, is not something to be taken lightly. Yet today, many married people put very little value in these words. These words have become meaningless, words without substance. So when we read the words of Jesus, we should know the course we must take.

Some Pharisees came to Jesus. They tried to make him say something wrong. They asked him, "Is it right for a man to divorce his wife for any reason he chooses?" Jesus answered,

"Surely you have read this in the Scriptures: When God made the world, 'he made people male and female.' And God said, 'That is why a man will leave his father and mother and be joined to his wife. And the two people will become one.' So they are no longer two, but one. God has joined them together, so no one should separate them."

Matthew 19:3–6 (ERV)

God ordained marriage from the time of Adam and Eve. He knew that man should not be alone, so He created woman as man's partner and helpmate. They were joined together by God's divine purpose for mankind. So now we find ourselves at odds with God's plan for a lifelong monogamous marriage relationship. Whether you are separated or divorced, we each have a choice to make. Do we ignore our marriage vows and stand in opposition to God's law, or do we stand with God for the restoration of our marriages? Standing for our marriages is a difficult road, a road many do not have the fortitude to follow. There comes a time for choosing. The following poem by Robert Frost says it well.

The Road Not Taken

Two roads diverged in a yellow wood,
And sorry I could not travel both
And be one traveler, long I stood
And looked down one as far as I could
To where it bent in the undergrowth;

Then took the other, as just as fair,
And having perhaps the better claim,
Because it was grassy and wanted wear;
Though as for that the passing there
Had worn them really about the same,

And both that morning equally lay
In leaves no step had trodden black.
Oh, I kept the first for another day!
Yet knowing how way leads on to way,
I doubted if I should ever come back.

I shall be telling this with a sigh
Somewhere ages and ages hence:
Two roads diverged in a wood, and I—
I took the one less traveled by,
And that has made all the difference.

I took the one less traveled by, and that has made all the difference. Yes, you and I, like this person, have taken the road *less traveled*. Through persistence, it *has made all the difference* in our lives. That difference is *eternal*, and that road is *the road less traveled.* It should be our only choice, our only course, our only destination. So stand firm!

Standing firm until parted by death.[10]

Standing Strong In Your Faith

While I was reading my devotional this morning concerning the Apostle Paul's conversion, it struck me that in many ways, Paul's experiences mirror many of my own struggles as I stand for my covenant marriage vows. For Paul, his experience with Jesus that day on the road to Damascus was his wake-up call. For many of us, our marriage problems became our own wake-up call, revealing where our lives were headed. Such was my own experience, and in my baby faith, I cried out to the Lord, "Why? Why am I in so much pain and emotional distress?" Even though it has now been over two years (this devotional was written in 2008) since Christian friends laid on hands and prayed over me and God's peace came upon my heart, still the pain remains. In my reading this morning, the Lord was speaking to Ananias and instructing him to go to Paul and lay hands on him so that Paul might receive baptism and the gift of the Holy Spirit. We read the following words of Jesus: "I will show him how much he must suffer for my name" (Acts 9:16, NIV 1984).

These words leaped off the page at me, a *rhema* statement, and I knew that the Lord was speaking to me and my own situation. For it is in suffering for our Lord that we each gain strength. I feel that God is in a teaching moment with me, and I see it in many of you as I listen to your day-to-day struggles with marital strife, separation, and even divorce. God is faithful, ever faithful to his people. And we *are* his people. He calls each of us to stand strong for our covenant marriage vows, even when the world laughs at us and when our spouses reject us and God's Word about marriage.

Further on in the book of Acts, we read Paul's account to King Agrippa of his encounter with Jesus.

> I said, "Who are you, Master?" The voice answered, "I am Jesus, the One you're hunting down like an animal. But now, up on your feet—I have a job for you. I've handpicked you to be a servant and witness to what's happened today, and to what I am going to show you. I'm sending you off to open the eyes of the outsiders so they can see the difference between dark and light, and choose light, see the difference between Satan and God, and choose God. I'm sending you off to present my offer of sins forgiven, and a place in the family, inviting them into the company of those who begin real living by believing in me." What could I do, King Agrippa? I couldn't just walk away from a vision like that! I became an obedient believer on the spot. I started preaching this life-change—this radical turn to God and everything it meant in everyday life—right there in Damascus, went on to Jerusalem and the surrounding countryside, and from there to the whole world.

> Acts 26:15–19 (MSG)

It struck me as I read these verses that as I stand, I am standing for and with Jesus. I am standing before a dark world, proclaiming that Jesus is Lord. He is sending me (and you) into this world, strong and steady in our faith, to proclaim the truth about our marriage vows, of their seriousness and their permanence. He is sending you and me into the dark world of Satan to open their spiritual eyes to the sin and horrors of divorce. There is no spiritual chasm that Jesus cannot bridge. We are his foot soldiers, his ambassadors. Through our own personal sufferings, we must stand tall. In doing so, there is no amount of sin against God or degree of hatred for God's Word about marriage and divorce that cannot be overcome by proclaiming Christ's love. His love is stronger than anything Satan can throw at us. So in our own personal sufferings, listen to Paul's message to the Corinthians.

> And lest I should be exalted above measure by the abundance of the revelations, a thorn in the flesh was given to me, a messenger of Satan to buffet me, lest I be exalted above measure. Concerning this thing I pleaded with the Lord three times that it might depart from me. And He said to me, "My grace is sufficient for you, for My strength is made perfect in weakness." Therefore most gladly I will rather boast in my infirmities, that the power of Christ may rest upon me. Therefore I take pleasure in infirmities, in reproaches, in needs, in persecutions, in distresses, for Christ's sake. For when I am weak, then I am strong.
>
> 2 Corinthians 12:7–10 (NKJV)

What is Paul's message? *For when I am weak, then I am strong.* Have you ever considered that our Lord and Savior, Jesus Christ, has given each of us a sacred mission—that of standing firm before a fallen world for our covenant marriage vows? Our marriage situation may well be our own personal thorn in our flesh sent directly from Satan to torment us. But our Lord tells us, "*My grace is sufficient for you, for My strength is made perfect in weakness.*" I know personally that it is by God's grace that I live in triumph day by day.

So, fellow standers, walk by faith and stand in faith, knowing that it is through your present sufferings that God's ultimate victory in your marriage will be accomplished.

Standing firm until parted by death.

As Standers, We Are Aliens

Have you ever given a thought to the fact that you and I are aliens? I don't mean undocumented visitors on US soil, nor do I mean a space creature or a Martian. I am speaking about our walk with Jesus Christ as we stand for our marriage and our covenant marriage vows. As we speak about our Christian walk, we soon realize that we are viewed differently by the world and by the Christian community. Yet that becomes our witness. Peter speaks to this in 1 Peter.

> Dear friends, I urge you, as aliens and strangers in the world, to abstain from sinful desires, which war against your soul. Live such good lives among the pagans that, though they accuse you of doing wrong, they may see your good deeds and glorify God on the day he visits us.

> 1 Peter 2:11–12 (NIV 1984)

The term *pagan* may seem harsh, but Peter was speaking about unbelievers. In the context of this devotional, the term *pagan* describes the views of many in the church today as they consider *covenant* and *divorce* and *remarriage.* We need to realize that these are weighty subjects that the world and most of our churches choose to ignore or not address. It is sad as so many families are fractured by divorce, and so many children are raised in an environment of unstable family structure and values. Thus, we are looked upon as *aliens* when we state that we are standing for our own dead or dying marriages. Is this a strange idea? It must be that the ideas are foreign, they are alien, and the world refuses to dig deep enough into God's Word for a clearer understanding.

As we live with our alien status, we must not become complacent. We must resist the urge to conform ourselves to others who are uncomfortable with our views and values. No one really likes being labeled an alien, an outsider. Yet many of us are made to feel like outsiders when we stand up and declare our views on covenant. We must resist the temptation of confining or isolating ourselves from the world. Just because our beliefs about covenant make others around us uncomfortable doesn't make it okay for us to hide our views. Study the words of Jesus shortly before his crucifixion as he prayed for his disciples.

> I have given them Your word; and the world has hated them because they are not of the world, just as I am not of the world. I do not pray that You should take them out of the world, but that You should keep them from the evil one. They are not of the world, just as I am not of the world. Sanctify them by Your truth. Your word is truth. As You sent Me into the world, I also have sent them into the world.
>
> John 17:14–18 (NKJV)

Jesus taught that we are aliens in this fallen world. We are aliens because of our commitment to covenant, and thus, we are not of this world. Do you see your challenge? Jesus is sending us out into the world, sanctified by the truth as found in the Word of God. As Jesus prays for each of us, he asks our Heavenly Father to protect us from Satan and his domain. Our message about covenant is strange as it does not follow the world's view, and it makes those of this world very uncomfortable. We are truly aliens in a world that is under the influence of Satan. In the Sermon on the Mount, Jesus tells us how we are to witness.

Here's another way to put it: You're here to be light, bringing out the God-colors in the world. God is not a secret to be kept. We're going public with this, as public as a city on a hill. If I make you light-bearers, you don't think I'm going to hide you under a bucket, do you? I'm putting you on a light stand. Now that I've put you there on a hilltop, on a light stand—shine! Keep open house; be generous with your lives. By opening up to others, you'll prompt people to open up with God, this generous Father in heaven.

Matthew 5:14–16 (MSG)

Our walk and our stand with Jesus is this: marriage is a lifelong commitment that ends only with the death of one of the partners. Thus, in this world, we are aliens with an alien message: the truth about covenant and covenant marriage vows. This journey we are on is a difficult one, but not an impossible one. Stand firm for your covenant marriage vows and for the rebuilding of your own marriage upon the Solid Rock of Jesus Christ. Do not give up or give in. Let your light shine forth as aliens in this sinful world.

Be proud of your identity! You *are* different. Your identity is this: you are a Christian and an alien with a message about the marriage covenant. So stand firm![11]

Standing firm until parted by death.

Point Of No Return

This phrase is one that we don't frequently hear today. In days gone by, people flying over the ocean would hear the pilot come on the PA system and state, "We have passed the point of no return." This was to inform the passengers that a point in their flight path had been reached where the destination was closer than their point of departure. It was significant because if problems existed with one of the passengers or crew or perhaps the aircraft itself, the nearest help was to be found at their destination, not where the flight started. Frequently, in those days, that meant that there was not enough fuel to turn around and take them back to where they started. There was no turning back, just pressing on. While this phrase still exists today, it is just not routinely broadcast to airline passengers.

This phrase can also be applied to events that occur in our everyday lives, especially in our relationships. More specifically, I am speaking about events in our marriages. When Adam fell in the garden, mankind became flawed. One of those flaws involves how we relate to our loved ones. No matter how well-adjusted we might be, interpersonal relationships between a husband and a wife leave much to be desired at times. Talk to any couple in a long-standing Christian marriage, and they will tell you that they got there by a lot of hard work. Marriage is a work in progress until the day we die. So to set the framework for a Christian marriage, let us look at Paul's message to the Ephesians as he explains how a man and woman are to relate in a Christian marriage.

> Submit to one another out of reverence for Christ. Wives, submit to your husbands as to the Lord. For the husband is the head of the wife as Christ is the head of the church, his body, of which he is the Savior. Now as the church submits to Christ, so also wives should submit to their husbands in everything. Husbands, love your wives, just as Christ loved the church and gave himself up for her, to make her holy, cleansing her by the washing with water through the word, and to present her to himself as a radiant church, without stain or wrinkle or any other blemish, but holy and blameless. In this same way, husbands ought to love their wives as their own bodies. He who loves his wife loves himself. After all, no one ever hated his own body, but he feeds and cares for it, just as Christ does the church— for we are members of his body. "For this reason a man will leave his father and mother and be united to his wife,

and the two will become one flesh." This is a profound mystery—but I am talking about Christ and the church. However, each one of you also must love his wife as he loves himself, and the wife must respect her husband.

Ephesians 5:21–33 (NIV 1984)

This is the *gold standard* of what a Christian marriage should look like. Yet so many of us have failed so miserably along the way, leading to dysfunctional marriages, separation, and more tragically, divorce. It is when the decision to pursue divorce enters our marriage that we have truly, from a relational point of view, reached the *point of no return.* But God has not had the last say-so. Those who are standing with God for the healing of their marriages know this one thing:

And looking at *them* Jesus said to them, "With people this is impossible, but with God all things are possible."

Matthew 19:26 (NASB)

Yes, when we humans find it impossible to mend our marriages, it is then that we feel that the point of no return has been reached; however, God can make the impossible possible. Thus, the underlying secret to marriage reconciliation is *God.* Without God in the picture, reconciliation is transient at best. And where does that reconciliation start? It starts with our own personal reconciliation to God. Through our reconciliation to God, our personal lives are changed. We have not reached that *point of no return* because God has intervened. However remember this, you and I cannot change our spouse, but God can. Our part in this pulling back from the *point of no return* in our marriages is to release our spouses into the capable hands of God through prayer. In Colossians, Paul writes the following.

> For God in all his fullness was pleased to live in Christ,
> and through him God reconciled everything to himself.
> He made peace with everything in heaven and on earth
> by means of Christ's blood on the cross.... Yet now he has
> reconciled you to himself through the death of Christ in
> his physical body.
>
> Colossians 1:19–20, 22a (NLT)

But God, he is our answer. He is the God of the resurrection, the God of healing, the Great Physician. With God, all things are possible. His timing is perfect despite our impatience. With God, there is no marriage relationship beyond redemption. With God, there is no *point of no return!* Put your trust in God. He will resurrect your marriage using the same powers he used to raise his Son, Jesus Christ, from the dead. If you believe in Easter and the miracle of the resurrection, believe in God's ability and powers to resurrect your own marriage.

So, fellow standers or potential standers, with God, *all things are possible*, and there is no *point of no return.*

Standing firm until parted by death.

Waiting For The Storm To Pass

Waiting for the storm to pass...a strange title for this devotional! It comes from a blog written by a Christian friend talking about his journey and fight to survive cancer. Being a cancer survivor myself, these words resonated volumes with me and should resonate in yet another way with each of us as we battle Satan in his relentless task of breaking up marriages and families. Place yourself in this statement:

> Life is not about waiting for the storm to pass; it's learning
> how to dance in the rain!

Yes, our lives (that is our dysfunctional marriages) aren't about waiting for the hammer to fall, then for the storm to abate, and finally for the sun to shine. Each of us finds ourselves caught in a whirling storm of life dealing with a dysfunctional marriage, separation, and/or divorce and the desolation of our family unit. Satan is hard at work, 24-7, to disrupt Christ's Church, His body—that is you and your family! Has your new situation resulted in financial hardship leading to (1) loss of your house and (2) not enough funds for food, medical care, clothing, and other basic necessities? We need to be proactive. Our God is here with you each step of the way. Thus, you need to *learn how to dance in the rain* while Satan is hard at work trying to discourage you.

> Keep a cool head. Stay alert. The Devil is poised to pounce, and would like nothing better than to catch you napping. Keep your guard up. You're not the only ones plunged into these hard times. It's the same with Christians all over the world. So keep a firm grip on the faith. The suffering won't last forever. It won't be long before this generous God who has great plans for us in Christ—eternal and glorious plans they are!—will have you put together and on your feet for good. He gets the last word; yes, he does.

> 1 Peter 5:8–11 (MSG)

God challenges us to *learn how to dance in the rain*. Waiting for the storm to pass leaves one in limbo. Living a Christian life involves being active in one's family, one's church, and one's community. When a Christian family fractures due to marital problems, one's participation in family, church, and community becomes strained; the future often looks bleak. God says to *learn how to dance in the rain*.

So what does one do when faced with marriage breakup? For the Christian, we seek God's help through prayer, the Word, and like-minded Christian friends and church leaders. These are friends and leaders who support you in saving your marriage and family, who do not advise running to the nearest lawyer, courtroom, and judge. Folks, divorce is not the answer. Jesus Christ is the answer!

A careful evaluation of almost every dysfunctional family reveals that Jesus Christ was not at the center of that family unit. What are we to do? A good Christian counselor will suggest that we should evaluate our own personal relationship with Jesus Christ. For myself, I realized that I was living with one foot in the world and one foot in the church. Personal study of the Word, personal prayer, and personal worship in my situation led to a personal decision to accept Jesus Christ as my Lord and Savior.

In dysfunctional families, there is almost always more than one family member at fault: both spouses, one or more of the kids, etc. Jesus Christ is missing as the central focus of that family unit. To see the sun shine, one needs to *learn how to dance in the rain.* Many hard decisions, actions, etc., have to take place before reconciliation and healing occurs. Jesus Christ is sifting you, molding you, preparing you for greater things.

> My friends, don't be surprised at the painful things that you are now suffering, which are testing your faith. Don't think that something strange is happening to you. But you should be happy that you are sharing in Christ's sufferings.... But if you suffer because you are a "Christ-follower," don't be ashamed. You should praise God for that name. It is time for judging to begin. That judging will begin with God's family. If it begins with us, then what will happen to those who don't accept the Good News of God? "If it is hard for even a good person to be saved, what will happen to the one who is against God and full of sin?" So if God wants you to suffer, you should trust your lives to him. He is the one who made you, and you can trust him. So continue to do good.
>
> 1 Peter 4:12–13a; 16–19 (ERV)

Survival after a family breakup is painful, very painful, yet you will survive. There is light at the end of the tunnel, a future based upon faith and hope. Consider the following scriptures as you *learn to dance in the rain* and weather the storm of your dysfunctional marriage.

> The fundamental fact of existence is that this trust in God, this faith, is the firm foundation under everything that makes life worth living. It's our handle on what we can't see.
>
> Hebrews 11:1 (MSG)

> Let not your heart be troubled; you believe in God, believe also in Me.
>
> John 14:1 (NKJV)

> "For I know the plans that I have for you," declares the LORD, "plans for welfare and not for calamity to give you a future and a hope. Then you will call upon Me and come and pray to Me, and I will listen to you. You will seek Me and find *Me* when you search for Me with all your heart."
>
> Jeremiah 29:11–13 (NASB)[12]

Standing firm until parted by death.

My Circumstances Are My Witness

Greetings. What a wonderful life each of you have! Each new day brings you both blessings and challenges. "Hey, wait a minute!" you exclaim. "Stop and rethink your statement." You ask, "What are you talking about? Did someone hit you on the head and confuse you? Here I am with my marriage and family falling apart, and you make a crazy remark about a wonderful life!" Yes, that *is* what I said. But before you start looking for something else to read, hear me out.

Yes, you do have a wonderful life because of one person. You have an awesome God who loves you more than you can ever imagine, whether you are a sinner or a saint. You have the opportunity to develop a unique relationship with this God, so keep on reading.

Our God planned before the beginning of time to send his only Son to live among us for a short time and allowed him to be crucified for your sins and mine. His Son thus took away the sting of death that we all face. He told us that if we believe in his Son, we will inherit Christ's righteousness and receive the gift of the Holy Spirit, thus gaining eternal life with our triune God.

> For God so loved the world, that He gave His only begotten Son, that whoever believes in Him shall not perish, but have eternal life. For God did not send the Son into the world to judge the world, but that the world might be saved through Him.
>
> John 3:16–17 (NASB)

Yes, you do have the opportunity for a wonderful life. The choice is yours. By accepting Jesus Christ as God's Son and your Savior and Lord, you can then seek his forgiveness for your personal sins. This ensures your eternal life with God. Yes, you can have a wonderful life. Failure to recognize Jesus Christ for who he is leads to an eternity without him; definitely not a good choice or a wonderful life.

Still you ask again, "How can I be having a wonderful life when my marriage and family are falling apart? Where can I get help?"

Oh, taste and see that the LORD is good; Blessed is the man who trusts in Him!

Psalm 34:8 (NKJV)

Other versions state "takes refuge in him or run to him." God is your Helper, your Counselor, your Refuge, and your trusted Friend when you are hurting. By accepting and trusting Jesus Christ as Savior and Lord, you become part of his royal family and experience the comfort that comes from that relationship. Those of you who have yet to accept the promise of John 3:16–17 need to consider seriously God's offer of salvation and eternal life.

A relationship with Jesus Christ leads to many blessings, yet some are strange in that they come to us through pain and various troubles (i.e., Satan's attacks on our marriages and families). It is at these times that those in Christ experience Christ's wisdom and comfort by trusting him. Trying to understand your situation in your own flesh will fail, but through trust, Christ through the Holy Spirit will come alive in you. In these special times, you will receive God's special peace, a peace that is beyond understanding. He offers it as part of the free gift of the indwelling of the Holy Spirit in your heart that you receive through baptism.

Jesus answered, "Believe me when I say that everyone must be born from water and the Spirit. Anyone who is not born from water and the Spirit cannot enter God's kingdom.

John 3:5 (ERV)

Through baptism, you share symbolically in Christ's death, burial, and resurrection. When you go under the water, you die to your old self. Under the water, you are buried with Christ. Then when you come up out of the water, you share in Christ's resurrection; you are born again (born of water). At that time, you receive a most wonderful gift from God, the gift of the Holy

Spirit who will dwell in your heart forever (born of the Spirit). He is a real person, just as Jesus and our Heavenly Father are real persons. The Holy Spirit is your Counselor, your Advocate, and your Guide. He empowers you, guides and directs you, teaches you, and makes you holy. While Jesus could only be with mankind physically but for a short time in a finite place some two thousand years ago, the Holy Spirit resides in your heart forever. He is not limited by time or space.

Now as to your troubles, in the Message, we read, "I've told you all this so that trusting me, you will be unshakable and assured, deeply at peace. In this godless world you will continue to experience difficulties. But take heart! I've conquered the world" (John 16:33, MSG).

Despite your troubles, you are a child of God, a bona fide member of God's royal family. You are coheirs with Jesus Christ to the kingdom of heaven. God's peace reigns in your heart. You know that you can trust him. Your witness is to live out Christ's love before your spouse, your family, and the world. Stand firm for your marriage vows. Know God's will for your life. To live in God's will is truly a wonderful life. Your daily circumstances filtered through your faith walk defines your witness. So stand tall. Remember, in Christ, you have been changed.

> And do not be conformed to this world, but be transformed by the renewing of your mind, that you may prove what *is* that good and acceptable and perfect will of God.
>
> Romans 12:2 (NKJV)

Standing firm until parted by death.

Running From God

Think about it. Running from God! Strange as it sounds, many people try to run from God. We can run away from our homes, run away from our friends, run from an accident, run away from the army, and also run from a murder or robbery, but run away from God? There are so many scenarios dealing with running, both physical and emotional. But run away from God? God our Creator, God our Heavenly Father, God our Provider, God our best Friend.

God knows all and sees all. Where can we hide? In a recent message, Andy Stanley made this statement: "You can run from God, but you cannot outrun God!" Who do we think we are fooling as we turn our backs on God and our spouse and walk/run away from our marriages? Didn't we promise before God and our spouse to be faithful to our covenant vows until parted by death? Yet now that sacred vow, that covenant vow spoken before God on our wedding day, is broken. God does not violate this covenant; our spouse does! And so as they break covenant, leaving the marriage, they are running from God and you and I. Little do they realize in the heat of the moment that they cannot outrun God.

When we look to Scripture, the most famous runner was Jonah. He was a prophet who ministered from 800 to 750 BC in the northern kingdom of Israel.

> The LORD gave this message to Jonah son of Amittai: "Get up and go to the great city of Nineveh. Announce my judgment against it because I have seen how wicked its people are." But Jonah got up and went in the opposite direction to get away from the LORD. He went down to the port of Joppa, where he found a ship leaving for Tarshish. He bought a ticket and went on board, hoping to escape from the LORD by sailing to Tarshish.
>
> Jonah 1:1–3 (NLT)

Notice the wording: "But Jonah...went in the opposite direction to get away from the Lord...hoping to escape from the Lord." Jonah was obviously not thinking straight, thinking that he could outrun God. After all, in that day and time, Tarshish and Nineveh were basically at the opposite ends of the known world. Perhaps he could get lost in that faraway city, dropping out of sight. But remember what is stated above. You can run from God, but you cannot outrun God. In Jonah's fear of the Ninevites, his thinking was scrambled.

We know the story of the terrible storm at sea that threatened to sink Jonah's ship. The sailors questioned Jonah. "Jonah told the men he was running away from the LORD. The men became very afraid when they learned this. They asked Jonah, 'What terrible thing did you do against your God?'" (Jonah 1:10, ERV).[13]

Is this not the same thing that happens when our prodigal spouses run out on our marriages? Here our prodigal spouses run not only from you and I, but they are also running from God. While we may not know our prodigal spouses' whereabouts, God does, and they cannot hide from Him. In the New Testament, the story of the prodigal son in Luke 15 tells a slightly different story in that the son wished to go live his life on his own terms. He was running away from his father's control. Circumstances were such that when his situation deteriorated, he returned home to his father. Here the father figure is God, and the prodigal son is mankind.

> When he finally came to his senses, he said to himself, "At home even the hired servants have food enough to spare, and here I am dying of hunger! I will go home to my father and say, 'Father, I have sinned against both heaven and you....' So he returned home to his father. And while he was still a long way off, his father saw him coming. Filled with love and compassion, he ran to his son, embraced him, and kissed him.
>
> Luke 15:17–18, 20 (NLT)

In these two stories, we can see our prodigal spouses running from a relationship, from authority, from a promise, running from God. Yet in the story of the prodigal son, we see the redemption that awaits our prodigal spouses as they return home to their covenant vows taken before God and before you and me. As God offers forgiveness to the prodigal son, we likewise must offer forgiveness to our prodigal spouses.

We often hear the stories from returned prodigals of the miserable situations they lived under while on the run. Remember, *you can run from God, but you cannot outrun God*. He will find the prodigals and, with love, redirect them home to their loving standing spouses.

So I say stand firm for your covenant marriage vows! God will honor your stand.

Standing firm until parted by death.

Plan B: Do I Need One?

Standers, it is time to take a personal inventory of your life. As you take stock of your marriage and your family and the status of your personal relationships that are in crisis, much confusion reigns. Well-meaning family and friends, your church family, colleagues at work, etc., offer a myriad of solutions and advice. Some are good and sound while others are worldly (full of pitfalls and disappointments). Divorce is mentioned most often. You ask yourself, "Which way do I turn?" The world would say, "Get on with your life. You deserve to find happiness. There is someone out there that is just right for you." With divorce rates at or over 50 percent of those professing to be Christian (essentially the same percentage as among nonbelievers), the road ahead definitely looks bleak. Basically, all this advice could be lumped into the category of *plan B*. But for the Christian, for the believer seeking Jesus Christ's truths about marriage and family relationships, there is no plan B.

Hold on! Are you saying that plan B and divorce are not options? What about my happiness? What about my rights? What about my freedom to get on with my life? What about finding that right person for me? Even my job, my retirement plans, and my investment plans have a contingency plan, a plan B. So why not my personal life? I deserve something better than what I have now. Divorce offers me an option, a way out! Or does it?

Think about the disruption of family ties, of family legacy. Think about the financial disruption of the family income when often there is just enough to get by when the family unit is together under one roof. And probably the most devastating consequences of divorce are the emotional scars on your children as the family unit breaks up. Despite statements that the kids will get over it, long-term studies show that those scars last a lifetime. Children from broken homes also have a higher incidence of failed marriage relationships as adults. Children (your children) need and deserve to be raised whenever possible in a two-parent family by their biological parents. So what are your options?

It appears that the divorce option must be out of the question. We know what God thinks of divorce.

> The LORD, the God of Israel, says, "I hate divorce, and I hate the cruel things that men do. So protect your spiritual unity. Don't cheat on your wife."
>
> Malachi 2:16 (ERV)

> "I hate divorce," says the God of Israel. God-of-the-Angel-Armies says, "I hate the violent dismembering of the 'one flesh' of marriage." So watch yourselves. Don't let your guard down. Don't cheat."
>
> Malachi 2:16 (MSG)

Doesn't that phrase from the Message hit you hard in your gut? "The violent dismembering of the *one flesh* of marriage." I had those feelings as I went through the death of my own marriage relationship. So what is the answer? The answer is Jesus Christ. You need to lean on him, look to him, pray to him, walk with him, and seek his advice in all your marriage and family problems. But you say, "Is he all that I have? I want more than that!"

Consider this: *when God is all you have, that is when you have all you need!* I repeat, *All* you need! Jesus Christ is the answer, first, last, and in between. He knows your needs.

> Come to me, all you who are weary and burdened, and I will give you rest. Take my yoke upon you and learn from me, for I am gentle and humble in heart, and you will find rest for your souls. For my yoke is easy and my burden is light.
>
> Matthew 11:28–30 (NIV 1984)

> Are you tired? Worn out? Burned out on religion? Come to me. Get away with me and you'll recover your life. I'll show you how to take a real rest. Walk with me and work with me—watch how I do it. Learn the unforced rhythms of grace. I won't lay anything heavy or ill-fitting on you. Keep company with me and you'll learn to live freely and lightly. Matthew 11:28–30 (MSG)

> Jesus answered, "I am the way and the truth and the life. No one comes to the Father except through me."
>
> John 14:6 (NIV 1984)

So understand this: in God's playbook for your life, there is no plan B! There is only him. So turn to Jesus Christ for your every need. *When God is all you have, that is when you have all you need!*

Standing firm until parted by death.

The Wilderness Road Walk

Take a moment and reflect upon your stand with Jesus Christ for the resurrection and healing of your marriage relationship. For many of us, it can be a time of great pain and unhappiness, a time filled with anger, distrust, betrayal, you name it. Yet for the Christian, it is a time when we are not in fellowship with our spouse, our one flesh mate. As we stand with our Lord and Savior, we need to reflect and understand the impact of this time apart from our spouse.

> And He was there in the wilderness forty days, tempted by Satan, and was with the wild beasts; and the angels ministered to Him.
>
> Mark 1:13 (NKJV)

We know from the Gospels that following Jesus Christ's baptism by John the Baptizer, Christ was led into the desert by the Holy Spirit for a time of reflection and maturing by his Father. And it was here that Christ showed his strength and wisdom in throwing off the temptations of Satan. In like manner, God led the Israelites on a forty-year sojourn in the wilderness to purify and strengthen his people for their destiny in the Promised Land. They had failed the first time under Moses, and God sent them into the desert for this time of wandering and his purification.

"I say this because I know the plans that I have for you."
This message is from the LORD. "I have good plans for

you. I don't plan to hurt you. I plan to give you hope and a good future. Then you will call my name. You will come to me and pray to me, and I will listen to you. You will search for me, and when you search for me with all your heart, you will find me.

Jeremiah 29:11–13 (ERV)

I often look at my own stand as a time in the desert, a walk down the wilderness road. It has been a time when I come face-to-face with my own eternity. It has been a time when I began to study deeply God's Word, to reflect, to pray, and to hear what God wishes to reveal to me. Unencumbered by the day-to-day distractions of conflict with my wife, it has been a time when I have come close to my Lord and Savior and my Heavenly Father. I have found great beauty and peace in my wanderings along that wilderness road.

In days gone by and even today, there are retreats or long sojourns to quiet places that allow each of us to come in touch with our Maker. In times of reflection, we hope to understand what has gone on before that has brought us to this present time in our lives. It is a time for setting realistic goals of spiritual and emotional growth, a time for making resolutions concerning our marriage relationships.

Wilderness road time is not wasted time, for as each day goes by, you and I are one day closer to victory in our personal walk with Christ and in the resurrection and healing of our marriage relationships. Wilderness road time allows us time to take baby steps, one step and one day at a time. While we may wish to shorten our wilderness road time, understand this: our marriages did not fall apart overnight, and they will not be healed overnight. Time is necessary for our personal growth with Christ and for the Holy Spirit to work on our spouse's heart. That frequently occurs on the other side of the mountain where we cannot see. Here is where great restraint is needed; here is where trust and faith in God's promises of healing of our marriages is paramount. It is in our wilderness road walk with God that he gives us the strength and wisdom to survive our stand. Use your time on your wilderness road walk to find out who you are in Christ. You will never be disappointed.

I know personally that my stand with my Lord and Savior is time that I would not trade for anything. It is here that I came to know God. And you can also. Many of us who profess to be Christians question our faith as our marriages disintegrate. We ask where God is in all of this. The wilderness road is the path to wholeness and freedom in Christ. Take it. Find out who you are in Christ, and you will never, never be sorry!

> So anyone who thinks they are standing strong should be careful that they don't fall…. But you can trust God. He will not let you be tempted more than you can bear. But when you are tempted, God will also give you a way to escape that temptation. Then you will be able to endure it.
>
> 1 Corinthians 10:12, 13b (ERV)

> So let us come boldly to the throne of our gracious God. There we will receive his mercy, and we will find grace to help us when we need it most.
>
> Hebrews 4:16 (NLT)

Your challenge is this: walk the wilderness road. Be quiet, listen, and you will find God's grace, and he will bless your stand.

Standing firm until parted by death.

Never Quit, Never Give Up

Love never fails.

—1 Corinthians 13:8a (NKJV)

Let's take a trip down memory lane. Once upon a time, a man and a woman were attracted to each other. They fell in love. As time progressed, the man proposed to the woman, and a marriage followed. Vows were exchanged in the presence of an official (minister, priest, elder, judge, etc.), but more importantly, in the presence of God. God was present even in a civil ceremony. One part of those vows so often overlooked or forgotten by the couple is *until parted by death.* This is part of most religious marriage ceremonies and also part of some secular marriage ceremonies. This reminds us that we made a marriage covenant before God and our spouse that ends only with death.

As we continue to stroll down memory lane, most if not all of us remember that we have experienced some turmoil from time to time in our marriages. If that turmoil gets serious and seems unresolvable and we take our problems to God and not to the world, we find healing solutions to those problems. However, the solution that the world offers us is that we should discard our current spouse and move on to the next one. What a sad commentary on the picture of marriage that God originally had in mind when he created marriage in the Garden for all mankind.

I give you a new command: Love each other. You must love each other just as I loved you.

John 13:34 (ERV)

Those who really love me are the ones who not only know my commands but also obey them. My Father will love such people, and I will love them. I will make myself known to them.

John 14:21 (ERV)

For those of us who seek God's will for our lives and marriages, there is so much more. The scriptures above suggest that if we have a love for our spouse like Jesus Christ has for each of us, then our marriages can survive and be healed. This is agape love, that special unconditional love and closeness that God has for his children (you and I). Jesus calls us to imitate his love.

So when we find ourselves in the throes of a dysfunctional marriage, we are to look to Jesus Christ, the only one who can fix and heal our relationship with our spouse. We are to hang in there, never quit, never give up. Why never give up? Because we took an oath, a vow before God and our spouse that we would see this marriage through until we are parted by death. Do you remember that you promised this on your wedding day? You are to persevere. And with God's help, you can.

You must be patient. After you have done what God wants, you will get what he promised you.

Hebrews 10:36 (ERV)

What has he promised? For the stander who is standing with Jesus Christ, it is your reconciliation with God and later the healing of your marriage relationship. You are not to quit or give up. Such healing may take weeks, months, or even years before you are reconciled with your spouse. However, God desires your reconciliation to himself first and then later will come your reconciliation with your spouse. Consider your marital problems as sin in the eyes of God; so look to him who can heal, Jesus Christ.

> We have all these great people around us as examples. Their lives tell us what faith means. So we, too, should run the race that is before us and never quit. We should remove from our lives anything that would slow us down and the sin that so often makes us fall. We must never stop looking to Jesus. He is the leader of our faith, and he is the one who makes our faith complete. He suffered death on a cross. But he accepted the shame of the cross as if it were nothing because of the joy he could see waiting for him. And now he is sitting at the right side of God's throne. Think about Jesus. He patiently endured the angry insults that sinful people were shouting at him. Think about him so that you won't get discouraged and stop trying.

> Hebrews 12:1–3 (ERV)

> And we say that those who accepted their troubles with patience now have God's blessing. You have heard about Job's patience. You know that after all his troubles, the Lord helped him. This shows that the Lord is full of mercy and is kind.

> James 5:11 (ERV)

So the message is this: don't quit or give up! Don't *grow weary and lose heart*. Seek God's help for the restoration and healing of your marriage relationship. Remember Job's perseverance. *The Lord is full of compassion and mercy.* God can and will heal your hurting marriage if you put your trust in him and don't give up. Final thought: *never quit, never give up!*

Standing firm until parted by death.

Set Apart

Today is a new day. Yesterday is gone, and as this new day dawns, it has the hopes (and fears) that yet another new day brings. Surely, we will find a new beginning today in all of our dreams and endeavors that represent our fragile marriage relationship. The blur of yesterday and the days, weeks, months, and perhaps years that have gone before are just that—a blur. The once utopian marriage that you entered into with your spouse is in that blur of the past. Your marriage relationship has now evolved into a dysfunctional mess of lies, fits of anger, perhaps violence, separation, and even divorce. What happened? Is there any hope that you can salvage your marriage relationship and your family? The good news is that there is hope in the Good News. That hope comes through a personal relationship with our Lord and Savior, Jesus Christ.

As you woke up this new day, there is hope of a better today and a still better tomorrow. As we strengthen or establish anew our ongoing personal relationship with Jesus Christ, he gives us hope. Hebrews says, "Now faith is being sure of what we hope for and certain of what we do not see" (Hebrews 11:1, NIV 1984). When we put our faith in our Creator, there is truly a new day and a new beginning. As we begin to study his Word, God's truths begin to make sense and take hold of our lives. Things begin to fall in place. As we begin to recognize the mistakes we made in the past, they become a blur. Yet each of us, as we seek God's solution for our lives, realize sooner or later that we are being set apart from the world. Our values are his and not those of the world. We realize that the blur of the past is due to being wrapped up in the things of the world and not in the things of God.

> Know that the LORD has set apart the godly for himself;
> the LORD will hear when I call to him.

> Psalm 4:3 (NIV 1984)

Set yourselves apart for a holy life. Live a holy life, because I am God, your God. Do what I tell you; live the way I tell you. I am the God who makes you holy.

Leviticus 20:7–8 (MSG)

Thus you are to be holy to Me, for I the LORD am holy; and I have set you apart from the peoples to be Mine.

Leviticus 20:26 (NASB)

Do this because you are a people set apart as holy to God, your God. God, your God, chose you out of all the people on Earth for himself as a cherished, personal treasure.

Deuteronomy 7:6 (MSG)

All these verses point to one extremely important fact: we have been set apart by God to be his special people. In much the same way, when each of us finds ourselves in the throes of marital discord, separation, or divorce, God speaks to each of his children who will listen. He calls us to stand for our marriage vows of *in sickness or in health, for richer or poorer, for better or for worse* and the one so many of us don't understand, *until parted by death*! We have been *set apart* by God as a special witness of our obedience to God's will. We are a chosen people, much like the Jewish nation was God's chosen people. He wanted them to demonstrate to the world what it means to be obedient to God's covenant. We are chosen by God to stand before the world saying that covenants (especially marriage covenants) are more important than short-term comfort or relationships. What we are doing is related to our eternal life and the eternal life of our spouse and our eternal destiny with Jesus Christ, God the Father, and the Holy Spirit. *We have been set apart!*

Yes, you and I have been set apart. We have been set apart by our Creator. We are a beacon of hope and a promise of eternal life with Jesus to a fallen world. We are special, set apart by divine appointment to stand for our marriage relationships. God has called us to partner with him in rebuilding our marriage relationships. *We have been set apart.*

We are special, set apart. Made in God's image and endowed with our own desire for a personal relationship with our Creator, we are indeed very special—*we have been set apart.*

Standing firm until parted by death.

Movin' On

Once upon a time, each of our lives looked simple. Times were good, and we were hopeful of a bright future as we turned away from the preacher or judge who married us and entered the world of *the married.* For some, life did proceed toward the good times, but for more than 50 percent of us, marital discord and divorce loomed upon the horizon. The world (Satan) beckoned to us, leading us down the path toward marital death. Family, friends, perhaps our spouse, and even sadly, many of our clergy suggested that we should move on. Movin' on is what many of us are inclined to do. When our life's dream of a happy marriage, of raising children, and of growing old together crumbles, movin' on seems like the only answer. However, God has a better plan: we need to put our trust in him to change each of us and mend our broken hearts and marriage. Movin' on in the world's dictionary (divorce, new spouse or spouses, etc.) is not in God's plan. However, God has his own movin' on plan. One of the most quoted passages in the Bible reveals his plan for movin' on is the twenty-third psalm (NIV 1984) quoted below, phrase by phrase.

The Lord is my shepherd, I shall not be in want.

When marital troubles arise, to whom should we look? Friends, family, our pastor, the world? While any of these may have a solution that seems plausible, might I suggest we turn to the one who created us, the *Lord*. He set the world in motion, and he has all our needs mapped out. Notice the first verse: "The Lord is my shepherd, I shall not be in want." He has our back covered. We can totally depend upon him. He is our Protector. Might I suggest that when marital troubles arise, we try movin' on with the Lord rather than with the world.

> He makes me lie down in green pastures, he leads me beside quiet waters, he restores my soul. He guides me in paths of righteousness for his name's sake.

When separation and/or divorce leave our situation uncertain, our Lord provides. By walking with him, he provides us with peace, hope, and comfort. He also intervenes by supplying our physical needs as many can attest. Our Lord starts healing our hearts as he guides us in paths of righteousness.

> Even though I walk through the valley of the shadow of death, I will fear no evil, for you are with me; your rod and your staff, they comfort me.

During these times, many worldly pressures will attack us. We truly are walking through a valley of death, the death of a relationship, the death of our marriage. But we have our *Big Brother* with us, our Lord and Savior. He is our Shield and Defender, and he puts his arm around us and pulls us close. If you listen closely, you can hear the heart of God speaking to you, "Never will I leave you; never will I forsake you" (Hebrews 13:5b, NIV 1984). He is our Heavenly Father, and Jesus Christ, his Son, is our *Big Brother*.

> You prepare a table before me in the presence of my enemies. You anoint my head with oil; my cup overflows.

Our Heavenly Father provides both physical needs and spiritual needs. Many of us who are without our spouse suffer from meager means to sustain our family. Yet God is our Provider. While we feel at times that our spouse is our enemy, our true enemy is Satan, who is manipulating our spouse. Our Lord invites us to share his table and anoints us with his blessings, showing us that we are his honored children. Our God is our Heavenly Father, yet he (Jesus Christ) is also our brother as we face our current and future situations. A cupful of blessings overflows for those who stand strong.

> Surely goodness and love will follow me all the days of my
> life, and I will dwell in the house of the LORD forever.

Our enemy, Satan, would have us just give up and move on into a new relationship. Such is often the advice of family, friends, and even Christian leaders. However, we surprise all of them for we are movin' on in our new relationship with Jesus Christ. When we look to Jesus for our future, the blessings of goodness and love will fill our lives both now and throughout all eternity as we dwell with our Father God, his Son Jesus Christ, and the Holy Spirit in heaven.

Yes, I am movin' on, and it is with Jesus Christ. Satan, you lost me for I am now on Jesus Christ's team for all of eternity!

Standing firm until parted by death.

This Pain Makes Me Stronger

In the stories of the thousands upon thousands of individuals who have experienced or who will experience marital discord, separation, or divorce, pain is a common denominator. I am not talking about physical pain (although it can manifest itself as physical pain), but a deep emotional pain stemming from a broken relationship with their spouse. Each situation has its own unique signs and symptoms. For some, the emotional pain is so intense that it can bring a strong man or woman to tears and to their knees. Such a situation responds best to one kind of therapy—the help of our Father God. Those of us who know our Heavenly Father have God on our side. He is our Great Physician. The Apostle Paul talks about a pain he experienced, one that is only described in the Bible as *a thorn in my flesh*. Much speculation has been made as to what discomfort Satan inflicted upon Paul. Yet Paul cried out to God for relief. Each of us might benefit from the response Paul received in his pleadings with God.

> And lest I should be exalted above measure by the abundance of the revelations, a thorn in the flesh was given to me, a messenger of Satan to buffet me, lest I be exalted above measure. Concerning this thing I pleaded with the Lord three times that it might depart from me. And He said to me, "My grace is sufficient for you, for My strength is made perfect in weakness." Therefore most gladly I will rather boast in my infirmities, that the power of Christ may rest upon me. Therefore I take pleasure in infirmities, in reproaches, in needs, in persecutions, in distresses, for Christ's sake. For when I am weak, then I am strong.
>
> 2 Corinthians 12:7–10 (NKJV)

In this often-quoted scripture, Jesus Christ (God) reminds Paul that his grace is sufficient for this attack from Satan and that his power is made perfect in Paul's weakness. Paul reveled in the knowledge that his discomfort resulted in an inner strength, a strength that can only come from God.

When we find ourselves in the throes of marital discord, know that Satan is at work to kill, steal, and destroy our one-flesh relationship. Like Paul, we too must suffer an emotional pain (and even perhaps physical pain) because our Heavenly Father knows what we need to become stronger warriors for the sanctity of our covenant marriage vows.

Often during Christ's ministry, he warned his followers about what was ahead. One example is found in the Gospel of John near the end of Christ's ministry. "I have told you these things, so that in me you may have peace. In this world you will have trouble. But take heart! I have overcome the world" (John 16:33, NIV 1984).

Christ was stating that following him would be difficult. In much the same way, living a godly marriage is impossible without Jesus in that marriage and in the hearts of the man and his wife. Satan is that trouble that Christ speaks of. However, by leaning on Christ and building our marriages upon the Solid Rock of Jesus Christ, the pain inflected by Satan (marital discord), which comes even in good marriages, makes us stronger. Isn't it great that even through marriage problems, our faith can be strengthened? For God says, "My grace is sufficient for you for My strength is made perfect in weakness." When our marriages experience turmoil, crying out to God for his help leads us to his grace. With his grace, God's power is made perfect. We find strength through a renewed relationship with Jesus.

So when the pain of marital discord occurs, look to Jesus Christ for his strength. He will never fail you! You can trust our Lord and Savior, Jesus Christ! One final thought: "For He Himself has said, 'I will never leave you nor forsake you'" (Hebrews 13:5b, NKJV).

Standing firm until parted by death.

Christ Jesus, My Spouse For A Season

As we pass through another holiday season (Thanksgiving, Christmas, and the New Year), many of us, or perhaps most of us, are spending this time of year without the presence of our *one-flesh* helpmate. For myself (at the time of writing this devotional), this is the fifth year in this situation. Yet while I am past the shock of the situation, it is nonetheless just as sad, painful, and heartrending as it was at the beginning of this journey of singleness. Still, this time alone for me has been a time of discovery, a time to be with God, and a time to know that he is ever present with me.

> *Be* content with such things as you have. For He Himself has said, "I will never leave you nor forsake you."
>
> Hebrews 13:5b (NKJV)

What a promise from God! *I will never leave you nor forsake you.* Now that is a promise you can take to the bank! Too often, when we feel abandoned by our spouse, we cry out, "Woe is me!" We seek solace wherever we can find it. Yet it is our God, our Heavenly Father, who lets us know, *I will never leave you nor forsake you.* We are God's children, and while we may stumble and fall, skinning our emotional knees, he is there as a loving parent to sooth our wounds. And wounds they are, emotional wounds cut deep into our very being by the breakdown of our marriage, the dissolution of our family, and the absence of our lifetime partner when we need them most. It is at this season of our lives that Christ Jesus steps in to be our spouse for a season, that time while our flesh-and-blood spouse is absent.

It was at this season of the year that I truly found Christ Jesus, and it has been the presence of the Holy Spirit in my own heart that has given me a sense of peace (a peace like none that I had ever experienced in my life). It is a peace that has supported me and carried me daily. It is a season in my life that I would not trade for anything for it has been and continues to be a time of discovery of who I am in Christ.

And this can be a time of discovery for any stander as they stand for their marriage and family relationships, walking alongside Christ Jesus, their spouse for a season. Remember these comforting thoughts about how God will take care of you during this season without your flesh-and-blood spouse.

For this reason I say to you, do not be worried about your life, *as to* what you will eat or what you will drink; nor for your body, *as to* what you will put on. Is not life more than food, and the body more than clothing? Look at the birds of the air, that they do not sow, nor reap nor gather into barns, and *yet* your heavenly Father feeds them. Are you not worth much more than they? And who of you by being worried can add a *single* hour to his life? And why are you worried about clothing? Observe how the lilies of the field grow; they do not toil nor do they spin, yet I say to you that not even Solomon in all his glory clothed himself like one of these. But if God so clothes the grass of the field, which is *alive* today and tomorrow is thrown into the furnace, *will He* not much more *clothe* you? You of little faith! Do not worry then, saying, 'What will we eat?' or 'What will we drink?' or 'What will we wear for clothing?' For the Gentiles eagerly seek all these things; for your heavenly Father knows that you need all these things. But seek first His kingdom and His righteousness, and all these things will be added to you. "So do not worry about tomorrow; for tomorrow will care for itself. Each day has enough trouble of its own.

Matthew 6:25–34 (NASB)

Christ Jesus, our spouse for a season, is our Provider, our Helpmate, our Companion. He says that he will always be there for you and for me. "I will never leave you nor forsake you" (Hebrews 13:5b, NKJV).

Standing firm until parted by death.

For Such A Time As This

Many of us who find ourselves dealing with a dysfunctional marriage and who are now standing with God for his healing of their marriage ask this one question: why? Why am I standing?

Are you standing because someone suggested it to you? Is it because you have a desire to honor your marriage vows? Is it that you still love and desire your spouse? Is it because of deep religious convictions about the permanence of your covenant marriage vows? Whatever the reason, well-meaning family, friends, or maybe even your own spouse will ask you why. Reflecting back on my own stand, I think back to biblical events where people took a stand. *Standing* is not easy for it is a commitment that often has far-reaching consequences.

The story of Esther tells of such a commitment, a moment in her own life where life or death of herself and others were in the balance, where her personal convictions outweighed personal comfort. Her decision could mean her own death, or it could save the whole Jewish nation. Read the words of her cousin Mordecai.

> Esther, don't think that just because you live in the king's palace you will be the only Jew to escape. If you keep quiet now, help and freedom for the Jews will come from another place. But you and your father's family will all die. And who knows, maybe you have been chosen to be the queen for such a time as this.

> Esther 4:13b–14 (ERV)

Reflect on this statement: "for such a time as this." You and I have had similar moments where there is but one right way to follow in dealing with those hard decisions in our marriages. When we got married, most of us never thought that we would experience serious marriage problems, let alone separation and/or divorce. Yet in such situations, decisions about our family's future must be made. By choosing to stand with God for his healing of our marriage, we are also standing for the salvation of our entire family, including our spouse.

Looking back, it was all worth the effort when we realize that we have been uniquely positioned *for such a time as this.*

We are standing in partnership with God for his healing of our marriages. When families fracture, everyone suffers: the husband, the wife, and the children. Divorce is sin because a covenant made in God's presence has been broken. Divorce was not in God's original plan for his children.

> He answered, "Haven't you read in your Bible that the Creator originally made man and woman for each other, male and female? And because of this, a man leaves father and mother and is firmly bonded to his wife, becoming one flesh—no longer two bodies but one. Because God created this organic union of the two sexes, no one should desecrate his art by cutting them apart."
>
> Matthew 19:4–6 (MSG)

The prophet Ezekiel wrote the Lord's words about Jerusalem's sins, saying, "This is what the Lord GOD says.… You have not put soldiers near the broken walls of the city. You have not built walls to protect the family of Israel. So when the day comes for the LORD to punish you, you will lose the war!" (Ezekiel 13:3a, 5, ERV).

Ezekiel goes on to prophesy, "I asked the people to change their lives and protect their country. I asked people to fix the walls. I wanted them to stand by those holes in the wall and fight to protect their city. But no one came to help!" (Ezekiel 22:30, ERV).

God's call to you to stand for your marriage was *to stand by those holes in the wall and fight to protect* (our marriages). God called us to stand in that gap and to declare that covenant trumps personal desires for freedom, desires of the flesh, or desires to move on with our lives with another who is not our covenant mate.

We have been called by God for *such a time as this* to *stand in the gap* for our covenant marriage vows and for the salvation of our spouses, our families, and even ourselves. God is a God of covenant. When we took our marriage vows, we took an oath, made a covenant. We need to abide by that oath. God has drawn a line in the sand, so the decision is ours. On which side of the line are you going to stand? Are you standing in the gap for your family, standing with God for the resurrection of your marriage in obedience to his will for your life? Or is it with Satan and the world? Whatever your decision, you should understand that you have been uniquely positioned *for such a time as this!*

Now back to my question. Why am I standing? One word: *obedience.* It is obedience to God's call upon my own life and my family. Therefore, each of us should reflect upon their own family situation and understand the ramifications of your stand. Do you find yourself like Esther uniquely positioned to stand with God for your marriage and your family *for such a time as this?*

In obedience to God's will for my life, I am...

Standing firm until parted by death.

Teach Me, Lord, To Wait!

Have you noticed we live in a world where almost everything is a product of immediate gratification? We frequent fast-food restaurants, self-serve gas stations, quick-lube stations for our cars, drive-through tellers at the bank, and the doc-in-a-box clinics when we are sick. Mega-stores support one-stop shopping. We travel between towns on high-speed freeways rather than taking the two lane scenic route with its stop signs and roadside parks. Life is in the fast-track mode. Today's world is not equipped for waiting. Yet when our lifestyle begins to crumble, when our marriages fall apart, waiting becomes a burden for some, while for others, waiting becomes a blessing. Let us see what the Bible says about waiting.

> And Moses said to the people, "Do not be afraid. Stand still, and see the salvation of the LORD, which He will

accomplish for you today. For the Egyptians whom you see today, you shall see again no more forever.

Exodus 14:13 (NKJV)

Trust in the LORD and wait quietly for his help. Don't be angry when people make evil plans and succeed.

Psalm 37:7 (ERV)

Be still, and know that I *am* God; I will be exalted among the nations, I will be exalted in the earth! The LORD of hosts *is* with us; The God of Jacob *is* our refuge.

Psalm 46:10–11 (NKJV)

Wait for the LORD, and he will save you.

Proverbs 20:22b (NKJV)

But we are hoping for something we don't have yet, and we are waiting for it patiently. Also, the Spirit helps us. We are very weak, but the Spirit helps us with our weakness. We don't know how to pray as we should, but the Spirit himself speaks to God for us. He begs God for us, speaking to him with feelings too deep for words.

Romans 8:25–26 (ERV)

Each of these scriptures is just a sample of the many times in the Bible that we are instructed to wait. In each if we work in our own power, we cannot overcome the issue at hand. For those who do not have a relationship with Jesus Christ as their personal

Lord and Savior, these scriptures have little meaning. Yet for many, when we realize that we cannot, in our own power, solve our marriage problems, we cry out to God, turning our lives and our marriages over to him. Each of the above scriptures reflects how our biblical forefathers approached their individual problems.

Moses entreated the Israelites to stand firm and not run at the sight of the Egyptians. When our marriages crumble, we need to stand firm with God for the sanctity of our marriage vows. As we stand, we draw closer to Jesus Christ, who is our example of sinless living. Many times during a stand, we have special moments alone with God that bring many blessings into our lives. Most standers come closer to Jesus Christ, and their faith is strengthened during this time of trial. Thus, this time is a blessing for those who are receptive.

The psalmist tells us to *be still* or *trust* as we wait on the Lord. We are not to fret but know that our God is all-powerful, that he is to be praised above all kings and leaders of nations of this earth. He is always with us, standing alongside us; he is our Fortress.

The writer in Proverbs calls us to wait for the Lord. He is our Deliverer. He will fight our battles for us if we just wait patiently on him.

Romans speaks of hope. As we stand in the gap for our families, our marriages, and our relationship with God, we hope for new beginnings. Our marriage and family situations did not occur overnight, and they will not be healed overnight. We need to be patient. The Holy Spirit must have time to work in each person's life. God's timing is not our timing, and in our rush-rush world, we get impatient. Impatience is probably one of the biggest obstacles we face as we stand with God for the healing of our marriages. Waiting for God's healing of our relationships becomes too much for some, yet it can be a blessing for others for God keeps his promises spoken to many standers. He has but one main agenda, and it is called repentance.

But do not forget this one thing, dear friends: With the Lord a day is like a thousand years, and a thousand years are like a day. The Lord is not slow in keeping his promise, as some understand slowness. He is patient with you, not wanting anyone to perish, but everyone to come to repentance.

2 Peter 3:8–9 (NIV 1984)

So, dear friends and fellow standers, the Lord calls each of us to wait as the Holy Spirit works in our loved ones and also in us to bring us all into a relationship with him. So *teach me, Lord, to wait!*

Standing firm until parted by death.

Finishing Well

I want to share with you some of the scriptures that I feel define who we are as Christians and as children of God. These are just a few that I have chosen. I am sure you can think of many more. Some are basic tenets of our faith while others explore our relationship with God and those around us. Put all together, it gets down to who we are when we meet our Creator on Judgment Day. *Finishing well* was summed up well by the Apostle Paul in 2 Timothy.

I have fought the good fight, I have finished the race, I have kept the faith. Finally, there is laid up for me the crown of righteousness, which the Lord, the righteous Judge, will give to me on that Day, and not to me only but also to all who have loved His appearing.

2 Timothy 4:7–8 (NKJV)

So let us look at a number of additional scriptures I have picked out, verses that can offer great comfort and reassurance that speak to one's walk here on earth this side of heaven. The Bible is full of many other scriptures with the same message of hope and reassurance; however, these are ones I have chosen. As you read them, pause and reflect upon each one, placing yourself in each of them. These are statements of faith in God and our Lord and Savior, Jesus Christ. Notice the principles of grace, forgiveness, hope, and love that are woven into these scriptures. Whether you are a strong Christian or a person on the fence or seeking the truth, each scripture are building blocks that you need to be a strong Christian.

> Yes, God loved the world so much that he gave his only Son, so that everyone who believes in him would not be lost but have eternal life. God sent his Son into the world. He did not send him to judge the world guilty, but to save the world through him. People who believe in God's Son are not judged guilty. But people who do not believe are already judged, because they have not believed in God's only Son. They are judged by this fact: The light has come into the world. But they did not want light. They wanted darkness, because they were doing evil things. Everyone who does evil hates the light. They will not come to the light, because the light will show all the bad things they have done. But anyone who follows the true way comes to the light. Then the light will show that whatever they have done was done through God.

John 3:16–21 (ERV)

> This is how we know what love is: Jesus Christ laid down his life for us. And we ought to lay down our lives for our brothers.

1 John 3:16 (NIV 1984)

But God demonstrates His own love toward us, in that while we were yet sinners, Christ died for us.

Romans 5:8 (NASB)

Trust in the LORD with all your heart, And lean not on your own understanding; In all your ways acknowledge Him, And He shall direct your paths.

Proverbs 3:5–6 (NKJV)

There is a way *that seems* right to a man, But its end *is* the way of death.

Proverbs 14:12 (NKJV)

When people sin, they earn what sin pays—death. But God gives his people a free gift—eternal life in Christ Jesus our Lord.

Romans 6:23 (ERV)

I mean that you have been saved by grace because you believed. You did not save yourselves; it was a gift from God. You are not saved by the things you have done, so there is nothing to boast about.

Ephesians 2:8–9 (ERV)

If we confess our sins, he is faithful and just and will forgive us our sins and purify us from all unrighteousness.

1 John 1:9 (NIV 1984)

Therefore, if anyone *is* in Christ, *he is* a new creation; old things have passed away; behold, all things have become new. Now all things *are* of God, who has reconciled us to Himself through Jesus Christ, and has given us the ministry of reconciliation, that is, that God was in Christ reconciling the world to Himself, not imputing their trespasses to them, and has committed to us the word of reconciliation. Now then, we are ambassadors for Christ, as though God were pleading through us: we implore *you* on Christ's behalf, be reconciled to God. For He made Him who knew no sin *to be* sin for us, that we might become the righteousness of God in Him.

2 Corinthians 5:17–21 (NKJV)

"For I know the plans that I have for you," declares the LORD, "plans for welfare and not for calamity to give you a future and a hope. Then you will call upon Me and come and pray to Me, and I will listen to you. You will seek Me and find *Me* when you search for Me with all your heart."

Jeremiah 29:11–13 (NASB)

So tell the family of Israel that this is what the Lord GOD says: "Family of Israel, you ruined my holy name in the places where you went. I am going to do something to stop this. I will not do it for your sake, Israel. I will do it for my holy name…. I will also put a new spirit in you to change your way of thinking. I will take out the heart of stone from your body and give you a tender, human heart. I will put my Spirit inside you and change you so that you will obey my laws. You will carefully obey my commands."

Ezekiel 36:22, 26–27 (ERV)

This is what the Lord said, "The time is coming when I will make a new agreement with the family of Israel and with the family of Judah. It will not be like the agreement I made with their ancestors. I made that agreement when I took them by the hand and brought them out of Egypt. I was their master, but they broke that agreement." This message is from the Lord. "In the future I will make this agreement with the people of Israel." This message is from the Lord. "I will put my teachings in their minds, and I will write them on their hearts. I will be their God, and they will be my people. People will not have to teach their neighbors and relatives to know the Lord, because all people, from the least important to the most important, will know me." This message is from the Lord. "I will forgive them for the evil things they did. I will not remember their sins."

Jeremiah 31:31–34 (ERV)

In the above scripture, the Lord says, "I will forgive them for the evil things they did. I will not remember their sins." This forgive-and-forget statement is the basis of the New Covenant that was ushered in by our Messiah. That is reflected in the following scriptures as they speak to the covenant that Jesus Christ brought to mankind.

For this *is* the covenant that I will make with the house of Israel after those days, says the Lord: I will put My laws in their mind and write them on their hearts; and I will be their God, and they shall be My people. None of them shall teach his neighbor, and none his brother, saying, 'Know the Lord,' for all shall know Me, from the least of them to the greatest of them. For I will be merciful to their unrighteousness, and their sins and their lawless deeds I will remember no more."

Hebrews 8:10–12 (NKJV)

These verses above from Hebrews reminds us of the great love that God, through Jesus Christ, has for his people. It reiterates the prophecy spoken to by the prophet Jeremiah listed above (Jeremiah 31:31–34).

God has said, "I will never leave you; I will never run away from you." So we can feel sure and say, "The Lord is my helper; I will not be afraid. People can do nothing to me...." Jesus Christ is the same yesterday, today, and forever.

Hebrews 13:5b–6, 8 (ERV)

Therefore, since we have a great high priest who has passed through the heavens, Jesus the Son of God, let us hold fast our confession. For we do not have a high priest who cannot sympathize with our weaknesses, but One who has been tempted in all things as *we are, yet* without sin. Therefore let us draw near with confidence to the throne of grace, so that we may receive mercy and find grace to help in time of need.

Hebrews 4:14–16 (NASB)

The teaching I gave you is the same that I received from the Lord: On the night when the Lord Jesus was handed over to be killed, he took bread and gave thanks for it. Then he divided the bread and said, "This is my body; it is for you. Eat this to remember me." In the same way, after they ate, Jesus took the cup of wine. He said, "This cup represents the new agreement from God, which begins with my blood sacrifice. When you drink this, do it to remember me." This means that every time you eat this bread and drink this cup, you are telling others about the Lord's death until he comes again.

1 Corinthians 11:23–26 (ERV)

"Do not let your heart be troubled; believe in God, believe also in Me. In My Father's house are many dwelling places; if it were not so, I would have told you; for I go to prepare a place for you. If I go and prepare a place for you, I will come again and receive you to Myself, that where I am, *there* you may be also. And you know the way where I am going." Thomas said to Him, "Lord, we do not know where You are going, how do we know the way?" Jesus said to him, "I am the way, and the truth, and the life; no one comes to the Father but through Me.

John 14:1–6 (NASB)

Finally, we need to look at Paul's description of marriage and how it all relates to Christ's church. Nowhere in God's Word is there a clearer description of the meaning of marriage than in this passage. Paul draws the comparison of the relationship of Christ to his body (the church of his believers) and his institution of marriage.

Be willing to serve each other out of respect for Christ. Wives, be willing to serve your husbands the same as the Lord. A husband is the head of his wife, just as Christ is the head of the church. Christ is the Savior of the church, which is his body. The church serves under Christ, so it is the same with you wives. You should be willing to serve your husbands in everything. Husbands, love your wives the same as Christ loved the church and gave his life for it. He died to make the church holy. He used the telling of the Good News to make the church clean by washing it with water. Christ died so that he could give the church to himself like a bride in all her beauty. He died so that the church could be holy and without fault, with no evil or sin or any other thing wrong in it. And husbands should love their wives like that. They should love their wives as they love their own bodies. The man who loves his wife loves himself, because no one ever hates his own body, but feeds and takes care of it. And that is what Christ does for the church because we are parts of his body. The Scriptures say, "That is why a man will leave his father and mother and join his wife, and the two people will become one." That secret truth is very important—I am talking about Christ and the church. But each one of you must love his wife as he loves himself. And a wife must respect her husband.

Ephesians 5:21–33 (ERV)

Marriage between a man and a woman was and is God's precious gift of love to his children. As mentioned in verses from Ephesians, our relationship with Christ is reflected in our marriages. Some translations use the word *submit* where the translation above uses *serve*. When marriages hit on hard times as so many do today and those relationships fall apart, Satan smiles and says, "I got another one." However, when we understand that our marriage is a work in progress until the day we die, then we begin to realize that we cannot do this alone. We need help, and who better than our Lord and Savior, Jesus Christ? Yet just as marriage is a work in progress until the day we die, reconciliation is likewise a work in progress until the day we die. Sounds like a hard job? Not really if we keep our eyes, minds, and hearts fixed upon Jesus. He is our example, and by following his example, we can fight off Satan as he tries to destroy our marriages.

There are so many more scriptures that I could mention. Space does not permit me to list more, but if interested, I refer you to God's Word, the Holy Bible. However, these verses listed here are just a starter. If you feel these scriptures describe your personal walk with Jesus Christ, you should feel certain that family and friends will say of you at the end of your days, "He [she] finished well."

Standing firm until parted by death.

Homecoming

But while he was still a long way off, his father saw him and was filled with compassion for him; he ran to his son, threw his arms around him and kissed him. The son said to him, "Father, I have sinned against heaven and against you. I am no longer worthy to be called your son." But the father said to his servants, "Quick! Bring the best robe and put it on him. Put a ring on his finger and sandals on his feet. Bring the fattened calf and kill it. Let's have a feast and celebrate. For this son of mine was dead and is alive again; he was lost and is found." So they began to celebrate.

—Luke 15:20b–24 (NIV 1984)

Anyone who has been exposed to the teachings of Jesus has heard of the parable of the prodigal son. In like manner, if you have been exposed to other Christians standing for the restoration of their respective marriages, you have heard that the spouse who is not standing for reconciliation is referred to as the prodigal. Each of us is standing with Jesus Christ for the restoration of his (her) marriage relationship, and we each wait expectantly for the *homecoming* of our prodigal spouse. I know in my own situation, I pray daily, sometimes multiple times a day, for the Holy Spirit to soften my wife's heart. I pray that she will come to understand the seriousness of breaking covenant and decide to come home. There she will find me waiting with open arms and unconditional love. Much like this father said in the parable, I will say, "For this wife of mine, the wife of my marriage covenant, was dead to our marriage and is now alive again, she was lost from our marriage relationship and now is found!" Oh, what rejoicing there will be in my household! Each of us who is standing for the restoration of our marriages is looking forward to that day when our respective prodigal spouse comes home.

Jesus Christ looks at each broken marriage relationship, and his heart cries out in anguish. Like you and I, he feels the pain of separation, desertion, and betrayal as he stands with us. It is through the work of the Holy Spirit that our prodigal's heart is softened, their wounds are mended, and our prodigal is directed homeward.

In the parable of the lost sheep, we see a similar story of homecoming.

> If a man has a hundred sheep and one of them gets lost, what will he do? Won't he leave the ninety-nine others in the wilderness and go to search for the one that is lost until he finds it? And when he has found it, he will joyfully carry it home on his shoulders. When he arrives, he will call together his friends and neighbors, saying, "Rejoice with me because I have found my lost sheep." In the same way, there is more joy in heaven over one lost sinner who repents and returns to God than over ninety-nine others who are righteous and haven't strayed away!
>
> Luke 15:4–7 (NLT)

Our Heavenly Father rejoices when a *lost* prodigal spouse returns home to their covenant marriage relationship. Each of us, both the stander and the prodigal spouse, must repent of our sinful lives that led to the breakup of our covenant marriage relationship. It is almost never just one spouse's fault because both spouses contribute in varying ways to the breakup. With the homecoming, the *new* marriage relationship must be built upon the Solid Rock of Jesus Christ for in the old marriage, Jesus Christ was not priority number 1, which led to that marriage's failure. With Jesus Christ at the center of a marriage relationship, marriages just don't fail. Jesus Christ taught us about ridding ourselves of our old sinful life and about reconciliation. Paul describes this in the scripture below.

Therefore, if anyone *is* in Christ, *he is* a new creation; old things have passed away; behold, all things have become new. Now all things *are* of God, who has reconciled us to Himself through Jesus Christ, and has given us the ministry of reconciliation, that is, that God was in Christ reconciling the world to Himself, not imputing their trespasses to them, and has committed to us the word of reconciliation. Now then, we are ambassadors for Christ, as though God were pleading through us: we implore *you* on Christ's behalf, be reconciled to God. For He made Him who knew no sin *to be* sin for us, that we might become the righteousness of God in Him.

2 Corinthians 5:17–21 (NKJV)

It is through the atoning blood of Jesus Christ that each of us is saved from the sinful lives of our old marriage. We must now look to Jesus Christ as we rebuild our new marriage relationship following the homecoming of our prodigal spouse.

So pray hard today and every day for a great homecoming harvest of prodigals around the world. May your prodigal be welcomed home with open arms, unconditional love, and understanding. Pray expectantly and boldly for your family's homecoming celebration. Jesus Christ will be there to celebrate it with you!

May God bless each of you in your stand as you pray for a joyous homecoming. As for me, I am standing firm until parted by death, looking expectantly to my wife's homecoming.

Standing firm until parted by death.

COVENANT

Covenant: What's It All About? (Part One)

"Promises. Pledged amidst spring flowers.
Cashed in February grayness."

Covenant—what's it all about? Webster's Dictionary defines it as "an agreement, usually formal, between two or more persons to do or not do something specified." The term appears throughout the Bible, and it forms the basis for our understanding of marriage vows and, likewise, our stand for those vows. I recommend reading chapter 14 on "Tough Promises" in Max Lucado's book *Facing Your Giants*. This reference speaks well of the situation we find ourselves in as we consider this principle that is so central to our faith and our marriages. The quote above comes from that chapter. We find that during our lifetime, we will make many promises to God, to our spouse, to our children, and to others that are so easy to make, yet in many cases, they are so much harder to keep.

One of the early examples of covenant in the Bible is the story of Noah.

> So God said to Noah, "I am going to put an end to all people, for the earth is filled with violence because of them. I am surely going to destroy both them and the earth. So make yourself an ark of cypress wood.... I am going to bring floodwaters on the earth to destroy all life under

the heavens, every creature that has the breath of life in it. Everything on earth will perish. But I will establish my covenant with you, and you will enter the ark—you and your sons and your wife and your sons' wives with you. You are to bring into the ark two of all living creatures, male and female, to keep them alive with you." Then God said to Noah and to his sons with him: "I now establish my covenant with you and with your descendants after you and with every living creature that was with you...I establish my covenant with you: Never again will all life be cut off by the waters of a flood; never again will there be a flood to destroy the earth." And God said, "This is the sign of the covenant I am making between me and you and every living creature with you, a covenant for all generations to come: I have set my rainbow in the clouds, and it will be the sign of the covenant between me and the earth. Whenever I bring clouds over the earth and the rainbow appears in the clouds, I will remember my covenant between me and you and all living creatures of every kind."

Genesis 6:13–14a, 17–19; 9:8–9, 11–15a (NIV 1984)

In the Bible (NIV 1984), the word *covenant* is mentioned 297 times. So you can see that it holds a very special place in the heart of God and in his teachings. We find covenant referenced again in a pivotal promise God made with Abraham:

As for me, this is my covenant with you: You will be the father of many nations. No longer will you be called Abram; your name will be Abraham, for I have made you a father of many nations. I will make you very fruitful; I will make nations of you, and kings will come from you. I will establish my covenant as an everlasting covenant between me and you and your descendants after you for the generations to come, to be your God and the God of your descendants after you.

Genesis 17:4–7 (NIV 1984)

God continued making covenants with Abraham. The following one has eternal implications for each of us. Following is Abraham's trip up the mountain to sacrifice his son Isaac:

> The angel of the LORD called to Abraham from heaven a second time and said, "I swear by myself, declares the LORD, that because you have done this and have not withheld your son, your only son, I will surely bless you and make your descendants as numerous as the stars in the sky and as the sand on the seashore. Your descendants will take possession of the cities of their enemies, and through your offspring all nations on earth will be blessed, because you have obeyed me."
>
> Genesis 22:15–18 (NIV 1984)

Here God swears to (promises to or covenants with) Abraham that through his seed Isaac would come one who would bless all nations on the earth. While not specifically mentioned here, we know that from Abraham's seed came the Messiah, Jesus Christ, our Lord.

Moving forward in time, we come to the story of David, his friend Jonathan, and Saul. King Saul realized that David was a threat to his throne. David had been anointed king by the prophet Samuel while Saul was still on the throne of Israel. Saul's son, Jonathan, befriended David, and they made a covenant of friendship, which transcended Jonathan's loyalty to his father. Jonathan protects David from his father's attempt to kill him, and he reminds David, "If I make it through this alive, continue to be my covenant friend. And if I die, keep the covenant friendship with my family—forever" (1 Samuel 20:14–15, MSG).

Time passes, and Saul and Jonathan are killed in a great battle with the Philistines. Jonathan has died, but the covenant he made with David does not die. Remember the story of Jonathan's son Mephibosheth. David remembers his promise, his covenant with Jonathan, and seeks out his crippled son, takes him in, and restores his family possessions to him. A promise is a promise! It is a covenant! Covenant does not say it better than in this story for only one person remained who was a part of that covenant: David. David chose to honor that covenant.

I could go on and on with examples of covenant from the Bible. To quote from Max Lucado, "God sets the standard for covenant keeping." The word *covenant* in Hebrew is *berit*, which means "a solemn agreement with binding force." God makes many promises to his people, and he never, ever breaks them. His track record of covenant runs throughout the Old and New Testaments. Again from Max Lucado: "Your eternal life is covenant caused, covenant secured, and covenant based." God, who always keeps his promises, should inspire you and me to keep our promises, our covenants.

So we come to the present day and our covenant marriage vows taken before God and our spouse. These vows involve a promise that we will be there for our spouse in the good times and the bad until parted by death. Covenant is not, I repeat, *is not* a contract that becomes null and void when one party backs out. Covenant still stands when only one person remains (remember David's covenant with Jonathan). So why should we honor our covenant marriage vows? We should do so to understand fully God's endless love for each of us. For he made the ultimate sacrifice of his great love for humanity as follows:

> For God so loved the world that he gave his one and only Son, that whoever believes in him shall not perish but have eternal life. For God did not send his Son into the world to condemn the world, but to save the world through him.

> John 3:16–17 (NIV 1984)

> For I received from the Lord what I also passed on to you:
> The Lord Jesus, on the night he was betrayed, took bread,
> and when he had given thanks, he broke it and said, "This is
> my body, which is for you; do this in remembrance of me."
> In the same way, after supper he took the cup, saying, "This
> cup is the new covenant in my blood; do this, whenever
> you drink it, in remembrance of me." For whenever you
> eat this bread and drink this cup, you proclaim the Lord's
> death until he comes.
>
> 1 Corinthians 11:23–26 (NIV 1984)

So you can see, covenant is God-ordained and God-blessed. It is not something that can be taken lightly. Our secular courts do not understand this as the alarming statistics on divorce can attest. Our wedding bands are a symbol of our covenant vows taken before God and our spouse. Stand firm for them through thick and thin! To quote from Max Lucado again: "Covenant-keeping enrolls you in the postgraduate school of God's love.... God calls on you to do the same. Illustrate stubborn love. Incarnate fidelity. God is giving you a Mephibosheth-size chance to show your children and your neighbors what real love does.... [Someday], someone may tell your story of loyalty to illustrate the loyalty of God."

> Know therefore that the LORD your God, He is God, the
> faithful God, who keeps His covenant and His loving-
> kindness to a thousandth generation with those who love
> Him and keep His commandments.
>
> Deuteronomy 7:9 (NASB)

May our merciful Heavenly Father bless each of you during this season of your life as you stand for the restoration of your marriage.[14]

Standing firm until parted by death.

Covenant: What's It All About? (Part Two)

I will be their God and they will be My people.

—Ezekiel 37:27b (NASB)

This basic theme found in numerous Scriptural references states the thematic unity of the Scriptures. As we study the Bible, covenant is the core concept, unifying the relationship between God and man. We, as standers for our covenant marriage vows, need to understand the various aspects of covenant in the eyes of God. It is obvious from our own personal situations that our prodigal spouses do not understand the importance of covenant. It is my hope that by the end of this devotional, you will have a better understanding of the many aspects of covenant and how important covenant is to God. Covenant, whether mentioned directly or implied, is found hundreds of times in the various translations of the Bible.

Covenant has been defined as an oath-bound promise where one party pledges certain things for the benefit of another party. Sometimes, certain conditions need to be met by the second party. However, often the promise is made unilaterally and is unconditional. In the Old Testament, the Hebrew for covenant is *berit*, coming from the verb *bara*, meaning "to bind." It is a binding of God and man and also between humans. While in some cases it has some of the characteristics of a mutual agreement or contract, it is much more as it is clearly a binding pledge.

Examples of biblical covenants that exist between humans include the covenant at Beersheba between Abraham and Abimelech on well ownership (Genesis 21) and the covenant of Jonathan and David recognizing David's right to the throne (1 Samuel 18 and 23). Covenants can be made against God's will (ill-advised), such as the covenant forged between the Gibeonites and Joshua where Israel would live at peace with and would protect the Gibeonites (Joshua 9). Solomon made a covenant of peace (ill-advised) with Hiram, king of Tyre, for trade purposes. The list goes on and on.

As far as you and I are concerned, the marriage covenant is central to our stand. Malachi speaks to this:

> You ask, "Why?" It is because the LORD is acting as the witness between you and the wife of your youth, because you have broken faith with her, though she is your partner, the wife of your marriage covenant."
>
> Malachi 2:14 (NIV 1984)

The marriage covenant is between one man and one woman who vow a lifelong commitment, which includes sexual union, sacrificial love, and mutual support.

> "Haven't you read," he replied, "that at the beginning the Creator 'made them male and female,' and said, 'For this reason a man will leave his father and mother and be united to his wife, and the two will become one flesh'? So they are no longer two, but one. Therefore what God has joined together, let man not separate."
>
> Matthew 19:4–6 (NIV 1984)

In the Bible, the divine covenants that God makes with man are most significant as they are the unifying principle for our understanding Scripture—the relationship of God and man, *God with us*.

> I will establish my covenant as an everlasting covenant between me and you and your descendants after you for the generations to come, to be your God and the God of your descendants after you. The whole land of Canaan, where you are now an alien, I will give as an everlasting

possession to you and your descendants after you; and I will be their God.

Genesis 17:7–8 (NIV 1984)

The first covenant God ever made was about redemption. It was made before the beginning of time. God the Father made a covenant with God the Son for the redemption of fallen mankind.

God gives us the strength to do that. God saved us and chose us to be his holy people, but not because of anything we ourselves did. God saved us and made us his people because that was what he wanted and because of his grace. That grace was given to us through Christ Jesus before time began. And now it has been shown to us in the coming of our Savior Christ Jesus. He destroyed death and showed us the way to have life. Yes, through the Good News Jesus showed us the way to have life that cannot be destroyed.

2 Timothy 1:8b–10 (ERV)

We are saved not by works but by grace planned for us *before the beginning of time*. This covenant was made with Jesus Christ so that he might save mankind that his Father had given to him.

All that the Father gives Me will come to Me, and the one who comes to Me I will certainly not cast out. For I have come down from heaven, not to do My own will, but the will of Him who sent Me. This is the will of Him who sent Me, that of all that He has given Me I lose nothing, but raise it up on the last day. For this is the will of My Father, that everyone who beholds the Son and believes in Him will have eternal life, and I Myself will raise him up on the last day.

John 6:37–40 (NASB)

Another covenant is the Edenic covenant (covenant of works), which God made with Adam (mankind), promising man in his state of innocence that he would grant him everlasting life on the provision of man's perfect obedience. This had to do with the Tree of Knowledge of Good and Evil. You know the story of how Adam and Eve broke the covenant, unleashing mankind's sinful nature. This was a covenant of works that had no provision for restoration, and once broken, the required perfection was lost. Mankind was without hope. Our hope came in the form of the covenant of grace mentioned above. This covenant is unconditional as God wished to rescue us from the curse of the covenant of works. In the New Testament, the covenant of grace comes to fruition in the redemptive work of Jesus at Calvary.

God makes many covenants throughout the Old Testament: with Noah, Abraham, Isaac, and Jacob. Following their time in Egypt, the covenant God made with the Israelites was the Mosaic covenant, which was the law, summarized in the Ten Commandments. God made an unconditional covenant with David, the Davidic covenant, that through him he would establish a perpetual kingdom. One of David's descendants would sit on the throne of Israel forever. God kept his side of this covenant even when many kings descended from David drifted into wickedness. The Davidic covenant came to fruition in New Testament times in our Lord Jesus Christ.

> My brothers, I can tell you for sure about David, our great ancestor. He died, was buried, and his tomb is still here with us today. He was a prophet and knew something that God had said. God had promised David that someone from his own family would sit on David's throne as king. David knew this before it happened. That is why he said this about that future king: 'He was not left in the place of death. His body did not rot in the grave.' David was talking about the Messiah rising from death. So Jesus is the one God raised from death. We are all witnesses of this. We

saw him. Jesus was lifted up to heaven. Now he is with God, at God's right side. The Father has given the Holy Spirit to him, as he promised. So Jesus has now poured out that Spirit. This is what you see and hear. David was not the one who was lifted up to heaven. David himself said, 'The Lord God said to my Lord: Sit at my right side, until I put your enemies under your power.' So, all the people of Israel should know this for certain: God has made Jesus to be Lord and Messiah. He is the man you nailed to the cross!

Acts 2:29–36 (ERV)

Finally, God establishes what we now call the New Covenant. Jeremiah first alludes to it:

"This is the covenant I will make with the house of Israel after that time," declares the LORD. "I will put my law in their minds and write it on their hearts. I will be their God, and they will be my people. No longer will a man teach his neighbor, or a man his brother, saying, 'Know the LORD,' because they will all know me, from the least of them to the greatest," declares the LORD. "For I will forgive their wickedness and will remember their sins no more."

Jeremiah 31:33–34 (NIV 1984)

In contrast with the Mosaic covenant, the New Covenant provides new birth, full forgiveness for our sins, an intimate knowledge of God, and the reassurance that it was unbreakable. The divine covenants link God and man, bringing fallen man into an intimate relationship with his Creator, God.

And I heard a loud voice from the throne saying, "Now the dwelling of God is with men, and he will live with them. They will be his people, and God himself will be with them and be their God."

Revelations 21:3 (NIV 1984)

May each of you stand firm for your covenant marriage vows.[15]

Standing firm until parted by death.

Covenant: Yet Another Aspect

Jonathan, out of his deep love for David, made a covenant with him. He formalized it with solemn gifts: his own royal robe and weapons—armor, sword, bow, and belt.

—1 Samuel 18:3–4 (MSG)

Jonathan, be kind to me. I am your servant. You have made an agreement [covenant] with me before the LORD.

—1 Samuel 20:8a (ERV) [Edited]

Those of us who are seeking God's help in the reconciliation of our marriages know that when we are standing for our marriage, we are standing for a covenant we took before God and before our spouse, our covenant marriage vows. The story of David and King Saul and his son Jonathan is one of those beautiful stories in the Old Testament that has become a benchmark for the meaning of covenant. I suggest you read the story of David and Jonathan in 1 Samuel starting in chapter 16 through the end of the book and continued in chapter 9 of 2 Samuel. I dare say that if the covenant marriage vows we each took at the time our respective marriages were honored as was this covenant that existed between David and Jonathan, divorce and the destruction of the family unit would be history.

As we look at this covenant between these two young men, we see a deeper meaning to covenant. From the Hebrew word *hesed* comes this deeper meaning. This word is often translated as *steadfast love* or *loving-kindness* or simply just *love*. This word is not just about warm feelings between two individuals, but it is about a deep loyalty, a devoted and compassionate affection. It is much deeper than merely a friendship. It is more like a contractual disposition of faithfulness toward one another. Don't misunderstand me. Covenants are not like the legal contracts we sign today. It is a contractual agreement that lives on when one party is no longer living or is no longer acknowledging the existence of the covenant. So in the above scripture, it might read, "As for you, show *hesed* to your servant, for you have brought him into a covenant with you before the Lord."

Is that not what we see in our covenant marriage vows, an image of covenant faithfulness? So what is our standard? *Hesed* covenant points toward our standard, a covenant that shows a stronger love reflected in God's covenant of faithfulness to his people. Several other scriptures also point this out.

> Then the Lord came down to him in a cloud, stood there with Moses, and spoke his own name. That is, the Lord passed in front of Moses and said, "Yahweh, the Lord, is a kind and merciful God. He is slow to become angry. He is full of great love [*hesed*]. He can be trusted. He shows his faithful love to thousands of people. He forgives people for the wrong things they do, but he does not forget to punish guilty people. Not only will he punish the guilty people, but their children, their grandchildren, and their great-grandchildren will also suffer for the bad things these people do.
>
> Exodus 34:5–7 (ERV) [Edited]

> For the LORD your God goes with you; he will never leave
> you nor forsake you.
>
> Deuteronomy 31:6b (NIV 1984)

That last scripture touches deep into my heart and my soul. *He will never leave you nor forsake you.* What comfort that gives me personally. Our God, our Heavenly Father, has a covenant with his people, a covenant that can best be translated as *hesed*. We in like manner have a covenant with him and with our spouse through our covenant marriage vows. So stand strong, being ever faithful to a covenant that can best be defined using the word *hesed*. Such is the covenant that exists between God, you, and your spouse as seen in his eyes. So stand strong!

Note: In the Greek, *agape* is the word used to describe God's love for mankind. It is rarely used in Greek outside of biblical context. It denotes God's unconditional love for each of us. *Hesed* is a Hebrew word for love as explained above. As my scriptural references are from the Old Testament, they are in Hebrew, not Greek.[16]

Standing firm until parted by death.

The Covenant Of The Rainbow

When you were just a little child, didn't you just marvel as I did at the sight of a rainbow? You were possibly told stories about a pot of gold being buried at the end of the rainbow. You strained hard to see where the end of the rainbow lies so you could go see for yourself. Or perhaps you saw the marvels of a double rainbow and got really excited. As you got older, you learned the scientific explanation of how sunlight is refracted though the raindrops in the air, giving the beautiful spectrum of colors that is projected upon the distant sky. If you were fortunate to get biblical teachings about the rainbow, you were told of the wonderful and fascinating story of Noah and the great flood recorded in the book of Genesis. In the ninth chapter of Genesis, we read about God's covenant made with all living creatures on earth. Following the great flood, God spoke to Noah and made a promise—an everlasting, irrevocable, unilateral covenant: the Noahic covenant.

> Then God spoke to Noah and to his sons with him, saying: "And as for Me, behold, I establish My covenant with you and with your descendants after you, and with every living creature that *is* with you: the birds, the cattle, and every beast of the earth with you, of all that go out of the ark, every beast of the earth. Thus I establish My covenant with you: Never again shall all flesh be cut off by the waters of the flood; never again shall there be a flood to destroy the earth." And God said: "This *is* the sign of the covenant which I make between Me and you, and every living creature that *is* with you, for perpetual generations: I set My rainbow in the cloud, and it shall be for the sign of the covenant between Me and the earth. It shall be, when I bring a cloud over the earth, that the rainbow shall be seen in the cloud; and I will remember My covenant which *is* between Me and you and every living creature of all flesh; the waters shall never again become a flood to destroy all flesh. The rainbow shall be in the cloud, and I will look on it to remember the everlasting covenant between God and every living creature of all flesh that *is* on the earth." And God said to Noah, "This *is* the sign of the covenant which I have established between Me and all flesh that *is* on the earth."

> Genesis 9:8–17 (NKJV)

Now, let us change our focus and look back at the creation story. God made man in his own image. He then found it was not good that man should be alone, so he created a helpmate for man: woman.

The Lord God said, "It is not good for the man to be alone. I will make a helper suitable for him....".But for Adam no suitable helper was found. So the Lord God caused the man to fall into a deep sleep; and while he was sleeping, he took one of the man's ribs and closed up the place with flesh. Then the Lord God made a woman from the rib he had taken out of the man, and he brought her to the man. The man said, "This is now bone of my bones and flesh of my flesh; she shall be called 'woman,' for she was taken out of man." For this reason a man will leave his father and mother and be united to his wife, and they will become one flesh.

Genesis 2:18, 20a–24 (NIV 1984)

And they became one flesh. The union of a man and a woman in marriage was ordained by God from the beginning of time. Marriage is precious in God's sight. When we got married, we took vows, solemn vows of mutual love, honor, and support before God and before our spouse. During the taking of those vows, each of us and our spouses exchanged (gave and received) a symbol of those vows, most commonly a ring. These rings symbolize our promises, a sign of our covenant marriage vows. These covenant vows are to last a lifetime until they are broken by the death of one of the spouses. When our spouses decide to leave our marriages, to break covenant, the covenant still remains between God and us. God still honors that covenant, and *no* secular court can break that covenant.

But at the beginning of creation God "made them male and female. For this reason a man will leave his father and mother and be united to his wife, and the two will become one flesh." So they are no longer two, but one. Therefore what God has joined together, let man not separate.

Mark 10:6–9 (NIV 1984)

You ask, "Why?" It is because the LORD is acting as the witness between you and the wife of your youth, because you have broken faith with her, though she is your partner, the wife of your marriage covenant. Has not the LORD made them one? In flesh and spirit they are his. And why one? Because he was seeking godly offspring. So guard yourself in your spirit, and do not break faith with the wife of your youth. "I hate divorce," says the LORD God of Israel...

Malachi 2:14–16a (NIV 1984)

The above quote from Malachi is often quoted about divorce. Yet over 50 percent of all marriages today end up in divorce. As divorced standers (or even as separated standers), many of us are confused about our wedding rings. Do we wear them, or do we take them off? If you believe in covenant as I do, then you should continue to wear your wedding ring. It is a sign of the covenant that still exists between you and God and you and your spouse. While just you and your spouse were the ones exchanging rings, God was and is a party to that covenant. In many marriage ceremonies, before the rings are exchanged, God's blessing is sought on these symbols (rings) of the covenant vows that were exchanged. In my view (belief) and those of many others who believe in covenant marriage vows, that one is still married in God's eyes despite what a secular court does in granting a divorce. By wearing your ring, you are saying to a fallen world that you are married and that you are in covenant with God and your spouse.

So where does the covenant of the rainbow fit into this story? You will remember that God placed the rainbow in the sky as a sign (symbol) of his covenant with all living creatures on earth. Your wedding ring is a symbol of your covenant vows taken before God and your spouse. When God sees a rainbow forming in the clouds over the earth, he is reminded of the covenant he made with all living creatures of earth after the great flood. In like manner, when I look at my wedding ring on my hand, it is a reminder to me and a testimony to others of my covenant marriage vows, those holy vows taken before the Lord and my spouse. So when I am asked about my wedding ring on my hand by people who know that I am divorced, I tell them it is my *rainbow* ring, my *covenant* ring. When they look confused, I relate to them the story of the Noahic covenant and the story of the rainbow; thus, the term of the "covenant of the rainbow." I am witnessing to them that I am a person of integrity, a person of faith, a person following God's will for my life.

So are you still wearing your wedding ring? As a stander, you should be. By standing, you are asking God to honor the covenant you made before him and your spouse. So remember the covenant of the rainbow and wear your wedding ring, your *rainbow* ring, your *covenant* ring! Be a witness to others of your faith, and trust in God to restore your marriage.

May God bless your stand.

Standing firm until parted by death.

Evidences Of God's Concern About Covenants

Before starting this devotional, read Psalm 105 in your favorite translation.

> O seed of Abraham, His servant, O sons of Jacob, His chosen ones! He is the LORD our God; His judgments are in all the earth. He has remembered His covenant forever, The word which He commanded to a thousand generations, *The covenant* which He made with Abraham, And His oath to Isaac. Then He confirmed it to Jacob for a statute, To Israel as an everlasting covenant.

Psalm 105:6–10 (NASB)

From cover to cover, the Holy Bible is about God's covenant with his children. It is a book of his everlasting love for mankind. In Genesis, God created man and woman with the plan that he would be in close relationship with his children throughout eternity. This is where mankind was introduced to covenant. A covenant implies promises or vows made that benefit all parties to those vows. Thus, we see that God covenanted with mankind from the beginning of time. Through his covenants with mankind, God has pledged his love and faithfulness for his children. He calls on mankind to promise theirs to him. (That was not the first covenant that God made. Before the beginning of time, God covenanted with his Son Jesus about his role in creation of the world and the salvation of mankind.) On a more personal basis, let me remind you that God was a participant in each of our marriages and was the primary witness to those spoken vows. Those vows were a *covenant* between God and the man and the woman as well as a *covenant* between the man and the woman. In other words, our *covenant* marriage vows constitute a three-way promise. Read again our scripture selection for today.

Here the psalmist writes about covenants being everlasting (more will be said about this below). Also, whether you realized it or not, you and I are descendants of Abraham, who is our spiritual father. We are Abraham's seed. For a few, we may even be biologically related. However, what is most important is that we are related spiritually through our faith in the one true God and his only Son, Jesus Christ. It is through God's covenants that we can believe (faith) and know that there is truth in the promise of eternal life with God if we accept his Son, Jesus, as our Lord and Savior.

Psalm 105, a psalm of praise written by King David, reminds us of God's mighty deeds for his people, Israel. The psalm gives a narrative of God's provision for his children as they were led by Moses out of Egypt and through the desert to the Promised Land. Evidence of God's covenant with his people, Israel, is present in every verse. Notice that in verse 10 he says that God's covenant is *everlasting*. The New Living Translation says God's covenant is *never ending*. From this one psalm, we should realize that God is in control and that his people will not perish from this earth. We can see this evidenced in our own lives if we just see how much he interacts in everything we do and say. In our troubled marriages, God seeks to heal as he guides us through his Word in the direction of healing. God's leading is further evidence of his love for us and of his part in our covenant marriage vows. The Israelites understood God's involvement in their lives, and they understood the concept of covenant.

> For He remembered His holy promise, *And* Abraham His servant.
>
> Psalm 105:42 (NKJV)

The New Living Translation uses the term "sacred promise to his servant Abraham" while the New American Standard Bible uses "holy word with Abraham his servant." These terms—*holy promise*, *sacred promise*, and *holy word*—all refer to God's covenant with Abraham. When we apply these views to our covenant marriage vows, we can see how concerned God is when he looks at our marriage vows spoken (taken) before him and our spouse and when one spouse chooses to ignore their covenant vows.

Look again at how God looks at the permanence of covenants or the promises we make in the ninth chapter of Genesis.

> God continued, "This is the sign of the covenant I am making between me and you and everything living around you and everyone living after you. I'm putting my rainbow in the clouds, a sign of the covenant between me and the Earth. From now on, when I form a cloud over the Earth and the rainbow appears in the cloud, I'll remember my covenant between me and you and everything living, that

never again will floodwaters destroy all life. When the rainbow appears in the cloud, I'll see it and remember the eternal covenant between God and everything living, every last living creature on Earth."

Genesis 9:13–16 (MSG)

The above version of the rainbow covenant story uses the term of *eternal* covenant. The NIV, the NKJV, and the NASB use the term *everlasting* covenant. Get the picture!

So there it is. The concept of covenant began before the beginning of time and continues to the present day and beyond. Covenant denotes a solemn promise made between the parties of that covenant. Covenants can be everlasting (eternal) as in the case of the unilateral covenant of the rainbow, or they can have a time limitation such as in our covenant marriage vows *until parted by death*. Covenant marriage vows do not go away when one party bails out. God will never bail out on them, so why should you? Stand firm with God and witness the restoration and healing of your marriage. You will never be sorry for standing with God. He will see you through these tough times. God will bless your stand.

Standing firm until parted by death.

Broken Covenants

Covenant is a term, a word, a fact of life that each of us in our marriage reconciliation ministry deal with each and every day. Perhaps I should say *broken covenants* for that is what exists when a spouse (or both spouses) willfully walk out of a marriage relationship that is sealed with a marriage covenant. A covenant is not a contract where if one person defaults, the deal is off. Covenants are unconditional, unilateral agreements built upon a *foundation of trust* and based upon the word of the one promising. Covenants are witnessed by God, with God being the Guarantor.

Covenants cannot be broken; they remain in place until the death of one of the parties (or beyond death where promises have been made that extend past death [i.e., the covenant made between Jonathan and David or even everlasting as in the Noahic covenant of the rainbow]). Our marriage covenants have only one biblical end: that is the death of one of the marriage partners, *until parted by death*. Remember that part of your marriage vows? So few do! So when one or both spouses willfully walk out of a marriage, the covenant still stands. God, a witness to those covenant vows made on your wedding day, is also a partner, a participant in those covenant vows. As such, he is standing for those covenant marriage vows. Let us look at those familiar verses from Malachi on divorce and marriage vows. Note that as you read this scripture, it really is not gender specific for it applies equally to both husband and wife.

> "This is another thing you do: you cover the altar of the Lord with tears, with weeping and with groaning, because He no longer regards the offering or accepts *it with* favor from your hand. Yet you say, 'For what reason?' Because the Lord has been a witness between you and the wife of your youth, against whom you have dealt treacherously, though she is your companion and your wife by covenant. But not one has done *so* who has a remnant of the Spirit. And what did *that* one *do* while he was seeking a godly offspring? Take heed then to your spirit, and let no one deal treacherously against the wife of your youth. For I hate divorce," says the Lord, the God of Israel, "and him who covers his garment with wrong," says the Lord of hosts. "So take heed to your spirit, that you do not deal treacherously."

> Malachi 2:13–16 (nasb)

Another aspect of covenants is that they are enforced by character with the focus on giving of one's self; thus, they are commitment based. As mentioned above, covenants between humans are until death, yet they remain in effect forever with God. On a more practical note, those in covenant are saying, "What can I give? I'm happy to do it. I accept responsibility. I'll be faithful forever. I'll give 100 percent. I am trusting. I want to, it's a relationship." On the other side of the coin, if we look at the marriage relationship as a contract, the participants may say, "What do I get? It's not my responsibility. It's not my fault. I'll be faithful for now. I'll meet you halfway. I am suspicious. I have to, it's a deal." Who in their right mind would go into a marriage with this second set of attitudes? But millions of us do enter into marriages with that attitude. Still others, not understanding the permanency of covenant, drift from the first set of attitudes into the second set of attitudes because their marriages are not based upon the Solid Rock of Jesus Christ. Let's face it, marriage is difficult because it requires two individuals who are different physically, psychologically, and emotionally and who are just *different* to come together in a close relationship of cooperation for a lifetime (thirty, forty, fifty, perhaps sixty years). Marriages require hard work from both participants; thus, they are a work *in progress* until one participant dies.

As we look at covenant, we recognize that our God is a God of covenant. The Bible, from Genesis to the book of Revelation, is the story of God's many covenants with mankind. Speaking to Abram (at the time God changed his name to Abraham), God said, "I will establish my covenant as an everlasting covenant between me and you and your descendants after you for the generations to come, to be your God and the God of your descendants after you" (Genesis 17:7, NIV 1984).

From this everlasting covenant, God established his everlasting relationship as our God and his everlasting relationship with us, his children. In like manner, the permanence and the importance of our covenant marriage vows can be seen in God's relationship with mankind. Secular courts cannot sever our covenant marriage vows. They can only sever man-made relationships, *not* relationships made by God. When God stands with us as a witness to the marriage vows we pledged to each other, he (God) becomes a party to those vows. That is why those of us who are standing and who are divorced in the in the eyes of secular courts state emphatically that in their heart, we are still married in God's eyes! Whose laws do you choose to follow, man's or God's?

> One day the Pharisees were badgering him: "Is it legal for a man to divorce his wife for any reason?" He answered, "Haven't you read in your Bible that the Creator originally made man and woman for each other, male and female? And because of this, a man leaves father and mother and is firmly bonded to his wife, becoming one flesh—no longer two bodies but one. Because God created this organic union of the two sexes, no one should desecrate his art by cutting them apart."
>
> Matthew 19:3–6 (MSG)

The Message states that man should not desecrate God's art (the two becoming one flesh) *by cutting them apart*. Very strong words, but you get the picture. Other translations quote Jesus as saying, "Let man not separate." The message is this: marriage is permanent! Man cannot separate what God has put together. However, many will take Jesus's next statement as their *escape hatch*. Let us look at it, examine it closely, and realize that it was written by a Jewish writer speaking to a Jewish audience in the first century.

> They said to Him, "Why then did Moses command to give a certificate of divorce, and to put her away?" He said to them, "Moses, because of the hardness of your hearts, permitted you to divorce your wives, but from the beginning it was not so. And I say to you, whoever divorces his wife, except for sexual immorality, and marries another, commits adultery; and whoever marries her who is divorced commits adultery."

Matthew 19:7–9 (NKJV)

What's this? Is Jesus talking about adultery? Just what is Jesus stating that constitutes a legitimate biblical reason for divorce? Let us look at how this *exception clause* is recorded in Matthew in the various commonly read translations of the Bible. The New International Version uses the word *marital unfaithfulness*, the King James Version uses *fornication*, the New Revised Standard Version uses *unchastity*, the New Living Translation uses *unfaithful*, and the New American Standard Bible uses *immorality*. From the original Greek, the word is *porneia*, which translates to "fornication." Many today feel that this word is loosely translated to be adultery, and therefore, adultery (sexual unfaithfulness in marriage) is grounds for divorce. But when we look at the Greek, we see the true meaning as originally spoken by Jesus was "fornication," which translates as a sexual act occurring outside the confines of a consummated marriage (sexual intercourse between unmarried people). Therefore, Matthew is not recording Jesus as speaking to us in the twenty-first century that adultery is biblical grounds for divorce. So what was Jesus stating?

Matthew was speaking to a Jewish audience in the first century AD, so we need to look at Jewish marriage customs in biblical times and in the first century AD. When a woman was pledged (betrothed) to a man, she was considered to be his wife. A betrothal contract of intent of marriage having been established, and it was as binding as marriage. She often came to live in his household, yet they did not come together sexually to consummate the marriage for at least a year, and only then after the final ceremony took place at the end of the betrothal period. Then, and only then, were they fully married and sexual contact was permitted and the marriage consummated. It was during this year of betrothal that a husband could sever the bonds of marriage pledged at the beginning of the betrothal period should the woman be sexually unfaithful (fornication). That is, he could divorce the woman. Remember the story of Mary and Joseph and the birth of our Lord and Savior, Jesus Christ.

> Now the birth of Jesus Christ was as follows: After His mother Mary was betrothed to Joseph, before they came together, she was found with child of the Holy Spirit. Then Joseph her husband, being a just *man,* and not wanting to make her a public example, was minded to put her away secretly. But while he thought about these things, behold, an angel of the Lord appeared to him in a dream, saying, "Joseph, son of David, do not be afraid to take to you Mary your wife, for that which is conceived in her is of the Holy Spirit…. Then Joseph, being aroused from sleep, did as the angel of the Lord commanded him and took to him his wife, and did not know her till she had brought forth her firstborn Son. And he called His name Jesus.

> Matthew 1:18–20, 24–25 (NKJV)

Joseph thought Mary was guilty of fornication and wished to divorce her quietly. But being a godly man, he listened to the angel of the Lord and understood the truth. Joseph did not divorce Mary. He took her as his wife, but he had no union with her until after the birth of Jesus, after the completion of the betrothal period. This part of the story of Jesus is based upon Jewish customs in the first century AD. It is in the light of Jewish marriage customs going back to the time of Moses that Jesus made his statement about fornication (commonly thought today to mean adultery) as recorded in Matthew's Gospel. Matthew was writing to a Jewish audience, so the statement applies only to a Jewish family and Jewish customs in biblical times. Nowhere else in the Gospels or in the writings of Paul is divorce said to be okay *for any reason!*

So each of us needs to think twice, thrice, or a thousand times or more before we break covenant with our spouse. Covenant breaking is a *sin* in God's eyes, and that should be reason enough for anyone to avoid doing it![17] [18]

Standing firm until parted by death.

Until Parted By Death

You and I have something in common. No, it is not that we are all human or that all of us are sinners who have fallen short of God's glory. No, it is not that we are seeking God's help and guidance in the healing of our broken marriages. While all of these things can be descriptors applied to each of us, the one thing we all have in common is that at the beginning of our married life, we all took covenant vows before God and our spouses. Those vows included a phrase that stated in substance, *until parted by death.* Too many young people (and older individuals also), in the throes of romantic love, seldom hear this phrase in their vows let alone understand what it means. In like manner, other phrases in our marriage vows such as *in sickness or in health, for richer or for poorer*, and *for better or for worse* just don't rise to the surface of our consciousness as we are caught up in the romantic excitement of the moment. What we often don't appreciate is the seriousness that God puts on these covenant vows we take when we are joined to our spouse in holy matrimony. So let us take a look at this critical vow taken before God and our spouses.

God ordained marriage to be a lifelong union between a man and a woman. Yet too many evangelical Christians, in excess of 50 percent, seek to terminate that union through divorce. From the Word, we find references to this union in Genesis, in the writings of the prophet Malachi, in the teachings of Jesus, and in the teachings of Paul. Each talks about the two (male and female, husband and wife) becoming one flesh.

> Therefore a man shall leave his father and mother and be joined to his wife, and they shall become one flesh.
>
> Genesis 2:24 (NKJV)

You can cry and cover the LORD's altar with tears, but the Lord will not accept your gifts. He will not be pleased with the things you bring to him. You ask, "Why are our gifts not accepted?" It is because the LORD saw the evil things you did—he is a witness against you. He saw you cheat on your wife. You have been married to her since you were young. She was your girlfriend. Then you made your vows to each other—and she became your wife. God wants husbands and wives to become one body and one spirit. Why? So that they would have holy children and protect that spiritual unity. Don't cheat on your wife. She has been your wife from the time you were young. The LORD, the God of Israel, says, "I hate divorce, and I hate the cruel things that men do. So protect your spiritual unity. Don't cheat on your wife."

Malachi 2:13–16 (ERV)

The Pharisees also came to Him, testing Him, and saying to Him, "Is it lawful for a man to divorce his wife for *just* any reason?" And He answered and said to them, "Have you not read that He who made *them* at the beginning 'made them male and female,' and said, 'For this reason a man shall leave his father and mother and be joined to his wife, and the two shall become one flesh'? So then, they are no longer two but one flesh. Therefore what God has joined together, let not man separate." They said to Him, "Why then did Moses command to give a certificate of divorce, and to put her away?" He said to them, "Moses, because of the hardness of your hearts, permitted you to divorce your wives, but from the beginning it was not so."

Matthew 19:3–8 (NKJV)

> The Scriptures say, "That is why a man will leave his father and mother and join his wife, and the two people will become one." That secret truth is very important—I am talking about Christ and the church.
>
> Ephesians 5:31–32 (ERV)

Note that the scripture from Malachi speaks of God being a witness to the union between a husband and his wife. In Paul's reference, he states that marriage is a human echo of the relationship of Christ and his *bride*, the church. From all four scriptures, we should glean that there is permanence in the marriage relationship. What better way to state this than to state from the onset of marriage that the only thing that terminates this relationship, these covenant vows, is death of one of the marriage partners. However, in the throes of romantic love and in the excitement of the moment, *until parted by death* gets little more than lip service and little or no commitment by either marriage partner. It is sad that so many God-fearing Christians just don't get it. People, we took covenant vows before God! Yes, I said before God! He was a witness to our wedding vows. We swore or affirmed these vows before God! It doesn't get more intense or serious. Yet greater than 50 percent of evangelical Christians thumb their nose at God (who they will stand before on Judgment Day) when they break covenant, leave a marriage, and seek divorce. Brothers and sisters, we took a vow, a solemn covenant vow! And it included only one termination clause: *until parted by death*. So look at your own situation and see where you stand.

Some of you are contemplating filing for divorce. Think again as this is sin, so don't go there. For those who are divorced and were the instigators of the action, repent of this sin, seeking God's forgiveness and that of your spouse. For those who are divorced (not by your own action), look at your own failings that led to this action by your spouse, and seek God's and your spouse's forgiveness. In like manner, pray for your spouse that the Holy Spirit will convict them of their rebellion and their departure from the marriage covenant.

Remember, covenant marriage vows are not a contract; they are covenant and have the permanence of covenant. Remember, there is only one termination clause: *until parted by death.*

Standing firm until parted by death.

Obedient To God's Will

As I pen this devotional, thousands upon thousands of couples around the world are getting married on this special day, 07/07/07. Not only is this an interesting group of numbers for a date, but on this special day, in each of these individual's lives, a monumental decision is being made. A marriage covenant is being established. That covenant will impact their lives and the lives of their families for generations to come. Often, young couples (and older couples also) do not understand the seriousness and the impact of their covenant marriage vows made before God and their spouse. Our wedding vows are a covenant made before God even when we don't realize that they constitute a covenant. Those vows include promises to remain faithful in sickness and in health, for better or for worse, and the far-reaching one: until parted by death. As I think back upon my own wedding, I remember repeating those vows and understood they meant until my wife and I were parted by death.

> "For I know the plans I have for you," declares the LORD, "plans to prosper you and not to harm you, plans to give you hope and a future. Then you will call upon me and come and pray to me, and I will listen to you. You will seek me and find me when you seek me with all your heart."

> Jeremiah 29:11–13 (NIV 1984)

Our Lord calls each of us to be obedient to his will. God's will for each of his people is to seek his face, to pray to him, and to keep our covenant marriage vows. A marriage covenant is not a contract; it is a solemn vow taken before God, and he is a witness to those vows. A covenant is similar to the blood oath of primitive cultures, becoming a *blood brother*, and it was sacred. Covenants are built upon a foundation of trust, upon unlimited responsibility, upon the word of the one who is promising. Covenants cannot be broken (they usually end only with the death of one partner). Covenants are unilateral agreements, are unconditional, and are witnessed by God. He is the Guarantor. Covenants are built upon the giving of one's self, upon relationship, upon commitment, upon promise, and are enforced by one's character, one's integrity.

Contracts, on the other hand, are basically built upon mistrust (covenants are built upon a foundation of trust). Contracts limit liability and can be voided by mutual consent. They are bilateral agreements, conditional, and are based upon the actions of both parties. Contracts are witnessed by other people, with the state being the guarantor, and are enforced by civil courts. They are written for a specific period and are predicated upon performance of the other party, not our own performance.

I cannot say it any clearer: marriage vows are a covenant, not a contract! God set forth marriage as a sacred ordinance between a man and a woman until parted by death! Our marriage vows were set up by God, and he considers covenant-breaking a sin. Sin separates us from God and his many blessings. Malachi spoke of this centuries before the coming of Christ.

> You can cry and cover the LORD's altar with tears, but the Lord will not accept your gifts. He will not be pleased with the things you bring to him. You ask, "Why are our gifts not accepted?" It is because the LORD saw the evil things you did—He is a witness against you. He saw you cheat on your wife. You have been married to her since you were young. She was you girlfriend. Then you made your vows

to each other—and she became your wife. God wants husbands and wives to become one body and one spirit. Why? So that they would have holy children and protect that spiritual unity. Don't cheat on your wife. She had been your wife from the time you were young. The LORD, the God of Israel, says, "I hate divorce, and I hate the cruel things that men do. So protect your spiritual unity. Don't cheat on your wife."

Malachi 2:13–16 (ERV)

[Jesus is speaking.] "But at the beginning of creation God 'made them male and female.' 'For this reason a man will leave his father and mother and be united to his wife, and the two will become one flesh.' So they are no longer two, but one. Therefore what God has joined together, let man not separate."

Mark 10:6–9 (NIV 1984)

So my question to you today is, whose will are you following? Is it man's, the will of the flesh, the call of Satan; or is it God's will, the obedience that comes from having a relationship with our Lord and Savior, Jesus Christ? Following the world's ways, Satan's will, leads to death—death of the soul. Following God's will leads to life eternal with him. We each make choices. Hopefully, we will be obedient to God's will. Even Jesus was obedient to his Father's will:

Then they came to a place which was named Gethsemane; and He said to His disciples, "Sit here while I pray." And He took Peter, James, and John with Him, and He began to be troubled and deeply distressed. Then He said to them, "My soul is exceedingly sorrowful, *even* to death. Stay here and watch." He went a little farther, and fell on the ground, and prayed that if it were possible, the hour might pass from Him. And He said, "Abba, Father, all things *are* possible for You. Take this cup away from Me; nevertheless, not what I will, but what You *will.*"

Mark 14:32–36 (NKJV)

Are you being obedient to the Father's will? Are you standing strong and tall in your call to stand by your covenant marriage vows? I hope so. This is a decision you need to make today, without fail! As I pen these thoughts, there is a funeral going on down the street at a small church for a nineteen-year-old man who died this week in an automobile accident. He left behind a wife and two small children. His obituary stated that he had made the decision to follow God's will for his life and that he loved God. Your walk with Jesus is the most important decision you will ever make in this life. Nearly as important is to remember your covenant marriage vows and to honor them. Our awesome God honors obedience to his will, and he will orchestrate the healing of your marriage in his perfect timing. May God bless you in your stand.[19]

Standing firm until parted by death.

Marriage, Separation, and Divorce

I Have A Dream

I have a dream today...

I have a dream that one day every valley shall be exalted, every hill and mountain shall be made low, the rough places will be made plain, and crooked places will be made straight, and the glory of the Lord shall be revealed, and all flesh shall see it together...

And when this happens, and when we allow freedom ring—when we let it ring from every village and every hamlet, from every state and every city, we will be able to speed up that day when all of God's children—black men and white men, Jews and Gentiles, Protestants and Catholics—will be able to join hands and sing in the words of the old Negro spiritual: "Free at last! Free at last! Thank God Almighty, we are free at last!"[20]

There is hardly any American alive today that has not heard of Rev. Martin Luther King Jr. and his "I Have a Dream" speech delivered on August 28, 1963. He gave this speech on the steps of the Lincoln Memorial in Washington, DC, bringing national attention to the civil rights movement. This speech was a pivotal moment in history and prompted the passage of the Civil Rights Act of 1964.

I *too* have a dream! I dream that one day, all of God's children will be so well-versed in the Holy Bible that Christian couples everywhere will have a clear understanding of the meaning of covenant and their covenant marriage vows taken before God and their spouse. Sadly, however, as attested in the staggering divorce statistics that are hovering around 50 percent in the American evangelical church, Christians (including many church leaders) don't understand or wish to understand the impact of covenant. I have a dream that Christian couples everywhere will enter into their covenant marriage vows understanding that there is only one thing that terminates a Christian marriage: that is the death of one of the partners. Even among Christians, *until parted by death* means so little today. Covenant vows are very important to God, and to break them is a sin. When covenant vows are broken, we must seek repentance and try to rectify the situation through reconciliation with our spouse if at all possible. Just because we didn't realize that covenant-breaking is a sin doesn't free us from the consequences. Just think of the situation of receiving a citation for exceeding a speed limit of 30 mph when we thought it was 45. Ignorance of the speed limit does not make your speeding any less serious. In like manner, ignorance of the significance of covenant marriage vows is not a valid argument for a Christian who seeks to follow God's will. So remember the work Christ did for us on the cross, and seek repentance for this sin.

I have a dream that *no-fault* divorce will become a thing of the past in the very near future. There needs to be a ground swell of realization in the Body of Christ that the Christian family is on the verge of collapse as this epidemic of divorce impacts our families and our children, often for generations down the line. Too often our church leaders choose to look the other way, tread lightly, or just ignore troubled marriages and the resultant divorce and the fracture of the family that occurs. When divorce is criticized from the pulpit, many in the congregation squirm but do little. Some may speak out against the message because it hits too close to home. Still others will leave the church fellowship altogether, while others seek a church more *tolerant* of divorce. Divorce fractures the Body of Christ, splits it, often leaving it wounded beyond reasonable repair.

I have a dream that the church, the Body of Christ (the church fellowship), will *circle the wagons* around a hurting marriage, loving the couple, mentoring the couple, and giving the couple a Christian arena where they can work through the problems in their marriage relationship. The church body needs to be equipped to provide tools for the couple to use as they seek to repair their marriage. I know this can be done as it is being done with great success by Pastor Leo Godzich in Phoenix, Arizona. The divorce rate in his church is a fraction of 1 percent in a congregation of over ten thousand members. Yes, it can be done when covenant marriage vows and Christ are unashamedly preached from the pulpits of our churches. For we all are called by Paul to the following standard in our marriages.

> Wives and Husbands. Be willing to serve each other out of respect for Christ. Wives, be willing to serve your husbands the same as the Lord. A husband is the head of his wife, just as Christ is the head of the church. Christ is the Savior of the church, which is his body. The church serves under Christ, so it is the same with you wives. You should be willing to serve your husbands in everything. Husbands, love your wives the same as Christ loved the church and gave his life for it. He died to make the church holy. He used the telling of the Good News to make the church clean by washing it with water. Christ died so that he could give the church to himself like a bride in all her beauty. He died so that the church could be holy and without fault, with no evil or sin or any other thing wrong in it. And husbands should love their wives like

that. They should love their wives as they love their own bodies. The man who loves his wife loves himself, because no one ever hates his own body, but feeds and takes care of it. And that is what Christ does for the church because we are parts of his body. The Scriptures say, "That is why a man will leave his father and mother and join his wife, and the two people will become one." That secret truth is very important—I am talking about Christ and the church. But each one of you must love his wife as he loves himself. And a wife must respect her husband.

Ephesians 5:21–33 (ERV)

Yes, I have a dream and a promise from God that in his own special timing, my own marriage will be resurrected and rebuilt upon the Solid Rock of Jesus Christ. Yes, I have a dream and a promise from God of a ministry with my wife (as husband and wife), teaching the principles of marriage reconciliation first to our children and grandchildren and then to others. Yes, I have a dream that a restored marriage can become a reality if I have faith in the promises of God. I have a dream! And this can be your dream too, a promise of a resurrected marriage for those who put their hope, their faith, and their trust in our Lord Jesus Christ.

Thus, I stand on a promise from God of a restored marriage. I have a dream of a modern-day miracle from God of a resurrected marriage, where God uses the same resurrection powers he used on Easter morning. Yes, I have a dream of an Easter-morning miracle, not only for my own marriage, but for all hurting marriages around the world. Then we all will be able to sing with Rev. King: "Free at last! Free at last! Thank God Almighty, we are free at last!"

Yes, I have a dream that all couples around the world will be free from the bondage of marital separation or divorce to worship Jesus Christ together as families, husbands with their wives and parents with their children. Yes, then we will be free in Christ, free to seek his face and his will in our resurrected and reconciled marriages.

Yes, I have a dream today.

May God bless you in your stand, and may your dream of a resurrected marriage become a reality.

Standing firm until parted by death.

The Deserts Of Our Lives

Have you ever had the thought that the world was just closing in on you? Circumstances in your life just couldn't get any worse! Is it arguments with your spouse? Is it finances? Kids? Your job? Could it be health and/or addiction issues? Or could it be family relationships, separation, or even divorce that has you at wits' end? What you are experiencing is one of the desert experiences of life that we all have from time to time. Don't despair for these are special times that our Lord uses to come close to us, to show us his glory and grace, to teach us, to possibly chasten us, and to help us grow in righteousness. For some of us, these desert experiences may be our first encounter with Jesus, and we find that he is faithful, always faithful. Even our Lord Jesus had desert experiences.

> At that time Jesus came from Nazareth in Galilee and was baptized by John in the Jordan. As Jesus was coming up out of the water, he saw heaven being torn open and the Spirit descending on him like a dove. And a voice came from heaven: "You are my Son, whom I love; with you I am well pleased." At once the Spirit sent him out into the desert, and he was in the desert forty days, being tempted by Satan. He was with the wild animals, and angels attended him.

Mark 1:9–13 (NIV 1984)

From this account, we see that Jesus had just experienced a mountaintop event, that of baptism and affirmation by his Father, before he entered into his desert experience. In our own lives, many of our mountaintop experiences will be followed by times of desert experiences. It is in the desert that we realize our need and dependence upon God. Here we grow as God teaches us. We needed something, an event, to get our attention so that God can have a teaching moment, a teaching season. Once again, let us look at Jesus.

> Then Jesus was led up by the Spirit into the wilderness to be tempted by the devil. And when He had fasted forty days and forty nights, afterward He was hungry. Now when the tempter came to Him, he said, "If You are the Son of God, command that these stones become bread." But He answered and said, "It is written, 'Man shall not live by bread alone, but by every word that proceeds from the mouth of God.'" Then the devil took Him up into the holy city, set Him on the pinnacle of the temple, and said to Him, "If You are the Son of God, throw Yourself down. For it is written: 'He shall give His angels charge over you,' and, 'In *their* hands they shall bear you up, Lest you dash your foot against a stone.'" Jesus said to him, "It is written again, 'You shall not tempt the Lord your God.'" Again, the devil took Him up on an exceedingly high mountain, and showed Him all the kingdoms of the world and their glory. And he said to Him, "All these things I will give You if You will fall down and worship me." Then Jesus said to him, "Away with you, Satan! For it is written, 'You shall worship the Lord your God, and Him only you shall serve.'" Then the devil left Him, and behold, angels came and ministered to Him.
>
> Matthew 4:1–11 (NKJV)

While there is just the dialog between Jesus and Satan, we know that Father God was at work in Jesus to give him the wisdom and strength to resist Satan. In like manner, when we are in our desert experiences, we need to lean on and listen to the Holy Spirit as he strengthens and nourishes our spirit. In her book *The Hiding Place*, Corrie ten Boom tells of the desert experiences of her sister and herself in Ravensbrück, a Nazi concentration camp during WWII. The ten Boom family, a Christian Dutch family, were part of the underground who were helping local Jews escape Nazi persecution. When their activity was discovered, they were arrested. In Ravensbrück, Corrie became very bitter, mired down in self-pity, feeling that God had forgotten them. Her sister, Betsie, reminded her "that there is no pit so deep that He [Jesus] is not deeper still!" Betsie implored Corrie to share their desert story after she got out of Ravensbrück of how Jesus was the victor in the concentration camps. Betsie went on to die in her desert place, yet in reality, she was on her own personal mountaintop as Jesus was there with her, ministering to her spirit. And he can minister to each of us in our desert places. Jesus will meet you in your desert to nourish you, to strengthen you, and to help you through your desert experience.

> Therefore, having been justified by faith, we have peace with God through our Lord Jesus Christ, through whom also we have access by faith into this grace in which we stand, and rejoice in hope of the glory of God. And not only *that*, but we also glory in tribulations, knowing that tribulation produces perseverance; and perseverance, character; and character, hope. Now hope does not disappoint, because the love of God has been poured out in our hearts by the Holy Spirit who was given to us. For when we were still without strength, in due time Christ died for the ungodly.

> Romans 5:1–6 (NKJV)

This passage shows that our sufferings lead to perseverance, character development, and lastly hope. Through faith, we accept Jesus as our Lord and Savior and that he is the Son of God. We further acknowledge that he died on the cross, taking upon himself God's wrath for our personal sins in exchange for his righteousness. So don't be distressed by your desert experiences. Be thankful for them. For in that desert, God lavishes his love and grace upon us as he teaches and strengthens us for what lies ahead.

Remember the Old Testament story of Joseph. His brothers threw him into a pit and then sold him into slavery. Later he was thrown in prison on false charges by Potipher's wife and he was forgotten. Being a patient, wise, and godly person, he rose to second-in-command of Egypt, just under Pharaoh. From his desert experiences, Joseph developed perseverance, character growth, and hope. Years later, his brothers came before him in Egypt, looking for food during a time of widespread famine.

> His brothers then came and threw themselves down before him. "We are your slaves," they said. But Joseph said to them, "Don't be afraid. Am I in the place of God? You intended to harm me, but God intended it for good to accomplish what is now being done, the saving of many lives."

> Genesis 50:18–20 (NIV 1984)

The New Testament contains passages of desert experiences, of humility, and of sufferings. For the early Christians, their desert experiences were persecution. But the Holy Spirit was with them, teaching, comforting, even convicting. The same is true for us today. I say convicting because many desert experiences are the result of our own personal wrong life choices. In these deserts, if our hearts are open, we are purified, and we emerge a better person, able to accept life's challenges as we witness to others what our Lord God has done in our lives. Remember Corrie ten Boom? She spent the next thirty-five years traveling the world, evangelizing to a fallen world that Jesus loves us all and that he died on a cross that we might have eternal life with him and the Father. She taught *forgiveness* and *reconciliation*.[21]

> Humble yourselves, therefore, under God's mighty hand, that he may lift you up in due time. Cast all your anxiety on him because he cares for you. Be self-controlled and alert. Your enemy the devil prowls around like a roaring lion looking for someone to devour. Resist him, standing firm in the faith, because you know that your brothers throughout the world are undergoing the same kind of sufferings. And the God of all grace, who called you to his eternal glory in Christ, after you have suffered a little while, will himself restore you and make you strong, firm and steadfast.
>
> 1 Peter 5:6–10 (NIV 1984)

"Will himself restore you and make you strong, firm, and steadfast." So don't resist your deserts. They have a purpose. May God bless you in your stand for Jesus Christ, in your stand for your marriage relationship, and in your desert experiences.

Standing firm until parted by death.

The Desert Of Your Love: The Empty Chair

Holidays are particularly troublesome when one or more of our loved ones are absent in our lives. One type of absence involves the fracturing of the family unit by separation and/or divorce. For many of us, we will have a sense of emptiness in our hearts because our one-flesh spouse is absent in the physical sense, but not absent in our thoughts or in our hearts. While that statement may sound contradictory, think about the emptiness in our hearts for a moment. It is true that if we have Jesus Christ in our lives, he can fill any emptiness that we may feel or experience in our hearts. Yet we humans are relational beings, and we thrive on relationships. We miss the physical presence of our spouses. God is also relational, and he understands our needs. So from the very beginning of time, he realized that man (Adam) should not be alone, so he created woman (Eve).

> Then the LORD God said, "I see that it is not good for the man to be alone. I will make the companion he needs, one just right for him...." The LORD God used the rib from the man to make a woman. Then he brought the woman to the man. And the man said, "Finally! One like me, with bones from my bones and a body from my body. She was taken out of a man, so I will call her 'woman.'" That is why a man leaves his father and mother and is joined to his wife. In this way two people become one.
>
> Genesis 2:18, 22–24 (ERV)

Now as the holidays approach, we see empty chairs where our spouses should be. As we are relational beings, God is also relational and does not desire to spend eternity without his children.

> For God so loved the world, that He gave His only begotten Son, that whoever believes in Him shall not perish, but have eternal life. For God did not send the Son into the world to judge the world, but that the world might be saved through Him.
>
> John 3:16–17 (NASB)

In summary, our God wishes to have eternal fellowship with all his children. That is why he sent his Son to die on a cross for us, bearing our sins upon his body. Through God's grace, we as believers can have the comfort of knowing that we will be in fellowship with God throughout eternity. We also believe that Jesus Christ is walking alongside us right now, feeling the pain we experience in the separation from our flesh-and-blood spouses. During this time, Jesus is our spiritual spouse in the absence of our physical (flesh-and-blood) spouses.

So as you look across the table during the holiday season and see an empty chair, realize that your Father in heaven has sent you into a desert, a desert of longing, a desert of uncertainty, yet a desert of love. It is in the desert that God reaches out to each of us, comforting us and teaching us about his endless love for us. Remember the desert experiences of Moses, of the Israelites during their forty years of wandering in the desert, of the prophets of old, and even of our Lord Jesus at the start of his ministry. Let your desert experience during the holiday season be a fresh encounter with your Lord and Savior, Jesus Christ. May you, like Paul, have the scales fall off your eyes as you experience a new and deeper relationship with your personal Jesus Christ. Jesus loves us with a love that defies understanding, and he, bearing our sins, chose to die on a cross in his desert (Golgotha) so that you and I might have fellowship with our Triune God for eternity. He extends that love to all who would believe in him as he spreads out his arms on that cross. In like manner, as we view our empty chairs during the holiday season, let us extend our love to and our prayers for our absent spouses.

Remember the words of the Apostle Paul in his letter to the Corinthian Church. He was explaining to them in just a few sentences who they were in Christ. So put yourself in these verses of this scripture that is the Gospel message in a nutshell.

When anyone is in Christ, it is a whole new world. The old things are gone; suddenly, everything is new! All this is from God. Through Christ, God made peace between himself and us. And God gave us the work of bringing people into peace with him. I mean that God was in

Christ, making peace between the world and himself. In Christ, God did not hold people guilty for their sins. And he gave us this message of peace to tell people. So we have been sent to speak for Christ. It is like God is calling to people through us. We speak for Christ when we beg you to be at peace with God. Christ had no sin, but God made him become sin so that in Christ we could be right with God.

2 Corinthians 5:17–21 (ERV)

Jesus will fill your every need, and he will fill your empty chair during this time in your life. Corrie ten Boom, in her book *The Hiding Place,* tells of her desert experiences as an inmate in Ravensbrück, a Nazi concentration camp during WWII. In her bitterness and self pity, her sister Betsie reminded her "that there is no pit so deep that He (*Jesus*) is not deeper still!" What a word of encouragement when we find ourselves mired in such self-destructive thoughts! Lean on Jesus Christ, he is our Lord and Savior. Our God's love has no limits as spoken by the Apostle Paul to the Ephesians.[22]

I pray that Christ will live in your hearts because of your faith. I pray that your life will be strong in love and be built on love. And I pray that you and all God's holy people will have the power to understand the greatness of Christ's love—how wide, how long, how high, and how deep that love is. Christ's love is greater than anyone can ever know, but I pray that you will be able to know that love. Then you can be filled with everything God has for you.

Ephesians 3:17–19 (ERV)

May our God bless you as you stand firm for your covenant marriage vows, and as you face your holidays, you will find the chair that once was empty is now filled with your loved one.

Standing firm until parted by death.

Gethsemane: Yours, Mine, And Christ's

The events that surround Christ's moments at Gethsemane impact us all. For Christ, Gethsemane became the pivotal moment in his earthly ministry. As I reread these moments, many thoughts and parallels come to mind as each of us stand for our covenant marriages. But first, let us look at the account found in Luke. (Other accounts are in Matthew 26:36–46 and Mark 14:32–42.)

> Jesus Prays Alone—Jesus left the city and went to the Mount of Olives. His followers went with him. (He went there often.) He said to his followers, "Pray for strength against temptation." Then Jesus went about 50 steps away from them. He knelt down and prayed, "Father, if you are willing, please don't make me drink from this cup. But do what you want, not what I want." Then an angel from heaven came to help him. Jesus was full of pain; he struggled hard in prayer. Sweat dripped from his face like drops of blood falling to the ground. When he finished praying, he went to his followers. He found them asleep, worn out from their grieving.

> Luke 22:39–45 (ERV)

As you can see from this account, Jesus was in great anguish. As he prayed, sweat came from him like drops of blood, falling to the ground. After all, he knew what lay ahead for him—the cross. While there would be physical pain, he knew that he must suffer excruciating agony in separation from his Father's love as he took the burden of humanity's sin upon his body. Jesus would experience hell for you and me. Little did his followers understand what was in store for him those next few hours. He pleaded with his Father to "take this cup from me," knowing what was ahead. This figure of speech (this cup) even in that day meant to "undergo or experience" an event. The NIV 1984 Study Bible footnotes for Mark's Gospel state that the cup was "the chalice of death and of God's wrath." Yet he said to his Father, "Not my will, but yours be done." Christ, even though he was fully God (and fully man), he willingly took a subordinate position and followed his Father's will.

As you and I look at our troubled marriages, our separations, or even our divorces, we have a decision to make. We are at a crossroads, our Gethsemane, in our Christian walk: do we follow the ways of the world and seek a relationship with another person, *or* do we follow Christ, the way of the cross? I do not mean literal death on a cross but the way of suffering and Christian growth that comes from following the example set by our Lord and Savior, Jesus Christ. Have you said to our Heavenly Father, "Not my will, Lord, but your will for my life and marriage be done"? If not, then you need to think again of the covenant marriage vows you took before God and your spouse. God does not take lightly the breaking of covenant.

Look back at the Old Testament and the story of the Israelites. God continuously honored his covenant with Abraham as he took special care of Abraham's seed throughout the ages. This included blessing them when they followed his commands and also included disciplining his children in love when they disobeyed. Is this not what happens in our own families with our own children? (At least that is what should happen.) God has called each of us to a special Christian walk to stand for our marriages in obedience to his will. Remember, a marriage is only biblically dissolved with the death of one of the partners. So what is your decision? Are you standing for your covenant vows? There is no higher calling than obeying God's will for your life and marriage.

Jesus, at Gethsemane, pointed us to the way to get help for our dilemma. It is prayer. It was his answer to his dilemma of the cross. So pray, pray hard, pray boldly, pray long, pray persistently— just pray! Our Heavenly Father is always available to hear and respond to our prayers. Remember what Mark said: "Watch and pray, lest you enter into temptation. The spirit indeed *is* willing, but the flesh *is* weak" (Mark 14:38, NKJV).

So I leave you with this final thought from Mark's Gospel, a passage that you know so well.

> But from the beginning of the creation, God "made them male and female. For this reason a man shall leave his father and mother and be joined to his wife, and the two shall become one flesh"; so then they are no longer two, but one flesh. Therefore what God has joined together, let not man separate.
>
> Mark 10:6–9 (NKJV)

Standing firm until parted by death.

A Cord Of Three Strands

Today, I am going to look at the wisest man who ever lived, King Solomon. In the book of Ecclesiastes, Solomon, identified as the teacher, the son of King David, speaks (as written below in three different translations).

> Though one may be overpowered, two can defend themselves. A cord of three strands is not quickly broken.
>
> Ecclesiastes 4:12 (NIV 1984)

> A person standing alone can be attacked and defeated, but two can stand back-to-back and conquer. Three are even better, for a triple-braided cord is not easily broken.
>
> Ecclesiastes 4:12 (NLT)

> An enemy might be able to defeat one person, but two
> people can stand back-to-back to defend each other. And
> three people are even stronger. They are like a rope that
> has three parts wrapped together—it is very hard to break.

Ecclesiastes 4:12 (ERV)

The ERV (Easy-to-Read Version) talks about a rope with *three parts wrapped together*. The NIV 1984 uses *a cord of three strands*, while the NLT uses *a triple-braided cord*. I wish to expand upon this three-stranded cord theme because it is a perfect example of what a Christ-filled marriage looks like. Our enemy, Satan, chooses to break up our marriages by separating us from our base, Jesus Christ. If he can separate us from Christ, then he has a good chance of breaking us into *a person standing alone* (NLT)—defenseless. As the verse says, that person *can be attacked and defeated* (NLT). That is Satan's goal, to put enough doubts, anger, violence, and distrust into our marriages that separation and/or divorce is seen as the only answer.

However, if a marriage relationship is struggling but they are seeking help, we see from the second part of the verse that the two working together (the husband and wife) can fight back.

Solomon speaks of yet another scenario: what works best is *a cord of three strands, a triple-braided cord*, or *a rope that has three parts wrapped together* because they exhibit great strength. When I was a Boy Scout, one of our craft projects was to take a thin cord, one that was easily broken, and twist it together with two other similar cords, making a rope that had greater strength than the combined strength of the three individual cords. There is a strength that is obtained when the three individual strands work in unison that is not seen when they are separated down to two or perhaps one single strand. As we dissect this verse and apply it in our lives, a Christ-filled marriage looks like the *cord of three strands*. The husband strand finds strength in his association with the other two strands, and the wife likewise finds her strand strengthened by the other two strands. And the third strand? You have probably figured it out already. The third strand is Jesus Christ (the Christ strand). He is the central strand around which the husband strand and the wife strand are twisted, braided, or wrapped together. On the surface, the Christ strand may look the same in size, but the Christ strand exerts that extra power (the power of God) to hold the husband strand and the wife strand together. The Christ strand is the glue, the cement, the bond that brings the *cord of three strands* into a greater strength to fend off Satan. The stronger the Christ strand is (our relationship with Jesus Christ), the stronger that marriage is. It can resist the pulls of the world. While the world may pull upon that *cord of three strands,* on *a triple-braided cord,* or on *a rope that has three parts wrapped together,* these cords (ropes) may stretch, but the Christ strand lends strength to the bond between the other two strands: the husband strand and the wife strand. This illustration is given to say that with Christ at the center of our cord or rope (our marriage), Satan has great difficulty separating the husband strand from the wife strand.

> He answered, "Haven't you read in your Bible that the Creator originally made man and woman for each other, male and female? And because of this, a man leaves father and mother and is firmly bonded to his wife, becoming one flesh—no longer two bodies but one. Because God created this organic union of the two sexes, no one should desecrate his art by cutting them apart."
>
> Matthew 19:4–6 (MSG)

In marriage, our Creator made man and woman to be in fellowship with each other. That fellowship, a holy marriage, consists of a bonding together of the man with his wife. So tight should that bond be that the Bible says that the two become one flesh. They become one in Christ. Christ created this bond with himself as the central strand, the glue that holds them together as one. Christ goes on to state in the Message that *no one should desecrate his art by cutting them apart.* When a divorce occurs, Christ's art (our one-flesh union) is cut apart. Yet if our union is strong (built upon Jesus Christ), our cord of three strands is strong, showing a resilience that comes from our relationship with Christ. *A cord of three strands is not easily broken.*

So, fellow standers, you know what you must do. Seek the help of the Lord Jesus as you rebuild your fellowship and relationship with your spouse. Seek the central strand, the Christ strand, as you make that new marriage rope that ties together your heart with that of your spouse. The resulting new relationship (marriage) will then have great strength to resist Satan because it is woven around the Christ strand, that central strand at the core of a Christ-filled marriage.

A cord of three strands (a triple-braided cord or a rope that has three parts wrapped together) is not quickly broken!

Standing firm until parted by death.

Therefore What God Has Joined Together

I am sure that most, if not all of you, who are reading this devotional know this verse and how it ends: "Therefore what God has joined together, let not man separate" (Matthew 19:6b, NKJV). Many of us heard this as we took our wedding vows with our spouses. The minister or person performing your marriage service finished it with these words of Jesus Christ. In the scripture below, Jesus was discussing marriage and divorce with some of the Pharisees of his day. I want to explore some of the broader ramifications of Christ's statement as I see it.

> And He answered and said to them, "Have you not read that He who made *them* at the beginning 'made them male and female,' and said, 'For this reason a man shall leave his

father and mother and be joined to his wife, and the two
shall become one flesh'? So then, they are no longer two
but one flesh. Therefore what God has joined together, let
not man separate."

Matthew 19:4–6 (NKJV)

Depending upon the Bible translation that you read, a
number of different words are used: *one flesh, joined, cleave, united,
one*. Whatever word or term or principle is used, it denotes that
there has been a change in the relationship between the man and
the woman. It entails a spiritual, emotional, and physical coming
together as husband and wife, a union, a joining, a cleaving. In the
King James Version, the old English term *cleave* is used. "And shall
cleave unto his wife" (Genesis 2:24b, KJV). While the dictionary
defines that word to mean "split or sever along a natural line,"
and also "to cling, adhere," I feel that it is used in this context to
represent a separation from the husband's parents and a joining
with the wife, in which the line between the man and woman is
obliterated as they become one flesh. The institution of marriage,
of becoming one flesh, dates back to Adam and Eve in the garden.

I want to look at several other aspects of Christ's statement in
Matthew as we think about what God has done for you and me
in creating the marriage relationship. We are all familiar with the
passages in Ephesians where Paul talks about Christians being
the Bride of Christ.

"For this reason a man shall leave his father and mother
and be joined to his wife, and the two shall become one
flesh." This is a great mystery, but I speak concerning
Christ and the church.

Ephesians 5:31–32 (NKJV)

In Christ, as in marriage, we are joined together as one in the Body of Christ. The Apostle Paul speaks of this: "There is one body and one Spirit, and God chose you to have one hope. There is one Lord, one faith, and one baptism. There is one God and Father of us all, who rules over everyone. He works through all of us and in all of us" (Ephesians 4:4–6, ERV).

This relationship of the church (the Body of Christ) to Christ is further laid out for us in Revelation where the Body of Christ is the bride of Christ. "Let us rejoice and be happy and give God glory! Give God glory, because the wedding of the Lamb has come. And the Lamb's bride has made herself ready" (Revelation 19:7, ERV).

Finally, I want to look at the seventeenth chapter of John. In this beautiful prayer, Christ prays for all believers. He lays out for us the oneness of Father God, Jesus Christ, and you and me (the Body of Christ).

> Father, I pray that all who believe in me can be one. You are in me and I am in you. I pray that they can also be one in us. Then the world will believe that you sent me. I have given them the glory that you gave me. I gave them this glory so that they can be one, just as you and I are one. I will be in them, and you will be in me. So they will be completely one. Then the world will know that you sent me and that you loved them just as you loved me.
>
> John 17:21–23 (ERV)

Thus, you can see both in marriage as well as in our Christian faith, God seeks a one-flesh relationship, a oneness, a unity in all our relationships. Anything less is not acceptable. When Christ states in Matthew that man should not destroy this relationship, I equate the word *man* with the word *world*, namely Satan and his influences. For when a divorce occurs, Satan has entered and destroyed that marriage relationship. It is only through the resurrection power of God that a dead marriage can be brought back to life and the marriage rebuilt.

Therefore what God has joined together.

Standing firm until parted by death.

RECONCILIATION AND FORGIVENESS

Enough Love For Us Both

At a recent marriage reconciliation conference, one of the speakers was sharing her testimony. She related that her prodigal was in the process of coming home when he expressed concern that he had no love left for their marriage relationship. Her response was filled with so much love, Christ's love, that it just melted my heart. "Dear, until such time as you can rebuild your love, I have enough love for us both!" What a profound statement from a stander! Her love, her unconditional love, was a love with no boundaries, a love so full that it was overflowing with excess. Oh, that each of us as standers could express that kind of love for our prodigals. Where do we look to find an example of such love? We need only to look to the cross. We ask, "Jesus, how much do you love me?" His answer is "This much," and he spread out his arms, and he died for you and me! Brothers and sisters, if we are to rebuild our marriages, we must have a heart full of sacrificial love, an unconditional love, for our spouse. We must have a heart like Jesus. Paul writes about love in chapter 13 of 1 Corinthians:

> Love is patient, love is kind. It does not envy, it does not boast, it is not proud. It is not rude, it is not self-seeking, it is not easily angered, it keeps no record of wrongs. Love

does not delight in evil but rejoices with the truth. It always protects, always trusts, always hopes, always perseveres. Love never fails.... And now these three remain: faith, hope and love. But the greatest of these is love.

1 Corinthians 13:4–8a, 13 (NIV 1984)

Max Lucado suggests we put our own name in the place of the words *love* and *it* or any place love is implied. When we do, we can see this passage in a different, more meaningful and personal light. "Ben is patient, Ben is kind. Ben does not envy, Ben does not boast..." and so on. How powerful this passage becomes! After all, the pure essence of God and Jesus Christ is love.[23]

For God so loved the world that he gave his one and only Son, that whoever believes in him shall not perish but have eternal life.

John 3:16 (NIV 1984)

Lest we not forget the rest of Christ's message from the third chapter of John:

For God did not send his Son into the world to condemn the world, but to save the world through him. Whoever believes in him is not condemned, but whoever does not believe stands condemned already because he has not believed in the name of God's one and only Son. This is the verdict: Light has come into the world, but men loved darkness instead of light because their deeds were evil. Everyone who does evil hates the light, and will not come into the light for fear that his deeds will be exposed. But whoever lives by the truth comes into the light, so that it may be seen plainly that what he has done has been done through God.

John 3:17–21 (NIV 1984)

God, our Father, expressed his unconditional love for mankind, for you and for me, that he sent his one and only son to die on a cross as an atonement for our sins. Jesus, loving us so much, willingly followed his Father's will when he went to the cross, bearing the burden of our sins and God's wrath as punishment for our sins. Jesus taught about love throughout his ministry.

> My command is this: Love each other as I have loved you. Greater love has no one than this, that he lay down his life for his friends.
>
> John 15:12–13 (NIV 1984)

Don't forget about the message found in 1 John 3:16 (NIV 1984): "This is how we know what love is: Jesus Christ laid down his life for us. And we ought to lay down our lives for our brothers."

Jesus Christ, out of love for you and me, laid down his life for us. Are you willing to lay down your life for your spouse? If you cannot answer this question with a resounding yes, then you are not ready to receive your prodigal home. Unconditional love is the key to reconciling a broken marriage. It is sacrificial. It is central to our Christian faith, our walk with Jesus Christ. Unconditional love is the only answer that a Christian has to divorce. Let us look back again to 1 Corinthians 13.

> If I speak with the tongues of men and of angels, but do not have love, I have become a noisy gong or a clanging cymbal. If I have *the gift of* prophecy, and know all mysteries and all knowledge; and if I have all faith, so as to remove mountains, but do not have love, I am nothing. And if I give all my possessions to feed *the poor*, and if I surrender my body to be burned, but do not have love, it profits me nothing.
>
> 1 Corinthians 13:1–3 (NASB)

Love is the cornerstone of our Christian faith. Without love, we are nothing. Love is patient and kind; it does not envy or boast. It is not proud or rude; it is not self-seeking or easily angered. It does not keep a tally sheet of wrongs nor does it delight in evil; it rejoices when truth wins out. Love always protects, trusts, and hopes; it always perseveres. *Love never fails!* How many of those aspects of love have you failed at in your marriage? Remember that your spouse is not the enemy. It is Satan. We need to extend sacrificial love to our spouses when they hurt and mistreat us, even when they do not return our love. Mark's Gospel speaks of this. "If anyone would come after me, he must deny himself and take up his cross and follow me" (Mark 8:34b, NIV 1984).

Are you willing to take up your cross for your marriage? When you deny yourself and take up your cross, that is sacrificial love. Oh, if we could just get our arms around this concept of love, our marriages and our relationships would be on the road to healing, and our lives would be so much fuller.

So I repeat my opening thought: do you have enough love for both your spouse and yourself until your prodigal can heal? Jesus had enough love for you and me when we were sinners and did not love him. Can you do less for your spouse? Are you walking in his will? Are you obedient to God's will?

> And now I plead with you, lady, not as though I wrote a new commandment to you, but that which we have had from the beginning: that we love one another. This is love, that we walk according to His commandments. This is the commandment, that as you have heard from the beginning, you should walk in it.
>
> 2 John 1:5–6 (NKJV)

Standing firm until parted by death.

Narrow Is The Gate That Leads To Marriage Reconciliation

All of us have struggled with the many sinful choices offered by the everyday world. Some of us who are strong in the Lord can resist these choices. Others of us fall victim as Satan works to pull us away from our Lord Jesus Christ. Anger, fits of rage, lying, hatred, slander, bitterness, unforgiveness, stealing, sexual immorality, profanity, drugs, and drunkenness are some of the sinful choices that come to mind. Sooner or later, any one of these can lead to troubles in our marriages, resulting in separation, possibly divorce, and various types of family disasters. For those of us who have fallen for Satan's lies, we hopefully become aware that there is a life model that is quite different from the ways of the world. This is what marriage reconciliation is all about. It involves following Jesus Christ and his teachings. We realize that Jesus's ways and our worldly ways are at odds. Jesus teaches us that if we follow his example, he will lead us down a narrow road and through a narrow gate (door) into the splendor of God's grace.

> Enter through the narrow gate. For wide is the gate and broad is the road that leads to destruction, and many enter through it. But small is the gate and narrow the road that leads to life, and only a few find it.
>
> Matthew 7:13–14 (NIV 1984)

The broad road and gate (door) are the ways of the world—the world of drugs, sex, various crimes, and murder with all its pseudo glamour, excitement, glitz, whistles and bells. But when you examine them closer, there is no joy; there is just bitterness, heartache, sadness, and despair. Those ways are full of emptiness, and they will lead to destruction and death of the soul.

> So Jesus said to them again, "Truly, truly, I say to you, I am the door of the sheep. All who came before Me are thieves and robbers, but the sheep did not hear them. I am the door; if anyone enters through Me, he will be saved, and will go in and out and find pasture. The thief comes only to steal and kill and destroy; I came that they may have life, and have it abundantly.
>
> John 10:7–10 (NASB)

Jesus goes on to say, "I am the good shepherd; the good shepherd lays down His life for the sheep," (John 10:11, NASB).

Here Jesus explains the parable of the shepherd and his flock. Jesus is the gate or door, the one and only way to salvation. Inside, there is safety, and all our needs are met. We need only to reach out to him in faith.

> And He was passing through from one city and village to another, teaching, and proceeding on His way to Jerusalem. And someone said to Him, "Lord, are there *just* a few who are being saved?" And He said to them, "Strive to enter through the narrow door; for many, I tell you, will seek to enter and will not be able. Once the head of the house gets up and shuts the door, and you begin to stand outside and knock on the door, saying, 'Lord, open up to us!' then He will answer and say to you, 'I do not know where you are from.' Then you will begin to say, 'We ate and drank in Your presence, and You taught in our streets'; and He will say, 'I tell you, I do not know where you are from; depart from Me, all you evildoers.' In that place there will be weeping and gnashing of teeth when you see Abraham and Isaac and Jacob and all the prophets in the kingdom of God, but yourselves being thrown out. And they will come from east and west and from north and south, and will recline *at the table* in the kingdom of God. And behold, *some* are last who will be first and *some* are first who will be last."
>
> Luke 13:22–30 (NASB)

Once again, our Lord Jesus lays out the path to salvation. In another scripture, he says, "I am the way and the truth and the life. No one comes to the Father except through me" (John 14:6, NIV 1984).

Here Jesus is reaffirming that he is the gate to eternal life. He is not one of many ways to God; he is the *only* way to God! In like manner, the road (the way) is narrow because his requirement to pass down this road and through the gate (door) is the forsaking of our sinful life (Adam's sin) and putting our faith in the saving grace of our Lord Jesus Christ.

Several weeks ago, I picked up a teaching principle at a Bible study I wish to share with you. As we talk about the Christian life, the narrow gate (door) and path that we must follow and the choices we must make to follow Jesus, the world (the sinful life) throws back all the things we have to give up. The world perceives Christianity as being negative, a series of *do nots*. We can't drink, swear, gamble, take drugs, view pornography, lust, covet, be sexually impure, etc.! Where is all the fun? Where are the good times? Where is the...? How many of you have had friends, acquaintances, or even strangers tell you that the costs to be a Christian and to follow Jesus are just too great?

> Now the deeds of the flesh are evident, which are: immorality, impurity, sensuality, idolatry, sorcery, enmities, strife, jealousy, outbursts of anger, disputes, dissensions, factions, envying, drunkenness, carousing, and things like these, of which I forewarn you, just as I have forewarned you, that those who practice such things will not inherit the kingdom of God.
>
> Galatians 5:19–21 (NASB)

The following statement (principle) will stimulate some thought and some wonder, so here it is: *Christianity is not about what we (you or I) have to give up when we choose to put our faith in Jesus Christ and follow him; it is about what we (you and I) do with what is left.* Let that sink in for a few minutes for it is very profound. After thinking about the narrow gate and the narrow road that leads to our Lord Jesus Christ, I realized that while the gate and road are initially very narrow, the road leads to an infinite number of godly choices. Christianity leads us into a new life of freedom, a brand-new life that is positive. As you ponder this definition of Christianity, you will realize that God has given us so much that we cannot even see the boundaries of his love and the pleasures he has provided for us. For everything we must give up (by not following Satan), our Lord Jesus Christ in turn has provided countless godly things for us if we will just follow him. We indeed have a new freedom in Jesus Christ since we no longer have our old sin nature we inherited from Adam.

> But the fruit of the Spirit is love, joy, peace, patience, kindness, goodness, faithfulness, gentleness and self-control. Against such things there is no law. Those who belong to Christ Jesus have crucified the sinful nature with its passions and desires. Since we live by the Spirit, let us keep in step with the Spirit.
>
> Galatians 5:22–25 (NIV 1984)

Jesus Christ is the answer to all of our troubles, all of our sorrows, and all of our pains as we face the reality of our floundering marriages, pending or final divorce decrees, and the resulting family disasters. Our hope must be and is in the one true God and his Son, our Lord Jesus Christ.

May our Lord Jesus Christ bless each one of you in your Christian walk of standing for your covenant vows taken before God and your spouse. It is a narrow walk, and narrow is the gate. Standing is a high calling, a difficult calling, a walk of faith with our Lord as we wait for the reconciliation and restoration of our covenant marriages. While God is reconciling each one of you to him, he is also reconciling our prodigal spouses to himself. When the timing is right, he will reconcile and rebuild our marriages based upon the Solid Rock of Jesus Christ. Be patient, walk in his will, put your complete trust in our awesome God, and he will never, never fail you.

Standing firm until parted by death.

Rock or Sand?

Jesus loved to teach his followers with parables. Much like we say a picture is worth a thousand words, Jesus painted word pictures that told stories to which those of his day could relate and we can also relate. Such was the story of the wise and foolish builders.

> Therefore everyone who hears these words of mine and puts them into practice is like a wise man who built his house on the rock. The rain came down, the streams rose, and the winds blew and beat against that house; yet it did not fall, because it had its foundation on the rock. But everyone who hears these words of mine and does not put them into practice is like a foolish man who built his house on sand. The rain came down, the streams rose, and the winds blew and beat against that house, and it fell with a great crash.
>
> Matthew 7:24–27 (NIV 1984)

This story is so simple that we all can understand the *surface* story. However, Jesus's parables had deeper meanings, and that is why he used them so often as he taught. I feel that it is the deeper meaning that he intended when he told this parable, so I ask you this question: what is Jesus saying to you in this parable as you come to the Lord, seeking the healing of your marriage? On the surface, the story here is about a construction project. On a deeper level, Jesus is speaking to you and me using metaphors. Depending on what your current personal situation is as you read this parable and study its deeper meanings, these metaphors may have different meanings.

The first metaphor I see is the word *house*. You and I can take the word *house* literally, or we can realize that here, Jesus is speaking to you and me that our marriage relationship is this *house*. Our marriage relationships, our *house*, is the sum total of all our words, our actions, and our deeds. After all, a house is supposed to provide us shelter, shelter from the storms of life. Isn't that what a marriage relationship is supposed to provide for the marriage partners? A shelter, a comfort zone, a place of quiet rest? Yet for each of us, our marriage relationships have fallen far short of being a shelter, a comfort zone, or a place of quiet rest!

The second metaphor I see is the word *foundation*. I think of a slab, footings, or piers and beams. I guess that is a *guy thing*. The ladies probably have a different connotation. Perhaps the ladies think of the first part of their facial makeup that they put on, the base or the *foundation* as it is often called. A foundation is an idea or object upon which something is built. Jesus is speaking at a much deeper level as he tells this parable. He is talking about what we see as true or what we feel is meaningful in our lives. He is speaking of the two basic commandments: *love God,* and *love your neighbor as yourself.*

> Jesus said to him, "'You shall love the Lord your God with all your heart, with all your soul, and with all your mind.' This is *the* first and great commandment. And *the* second *is* like it: 'You shall love your neighbor as yourself.' On these two commandments hang all the Law and the Prophets."
>
> Matthew 22:37–40 (NKJV)

This is the true foundation Jesus is talking about, and it is on this foundation that our marriages need to be built.

The third metaphor I see is the word *wise*. The usual or common meaning doesn't go deep enough. If you think deeper, the question is, what does it mean in the context of a marriage? I am thinking about a marriage between two committed Christians who are in the Word together on a daily basis and who are also in prayer together on a daily basis. I know for a fact that if I (and my wife) had been *wise*, our marriage would have survived the storms of life that Satan put along our path.

In like manner, the fourth metaphor I see is the word *foolish*. Here, I tend to take this word at its face value. Perhaps this describes each of us, we who are in the process of standing for our troubled marriages. *If* we had not been so foolish, *if* we had based our marriage relationship upon the teachings of Jesus, *if* we had been in the Word and prayer on a daily basis, and *if* we had applied Christ's teachings in our daily lives, our marriages could have weathered the storms. So many *ifs*. Yet in our foolishness, we allowed the ways of the world to destroy our marriage relationship, leading to arguments, fighting, abuse (of various kinds), separation, and possibly divorce.

Last, I see a set of metaphors: the words *rains*, *streams*, and *wind*. These three constitute the storms of life that Satan cooks up for each of us in the hope that we will stumble and fall.

But take heart for there is a light at the end of the tunnel. That *light*, a metaphor in itself, is a name for Jesus Christ, our Lord and Savior. It represents a faith and commitment we each must develop. Jesus is our rock, our foundation, our hope, and our future as we seek God's help in the reconciliation and rebuilding of our troubled marriages. Had we been wise and not foolish, Jesus Christ would have been at the center of our marriages. Jesus is asking for obedience. It is Jesus Christ who needs to be on the throne of our lives and be number 1 priority in our marriages if our marriages are to survive Satan's attacks.

So I challenge each of you, are you rebuilding your life and your *new* marriage on a firm foundation? That foundation is Jesus Christ who is our Rock. Or have you allowed your marriage to flounder and be shaken to the ground as if on a foundation of sand, falling victim to the ways of the world and Satan? The choice is yours.

Standing firm until parted by death.

The Cross: A Look Back At Its Lessons

As the season for remembering and celebrating the events of the Crucifixion and the resurrection of our Lord and Savior Jesus Christ passes, we need to reflect on the lessons we can learn from the events that occurred at the cross. The events of two thousand years ago reflect the ultimate example of reconciliation: that of God's reconciliation of his fallen children (you and me) to himself. For it was on the cross that Jesus Christ suffered and died, taking upon his personage the wrath of God's judgment and punishment for man's sin.

> For He made Him who knew no sin *to be* sin for us, that we might become the righteousness of God in Him.
>
> 2 Corinthians 5:21 (NKJV)

On the cross, Jesus was stripped bare of his righteousness, that righteousness that he received from his Father. He suffered separation from the Father, and by his sacrifice on the cross, we can inherit and put on his *robe of righteousness* so that we might approach a Holy God. That is the requirement for you and me to come into the presence of a Holy God: we are clothed in righteousness like his one and only Son, Jesus Christ. This unselfish action by Jesus and our Father God is the ultimate form of reconciliation, an act of unconditional love for all mankind. Our reconciliation to God is the basis of and the essential requirement for marriage reconciliation.

On Good Friday, I attended a prayer service at one of our local churches. The service was titled "Seven Last Words of Jesus." I wish to reflect on the lessons Jesus presents to us from the cross.

The First Word: Forgive

And when they had come to the place called Calvary, there they crucified Him, and the criminals, one on the right hand and the other on the left. Then Jesus said, "Father, forgive them, for they do not know what they do."

Luke 23:33–34a (NKJV)

Half-dead, in unbelievable physical and spiritual pain, nailed to the cross with spikes, Jesus cried out to his Father to forgive those who put him there on the cross. As I reflect upon this plea from our Lord, I realize that it was you and I who put Jesus on that cross. Yet through his immeasurable love for us, he asked his Father to forgive us. As you and I reflect on the cross and our failed marriages, have we forgiven our spouses? Have we forgiven ourselves?

The Second Word: Remember

Then he said to Jesus, "Lord, remember me when You come into Your kingdom." And Jesus said to him, "Assuredly, I say to you, today you will be with Me in Paradise."

Luke 23:42–43 (NKJV)

One of the thieves who hung on a cross next to Jesus hurled insults at him. The other thief realized that he was on his cross because of his sinful life but that Jesus was without sin. Recognizing Jesus's deity, the second thief sought forgiveness and asked Jesus to remember him when he was enthroned in his kingdom. Which thief represents you and me? Have you and I willingly laid our sins at the foot of the cross?

The Third Word: Others

When Jesus therefore saw His mother, and the disciple whom He loved standing by, He said to His mother, "Woman, behold your son!" Then He said to the disciple, "Behold your mother!" And from that hour that disciple took her to his own *home.*

John 19:26–27 (NKJV)

As Jesus hung there on the cross, his thoughts were on others who were there at the cross, witnessing the horror of the Crucifixion. His compassion and love poured out to his family and his friends. His compassion and love was also poured out for you and me. He was tying up loose ends before the inevitable. As we stand at the foot of the cross, will you, will I receive his love and compassion expressed by his death on the cross?

The Fourth Word: Godforsaken

And at the ninth hour Jesus cried out with a loud voice, saying, "Eloi, Eloi, lama sabachthani?" which is translated, "My God, My God, why have You forsaken Me?"

Mark 15:34 (NKJV)

As our Lord Jesus Christ hung on the cross, he was stripped bare of his righteousness needed to come before a Holy God. He was deserted, without hope, desperate. He was abandoned by his Father. He was truly in hell. He was forsaken! Shouldn't you and I be giving thanks to Jesus for the robe of righteousness that he has given us? This righteousness is what we need to put on, to clothe ourselves, to cover ourselves if we wish to come into the presence of a Holy God.

The Fifth Word: Thirst

After this, Jesus, knowing that all things were now accomplished, that the Scripture might be fulfilled, said, "I thirst!"

John 19:28 (NKJV)

I can only imagine the agony Jesus suffered on the cross. There in the heat of the day, with his lifeblood flowing out of his body, his thirst must have been intense. What did the soldiers offer him? They lifted to his lips a sponge on a hyssop stalk that was soaked in wine vinegar. When Jesus (or perhaps a stranger) comes to our door seeking a drink of cool water, do we offer him a bitter drink? How often have our actions to our spouse been like wine vinegar in their mouths?

The Sixth Word: Anger

And when Jesus had cried out with a loud voice, He said, "Father, 'into Your hands I commit My spirit.'" Having said this, He breathed His last.

Luke 23:46 (NKJV)

Can't you hear the anger and frustration in Jesus's words? He had spent three long years teaching the people a message of love and peace. How did they respond? They crucified him! All they wanted from him was a warrior king, a king to lead them and an army to drive out the Roman conquerors and free themselves of the oppression of the Jewish rulers. His anger and frustration is aimed at the world that is full of sin, the sin that started in the Garden of Eden, and the sin that exists today in each of us. Have you, have I, made the decision to lay our sins at the foot of the cross so that Jesus can deal with them? If not, that is priority number 1. Without you and me becoming reconciled to God through the cross of Jesus, we cannot come before the throne of a Holy God, and we cannot become reconciled to our spouses.

The Seventh Word: Everything

When he tasted the wine, he said, "It is finished." Then he bowed his head and died.

John 19:30 (NKJV)

When the ninth hour came, Jesus cried out, "It is finished." Everything that he had come down from heaven to do had been accomplished. He had taught his Gospel of love and peace. He had performed miracles. He had trained his apostles. He had set in motion the greatest revolution the world would ever see. Everything was in place. The job was finished, and now Jesus looks at you and me. Do we have our lives in order? What about your salvation? What about my salvation? Only you and I can take the necessary steps toward the cross with our sins. Only you and I can choose to exchange our sinful lives for the righteousness of Christ and become one of his followers. Remember, marriage reconciliation starts with our first step toward the cross. You and I must put our trust in God, and he will see us through our marriage problems. As for our spouses, we must pray for them and leave God to deal with them. After all, he knows what they need.

Therefore, if anyone *is* in Christ, *he is* a new creation; old things have passed away; behold, all things have become new. Now all things *are* of God, who has reconciled us to Himself through Jesus Christ, and has given us the ministry of reconciliation, that is, that God was in Christ reconciling the world to Himself, not imputing their trespasses to them, and has committed to us the word of reconciliation. Now then, we are ambassadors for Christ, as though God were pleading through us: we implore *you* on Christ's behalf, be reconciled to God.

2 Corinthians 5:17–20 (NKJV)

May we each embrace the cross, the message of reconciliation, and God's resurrection power. May God bless each of us as we stand for our covenant marriage vows.[24]

Standing firm until parted by death.

Separated From God

Have you ever felt separated from God? I would imagine that, in most believers' lives, there have been times that God felt distant. Times of illness, death of a loved one, relationship problems, and loss of a job are a few that come to mind easily. These are physical and spiritual deserts that many of us may experience during our lifetime. However, this is not the separation from God that I am talking about. I am referring to the *sin* in our lives that separates us from God. Sin and God are incompatible. Like oil and water, they don't mix. Sin and God cannot coexist in the same place. Sin angers God so much that we cannot come into the presence of a Holy God, our Father, clothed in our sin. Yet God longs to have fellowship with us, his adopted children, for all eternity. Thus sin needs to be cleansed from our lives and deserves punishment. God knows us well enough (after all, he created us) to know that his wrath because of our sin problem is more than we could ever bear. His perfect solution: he sent his one and only Son to be sin for us, trading our sins for Christ's righteousness at Calvary so that we, his adopted children, might come into his presence free of sin.

Yes, God loved the world so much that he gave his only Son, so that everyone who believes in him would not be lost but have eternal life. God sent his Son into the world.

He did not send him to judge the world guilty, but to save the world through him. People who believe in God's Son are not judged guilty. But people who do not believe are already judged, because they have not believed in God's only Son. They are judged by this fact: The light has come into the world. But they did not want light. They wanted darkness, because they were doing evil things. Everyone who does evil hates the light. They will not come to the light, because the light will show all the bad things they have done. But anyone who follows the true way comes to the light. Then the light will show that whatever they have done was done through God.

John 3:16–21 (ERV)

God made him who had no sin to be sin for us, so that in him we might become the righteousness of God.

2 Corinthians 5:21 (NIV 1984)

In Christ, he chose us before the world was made. He chose us in love to be his holy people—people who could stand before him without any fault. And before the world was made, God decided to make us his own children through Jesus Christ. This was what God wanted, and it pleased him to do it.

Ephesians 1:4–5 (ERV)

So, brothers and sisters, as we seek reconciliation with our spouse, God seeks reconciliation with us through his Son, Jesus Christ. Jesus took our sins upon his body at Calvary so that we might have fellowship with God (not separated from God) for eternity. Praise be to God and his Son, Jesus Christ!

Standing firm until parted by death.

Our Great Physician

Many of you who have read my devotionals do not know that in real life, I am a physician. Retired, yes, but still a physician. Upon receiving my degree almost fifty years ago, I, like many new physicians of that day, took the Oath of Hippocrates. An ancient oath, it states that as a physician, I am honor-bound by *oath and covenant* to help and protect from harm those who seek my counsel or help. Today, this oath is not taken as originally written as many young physicians feel the wording is outdated and expresses ideas, values, and procedures that do not apply in today's world of medical practice. That said, most graduating medical school students today swear to some form or version of the oath upon graduation. The taking of such oaths in recent decades in US medical schools administering an oath has risen from 24 percent in 1928 to nearly 100 percent today.

It is an oath that basically states, "Physician, first, do no harm!" It calls on all physicians to seek with all their ability to heal the body and to refrain from that which might do harm, both to the body or to the soul of their patients. It describes a trust, a covenant, that exists between a patient and their physician. I am a *physician*, not merely a *doctor* healing the body, but one who sought to heal the whole person to the best of my abilities and knowledge.

We each have another physician, our Great Physician. He is our triune God: Father, Son, and Holy Spirit. He seeks to heal the wholeness of our person, not just our physical body. The Apostle Peter speaks about the Son.

> He never did one thing wrong, not once said anything amiss. They called him every name in the book and he said nothing back. He suffered in silence, content to let God set things right. He used his servant body to carry our sins to the Cross so we could be rid of sin, free to live the right way. His wounds became your healing. You were lost

sheep with no idea who you were or where you were going. Now you're named and kept for good by the Shepherd of your souls.

1 Peter 2:22–24 (MSG)

Is this not what we want from our God? He seeks healing of our heart and our soul. Other translations state "live for righteousness." He is our Shepherd. He is our Great Physician!

God calls us to live in harmony with those around us, and that includes our spouses. When our marriages break down, we are out of harmony with our spouses and also with God. That harmony can be summed up by the Apostle Paul.

Love is patient and kind. Love is not jealous, it does not brag, and it is not proud. Love is not rude, it is not selfish, and it cannot be made angry easily. Love does not remember wrongs done against it. Love is never happy when others do wrong, but it is always happy with the truth. Love never gives up on people. It never stops trusting, never loses hope, and never quits. Love will never end.… So these three things continue: faith, hope, and love. And the greatest of these is love.

1 Corinthians 13:4–8a, 13 (ERV)

We read and sing that God is love. As you come to know God, you soon realize that he is pure love! It is through that love that he heals our hearts, our minds, our souls, and our bodies. We call upon him to heal our fellowships and relationships with our spouses. That process is called reconciliation. We first become reconciled to God, then to self, and finally to our spouses. However, we cannot do this alone. We need divine intervention; we need healing that comes from our God. He is our Great Physician!

There are many other names that we use as we speak about our God. He is our Creator, our Sustainer, our Alpha and Omega.

He is our Jehovah-Rapha, the Lord who heals. Jehovah-Rapha is a name of God that speaks to us and to our needs daily. We live stressful lives in this fallen world and society. Everyday problems confront us, and we bend under the load of what we see as unsolvable problems. Jehovah-Rapha can heal all our problems and sicknesses; he heals our souls. He is our Great Physician!

O LORD my God, I cried to You for help, and You healed me.

Psalm 30:2 (NASB)

He said, "If you will listen carefully to the voice of the LORD your God and do what is right in his sight, obeying his commands and keeping all his decrees, then I will not make you suffer any of the diseases I sent on the Egyptians; for I am the LORD who heals you."

Exodus 15:26 (NLT)

All praise be to God for he is our Healer. He is our Great Physician!

Standing firm until parted by death.

Bowl and Towel

Bowl and towel? An odd choice of words. Why these words? How do they fit into the scheme of things as we look at our lives through the lens of fractured family relationships? Reconciliation of family relationships begins with the establishment of a firm relationship with our Lord and Savior, Jesus Christ. I am going to look at two events in the life of Jesus during the final hours of his life before his crucifixion and show how these events impact our marriage relationships.

Reconciliation of our family relationships begins first with our reconciliation with God. What better way to do this than emulating Jesus Christ's life?

> It was almost time for the Jewish Passover festival. Jesus knew that the time had come for him to leave this world and go back to the Father. Jesus had always loved the people in the world who were his. Now was the time he showed them his love the most.... So while they were eating, Jesus stood up and took off his robe. He got a towel and wrapped it around his waist. Then he poured water into a bowl and began to wash the followers' feet. He dried their feet with the towel that was wrapped around his waist.... When Jesus finished washing their feet, he put on his clothes and went back to the table. He asked, "Do you understand what I did for you? You call me 'Teacher.' And you call me 'Lord.' And this is right, because that is what I am. I am your Lord and Teacher. But I washed your feet. So you also should wash each other's feet. I did this as an example for you. So you should serve each other just as I served you.
>
> John 13:1, 4–5, 12–15 (ERV)

The setting: the Last Supper. The message: like Jesus Christ, mankind was placed on earth to serve, not to be served. Jesus says it himself in the last two sentences above: "I did this as an example for you. So you should serve each other just as I served you." Embracing this core Christian concept (that of a servant) is crucial to our personal walk with Christ. This is often a chief factor in the breakdown of our families and of our relationships with our spouses. Both male and female are meant to serve, each with specific roles related to gender. Jesus Christ is our model. It isn't difficult, but it requires humbling ourselves by putting others first. Do you have a servant heart? Would Jesus be proud of you? How do you measure up?

Modern-day western society rules have led to blurring of gender lines. But the basic message is the same: love and service to our fellow man by both the husband and the wife. Relationships and families fracture when one or more of the parties put themselves first. Selfishness is a sure sign of problems brewing on the horizon.

Further on in this story of contrasts, we see Jesus standing before Pilate. The Jewish authorities have already condemned Jesus. Now standing before Pilate, his body broken and bleeding from the scourging ordered by Pilate, Jesus is asked if he understands his situation. In his silence, Pilate offers him freedom as he can find nothing in him to warrant further punishment. However, the crowds cry, "Crucify him, crucify him." Still seeking a way out for himself, Pilate asks Jesus further questions while continuing to question the crowd.

> When Pilate saw that he was accomplishing nothing, but rather that a riot was starting, he took water and washed his hands in front of the crowd, saying, "I am innocent of this Man's blood; see to that yourselves.... But after having Jesus scourged, he handed Him over to be crucified.
>
> Matthew 27:24, 26b (NASB)

Faced with probably the single most important decision of his life as the Roman governor, Pilate folded. While he had the civil authority to release Jesus or have him crucified, he abdicated his position. He took water and poured it over his hands, symbolically washing his hands of the whole situation. He allowed Jesus to be turned over to the Jewish mob to be crucified with the help of the Roman soldiers. Does this situation sound familiar? Faced with our own tough family relationship questions, we often fold, washing our hands of the situation. We take the easy way out. Rather than making the tough decisions, we turn and walk or run away. Faced with tough decisions, we fail to go to God for his wisdom and guidance. In the weakness of our flesh, we abdicate our responsibility by symbolically washing our hands of the situation.

Bowl and towel: In which scenario will your hands get wet?

Standing firm until parted by death.

God Rests When You Work

Marital discord. It is so common these days. As we face these problems in our family, we seek ways to try to fix the problem. We want the associated pain to go away. It is just human nature. When a lightbulb in our residence burns out, we exchange it for one that is functional. Our car breaks down, we take it to the mechanic. If the yard needs mowing, we just go and do it. Just think of all the things that you fixed today, and you get the picture. But when it comes to fixing the things dealing with relationships, spiritual things, etc., we usually fail. We try to fix things in the *flesh* and forget that we have one who walks alongside of us every day, one whom we can look to and depend on: Our Lord and Savior, Jesus Christ.

Some of you may already be acquainted with the various twelve-step programs that deal with drugs, alcohol, and gambling. What I remember about such programs was a cliché: *let go and let God*. I know that early in my stand for my marriage, a wise friend who had walked this path before me told me that I needed to step aside, to get out of God's way so that he could do the work necessary in my wife's life as well as the work needed in my own life. Like so many of us do, I just wanted a certain person to talk to my wife, to straighten her out. I feel that many of you have been down this same path and understand this. God is content to stand aside while you and I are frantically trying to fix our marriages using the world's way. We humans are just that stubborn. We are reluctant to admit that a problem is beyond our skills to fix. So God, in his infinite wisdom, is willing to let us struggle and fail time and time again until we admit to him that we are powerless without him; we finally turn to him.

How often have you said, "When all else fails, let's pray about it." Wrong! Going to God in prayer should be our first line of attack, not our default setting when we have a problem. Prayer should be used whether it is a little problem or a huge problem. Go to God first!

> "For I know the plans that I have for you," declares the LORD, "plans for welfare and not for calamity to give you a future and a hope. Then you will call upon Me and come and pray to Me, and I will listen to you. You will seek Me and find *Me* when you search for Me with all your heart."
>
> Jeremiah 29:11–13 (NASB)

God knows our deepest thoughts and desires. When you seek his face (counsel, help, etc.), he will always be there for you. Sometimes God may answer *no* or *not now*, but be assured that God has your best interests on his heart and mind as he deals with your problem. No problem is too big for God. "Jesus looked at them and said, 'This is something that people cannot do. But God can do anything'" (Matthew 19:26b, ERV).

Back to the title of this devotional, "God Rests When You Work." You probably figured out the second part of this statement: God works when you rest. When we are in God's way, trying to fix the problem in the flesh (the world's way), God steps aside to allow us time to realize that we are powerless without him. God sees the big picture. He can fix our messes if we will just get out of his way. We need to rest. It sounds so simple, but it is *oh, so hard!* We need to eat some *humble pie* as we look to God for his solution.

So remember this simple thing: God loves to solve our messes, but we need to step aside as he performs one of those modern-day miracles of marriage reconciliation and restoration.

As you pray for your marriage, your part in this process is to align yourself with God and leave your spouse totally to God. When the timing is right, God will bring you and your spouse together again, showing you what each of you need to do under God's guidance to bring about reconciliation and restoration. It will take time to clean up the mess you and your spouse made. But know this: God will never fail you if you put him first—first in your marriage and first in your relationship with your spouse. Our God is a jealous God, not wanting to share *top billing* in your marriage with anyone or anything. He wants to be *number 1* in your life and your marriage. Never forget that. Put him first, and your life will always be on the right track.

> And we know that all things work together for good to those who love God, to those who are called according to His purpose.
>
> Romans 8:28 (NIV 1984)

The watch words for today, tomorrow, and from now on are the following: *God rests when you work. God works when you rest.* Standing firm until parted by death.

Through Our Father's Compassion, Feel Forgiven

I would imagine that most people that come from a Christian heritage, be they a professing Christian or a non-Christian, have a familiarity with Jesus's parable of the prodigal son found in the fifteenth chapter of Luke's Gospel. We remember how the younger son squandered his inheritance (not really due him because his father was still living), yet this son was accepted back home unconditionally by his father. In a deeper sense, this is a parable or story about our own Heavenly Father, our Abba

Father, and his unconditional love for his sinful children, you and me. Let us look at one of the lines from this story as told by Jesus. "But when he was still a great way off, his father saw him and had compassion, and ran and fell on his neck and kissed him" (Luke 15:20b, NKJV).

This parable speaks of the compassion of the prodigal's father or, in a deeper sense, the compassion of our Abba Father for you and me. This father did not condemn his son but, in gladness and in love, welcomed his prodigal home. We too are like the prodigal, sinners who have all fallen short of the glory of God (see Romans 3:23). We have fallen short of our Abba Father's expectations of us. Yet God, our Abba Father, has mercy and compassion for us as sinners and welcomes home all who come humbly to him. This is the story of the radical message of God's unconditional love, of God's forgiveness. This is about God's grace for all mankind.

From the beginning of time, God desired to have fellowship with man. Yet with the fall of man in the garden, that fellowship became hindered by man's sin. God, through his great love and compassion for mankind, took the next step to seal that fellowship with him by sending his one and only Son as atonement for man's sin.

> But God demonstrates his own love for us in this: While we were still sinners, Christ died for us.
>
> Romans 5:8 (NIV 1984)

I know that in my own walk with Jesus Christ, as I began to understand the depth of God's love for me, a sinner, I came to understand God's unmerited gift of grace to me. Realizing that if I was the only sinner in the whole world, Jesus Christ would have and indeed did go to the cross just for me and me alone. It was an act or action by God motivated out of his pure love for me, an act of grace and his desire for eternal fellowship with me. My forgiveness is thus an unmerited gift (grace) from God. (Jesus

Christ did go to the cross for *all* mankind. Through a paradigm shift in our own thinking, we can understand that Christ would and did go to the cross just for each one of us alone. What a Savior we have in Christ!)

Each of us who have accepted this gift of love, forgiveness, and compassion from our Abba Father need to pass it on to all whom we meet. That starts with our spouses and our families. Reconciliation of marriage or family relationships begins with compassion, with forgiveness. Just as our Abba Father forgave us, we likewise must forgive others. Notice that there was total forgiveness offered by this father to his younger son. No retribution, no condemnation, just mercy and love (grace) poured out by a loving father. So, fellow standers, feel forgiven by your Abba Father as you show forgiveness to all those you come in contact with, especially your spouses and your families. God is a God of compassion, forgiveness, and love. Feast upon it, and draw it deep within your soul so that you might reflect the love and forgiveness of Jesus Christ and our Abba Father in your daily walk.

Standing firm until parted by death.

Forgiveness: The Gateway To Marriage Reconciliation

In the confusion and turmoil of the death of a marriage relationship, forgiveness, more often than not, takes a backseat. There are hurts, accusations, betrayals, and even physical violence. How can forgiveness be at the forefront of our thoughts or actions in such situations? Our human nature causes us to respond by putting up our defenses. We fire back, and the battles rage! Those of us who have been down this path know the futility of those actions. Somewhere along this road to destruction, if we are lucky and our minds are not totally shut down, God will get our attention. It is here that even nonbelievers realize that there must be a better way, and many begin to perceive God's nudging. Something has to give, but where do we start? We need only to look to the cross and Jesus Christ, the only sinless human to walk on this earth, and remember his spoken words as he hung there on the cross.

> Jesus said, "Father, forgive them, for they do not know what they are doing."
>
> Luke 23:34a (NIV 1984)

Even Jesus Christ, the Son of God, recognized where reconciliation (peacemaking) had to begin; it is through forgiveness that we offer. Jesus knew that his ministry to a fallen world came through forgiveness.

> God sent his Son into the world not to judge the world, but to save the world through him. "There is no judgment against anyone who believes in him. But anyone who does not believe in him has already been judged for not believing in God's one and only Son. And the judgment is based on this fact: God's light came into the world, but people loved the darkness more than the light, for their actions were evil. All who do evil hate the light and refuse to go near it for fear their sins will be exposed. But those who do what is right come to the light so others can see that they are doing what God wants."
>
> John 3:17–21 (NLT)

God, in his infinite wisdom, knew that it was through forgiveness that the world could be reconciled to himself. That reconciliation begins at the cross. It is a scandalous message, the message of the cross, a message that most find hard to accept. But it is at the cross that forgiveness begins and reconciliation of the world to Jesus Christ and God takes place.

Just what is forgiveness? A simple definition: "a willingness to set aside punishment; a pardon for a wrong [sin] committed." That is the reason for the cross. Punishment for your sins and mine was and is necessary, a just judgment from a Holy God. Yet Jesus Christ, through his great compassion for his brothers and sisters (you and me) and being God, took that punishment on the cross. He offered forgiveness to those who believed in him as God's one and only Son and who sought his forgiveness. That is the scandalous message of the cross: death to self and death to our sins in exchange for life eternal with God. God was reconciling mankind to himself.

> And all of this is a gift from God, who brought us back to himself through Christ. And God has given us this task of reconciling people to him. For God was in Christ, reconciling the world to himself, no longer counting people's sins against them. And he gave us this wonderful message of reconciliation.
>
> 2 Corinthians 5:18–19 (NLT)

Now back to the original statement, reconciliation begins with forgiveness. As seen in the scripture above, God has committed us to reconciliation with our fellow man (that includes your spouse). Jesus often spoke about forgiveness.

> If you forgive those who sin against you, your heavenly Father will forgive you. But if you refuse to forgive others, your Father will not forgive your sins.
>
> Matthew 6:14–15 (NLT)

How much plainer does it need to be said? Forgiveness is the gateway to greater blessings. When we ask our Heavenly Father to heal our marriages, he looks first at our repentant hearts to see if we are ready for reconciliation.

One final thought: don't forget to forgive yourself for your part in the breakdown of your marriage relationship (or any other relationship where you are seeking reconciliation). Remember that the second step in the reconciliation process in reconciliation is to self, so forgive yourself.

I leave you with this thought: *forgive them!* Reconciliation begins with forgiveness.

Standing firm until parted by death.

Finding Freedom In Forgiveness

Forgiveness. It is a concept most of us struggle with from time to time. Webster defines forgiveness as "the act of granting a pardon or the act of giving up on wanting to punish another human being for actions taken against us." Those of us struggling with our marriage and/or family relationships are familiar with this concept but often struggle with implementing it in our own lives. Our Lord and Savior Jesus Christ knew about forgiveness but didn't struggle with it when he prayed.

> When they came to the place called the Skull, there they crucified him, along with the criminals—one on his right, the other on his left. Jesus said, "Father, forgive them, for they do not know what they are doing."
>
> Luke 23:33–34a (NIV 1984)

Treated as a common criminal, beaten and essentially half-dead, abandoned by many of his day-to-day followers, Jesus hung on the cross and prayed to his Father to grant the world *forgiveness*. Forgiveness is part of the very nature of God. He has been forgiving mankind since the beginning of our existence here on earth. His forgiveness in the Old Testament was primarily directed toward his covenant people, the Israelites. Although God is a God of forgiveness, he does not let the guilty go unpunished. This fact is demonstrated in his message to Moses.

> That is, the LORD passed in front of Moses and said, "YAHWEH, the LORD, is a kind and merciful God. He is slow to become angry. He is full of great love. He can be trusted. He shows his faithful love to thousands of people. He forgives people for the wrong things they do, but he does not forget to punish guilty people. Not only will he punish the guilty people, but their children, their grandchildren, and their great-grandchildren will also suffer for the bad things these people do."
>
> Exodus 34:6–7 (ERV)

Throughout the Old Testament, when God's chosen people disobeyed or failed to trust the Lord, there were consequences: defeat in battle, pestilence, captivity by a foreign power, destruction of the temple, just to name a few. Our God is a fair God, full of love and compassion, yet he is also a just God for he tells his people what to expect when they are disobedient. Because he is a God of love, forgiveness is central to his nature. God has been teaching mankind throughout the ages how to forgive, sometimes with success and sometimes without success. Jesus speaks about this in the Sermon on the Mount.

> For if you forgive men when they sin against you, your heavenly Father will also forgive you. But if you do not forgive men their sins, your Father will not forgive your sins.
>
> Matthew 6:14–15 (NIV 1984)

Here Jesus lays down a very important biblical principle. Unless we are willing to forgive those who sin against us, our

Heavenly Father cannot forgive us of our sins. It is through God's grace that we are forgiven at the cross. God places great emphasis on horizontal forgiveness, that is, human to human. We see this in the Lord's Prayer as he speaks about forgiveness. His message to you and me is one of forgiveness toward those who have hurt us. And of course, there is the concept of redemption when we seek forgiveness from Jesus for our own sins.

Those of us seeking reconciliation with our spouses, family members, or even friends need to take to heart Jesus's words from the Sermon on the Mount. Without forgiveness from Jesus and our Heavenly Father, we cannot come before a Holy God. Plain and simple. We ask Jesus to forgive us of our many sins, yet if we do not forgive others, we are still bound up in our own sin. Yet when we find in our hearts to forgive another person who has wronged us, we find freedom. Otherwise, we become a prisoner in our own private jail, a jail built by anger, hatred, hurt, and fears related to various injustices done to us. When we forgive, there is a healing power that sets us free to love God, to love life, and to love mankind. When asked about the most important commandments of God, Jesus responded that we are to love God with our total being. Then he said, "The second most important command is this: 'Love your neighbor the same as you love yourself'" (Mark 12:31a, ERV).

When we love our neighbor as ourselves, we have no issues with our neighbor. If we did, we would need to extend to them our forgiveness and also seek their forgiveness. There is healing power for our relationships when we can forgive. And when you forgive another human being, he becomes your neighbor, and you are to love him as yourself.

Several days ago, I heard the true story of Jennifer Thompson-Cannino and Ronald Cotton. In 1984, Jennifer identified Ronald as the man who had raped her only to find out some eleven years later that her identification was in error. Ronald was exonerated through DNA evidence. For over eleven years, as Ronald sat in prison, Jennifer thought of him as a monster, even praying that he would die. She found herself in a prison of her own making, a prison of anger and hatred. When she found out her error, it was almost unbearable. She found it was almost impossible to forgive herself. In prison, Ronald was an angry man and had come to live with the injustices he was experiencing. However, Ronald knew inside that things had to change. Jennifer and Ronald were victims of a crime perpetrated by another man. Ronald, in his own words, stated, "Letting go of my anger toward the other man was hard, but staying free in my heart was a choice only I could make."

In the ensuing months after his release from prison, Ronald and Jennifer met face-to-face, and she stated, "I asked Ron if he could ever forgive me. And with all the mercy in the world, he took my hands, and with tears in his eyes, he told me he had forgiven me a long time ago. At that moment, I began to heal. Ronald taught me how to let go of all that pain. His forgiveness set me free." She went on to say, "I did not want to be a prisoner of my own hatred." Ronald related, "Jennifer and I are friends. Together we were able to help each other heal through this shared experience. I could choose to be bitter. I could hate the prison guards and the system. But I chose to forgive them all so that I can stay free and not be a prisoner for the rest of my life."

Both of these people found themselves in a prison of their own making: hatred, anger, hurt, etc., resulting from those events so many years before. Yet when the truth became known, Jennifer sought forgiveness. Deep in her heart, she knew she needed to be set free. This story shows that two hurting people can find freedom in forgiveness. Such is the power of forgiveness in God's redeeming love. Jennifer and Ronald have gone on to write a book together about their journeys that led to their finding freedom in forgiveness. Their memoir is called *Picking Cotton*. They frequently speak on judicial reform.

There is freedom in forgiveness. Each of us needs to seek this freedom as we become reconciled to God and to our spouses, families, and friends. When we receive forgiveness and extend forgiveness to others, there is peace and a freedom that invades our hearts. I found it, and so can you. So, fellow standers, offer forgiveness to your spouse, your family, and your friends. You will never be sorry you did.

There is freedom in forgiveness![25]

Standing firm until parted by death.

GRACE

Redeemed Through Grace

Have you ever given much thought to the term *grace*? Until recently, this was not a term that permeated my brain when speaking about God and salvation. Although I have been churched my whole life, grace was not taught much in the denomination in which I grew up. And I don't think I was asleep at the wheel. I never got into Bible study with any intensity until about five years ago, and even then, grace did not sink in right away. *Holman Illustrated Bible Dictionary* defines grace as "undeserved favor given by a superior to an inferior." Holman goes on to state that "it is the redeeming activity of God that manifests itself in the redemptive work of Christ by which sinners are forgiven and accepted by God." God abhors sin. Man was born with a sinful nature, which we inherited from our ancestor, Adam. Yet we are God's adopted children, and he wants more than anything to have fellowship with us both here in this life and, more importantly, in eternity. Unfortunately, we cannot come before a Holy God, our Heavenly Father, clothed in our sin. But he had a plan.

> Therefore, if anyone *is* in Christ, *he is* a new creation; old things have passed away; behold, all things have become new. Now all things *are* of God, who has reconciled us to Himself through Jesus Christ, and has given us the

ministry of reconciliation, that is, that God was in Christ reconciling the world to Himself, not imputing their trespasses to them, and has committed to us the word of reconciliation. Now then, we are ambassadors for Christ, as though God were pleading through us: we implore *you* on Christ's behalf, be reconciled to God. For He made Him who knew no sin *to be* sin for us, that we might become the righteousness of God in Him.

2 Corinthians 5:17–21 (NKJV)

This is a passage full of theology, but what Paul is talking about here is grace. To Paul, the Christian life can be summed up in the term *grace*, the grace of God. Salvation from beginning to end is all about grace. This theme permeates all of Paul's letters. Peter speaks of this also:

For Christ died for sins once for all, the righteous for the unrighteous, to bring you to God.

1 Peter 3:18a (NIV 1984)

To rephrase this, Jesus was not guilty of any sin, yet he suffered and died on a cross at Calvary for all sinners (you and me) to bring us to God. Oh, how wonderful it is that God loves us so much that he would die for us to cleanse us of all unrighteousness! Do you realize that when Christ died for you and me, he did not die like a sinner but *as* a sinner? [26]

God made him who had no sin to be sin for us, so that in him we might become the righteousness of God.

2 Corinthians 5:21 (NIV 1984)

So as we ponder these things, we see that our Father God doesn't condone our sin, nor does he compromise his standards.

He realizes that we are rebellious, and he does not relax his demands for us to be sin-free in his presence. He assumes our sinful nature, and wonder of wonders, he pronounces sentence upon himself. Max Lucado, in his book *In the Grip of Grace*, states the following: "God's holiness is honored. Our sin is punished. And we are redeemed. God is still God. The wages of sin is still death. And we are made perfect." Hebrews 10:14 (NIV 1984) states, "Because by one sacrifice he has made perfect forever those who are being made holy." Praise be to God who redeems us through grace in Christ Jesus. [27]

Standing firm until parted by death.

My Grace Is Sufficient

Because of the surpassing greatness of the revelations, for this reason, to keep me from exalting myself, there was given me a thorn in the flesh, a messenger of Satan to torment me—to keep me from exalting myself! Concerning this I implored the Lord three times that it might leave me. And He has said to me, "My grace is sufficient for you, for power is perfected in weakness." Most gladly, therefore, I will rather boast about my weaknesses, so that the power of Christ may dwell in me. Therefore I am well content with weaknesses, with insults, with distresses, with persecutions, with difficulties, for Christ's sake; for when I am weak, then I am strong.

2 Corinthians 12:7–10 (NASB)

The Apostle Paul knew our Lord and Savior Jesus Christ and followed his will for his life. Yet with his human faults and shortcomings, he found himself tormented by a messenger of Satan. So he pleaded with the Lord to remove the thorn in his flesh. We don't know what it was, but the Lord told him, "My grace is sufficient for you." Paul accepted this in time, knowing that the Lord was all-sufficient for him. Now, what about you? What is the thorn in your flesh? Is it separation from your spouse, a divorce, another person in your spouse's life, alienation of family members, loss of your job, etc.? Cry out to the Lord! Seek his face and his will for your life. Jesus Christ is the answer. His grace is sufficient if you will just follow his will for your life.

I know in my own walk with Jesus, I often look to one of my favorite passages from the Old Testament for reassurance:

> "For I know the plans that I have for you," declares the LORD, "plans for welfare and not for calamity to give you a future and a hope. Then you will call upon Me and come and pray to Me, and I will listen to you. You will seek Me and find *Me* when you search for Me with all your heart."
>
> Jeremiah 29:11–13 (NASB)

So, fellow standers, seek the Lord with all your heart, and you will find his grace *is* sufficient! For when you are weak, it is in those times that you are strong through the power of your Lord and Savior, Jesus Christ.

Standing firm until parted by death.

Understanding Grace: A Further Examination

Previously, we have examined grace and found that (1) we are redeemed through grace, and (2) his grace is sufficient. Today we will look at the relationship of grace and righteousness and faith.

> What the law says is for those who are under the law. It stops anyone from making excuses. And it brings the whole world under God's judgment, because no one can be made right with God by following the law. The law only shows us our sin. But God has a way to make people

right, and it has nothing to do with the law. He has now shown us that new way, which the law and the prophets told us about. God makes people right through their faith in Jesus Christ. He does this for all who believe in Christ. Everyone is the same. All have sinned and are not good enough to share God's divine greatness. They are made right with God by his grace. This is a free gift. They are made right with God by being made free from sin through Jesus Christ.

Romans 3:19–24 (ERV)

In this passage, Paul is speaking about observing the Mosaic Law. He says that act, in and of itself, does not lead to our justification. Observing the law points our sin out to us. This is where righteousness and grace interact. We cannot come before a Holy God covered in our sin. In the *great exchange* at Calvary, Jesus Christ took on the burden of our sins and their merited punishment upon his person. In accepting Jesus as our Lord and Savior, Jesus covered our sins with his righteousness, his blood, the blood of the Lamb. Jesus was the perfect sacrifice. Thus, we are made right with God through faith in his Son, Jesus. Observing (obeying) the law just doesn't do it. It is through God's grace, his free gift to you and me, that we are justified. Our justification is a gift from our Father God.

Max Lucado says that when we become aware of grace, it "fosters an eagerness for good. God's trust makes us eager to do right. Such is the genius of grace." When we look at the Mosaic Law, it shows us what we are doing wrong, but it fails to make us eager to do what is right. However, grace can! Notice this amazing difference![28]

I mean we are made right with God through faith, not through what we have done to follow the law. This is what we believe.... So do we destroy the law by following the way of faith? Not at all! In fact, faith causes us to be what the law actually wants.

Romans 3:28, 31 (ERV)

Paul states in Romans 3:31, "Faith causes us to be what the law actually wants." Remember Abraham? What made him right with God was his faith, not his works. And it was accounted to him as righteousness. The Message says, "He trusted God to set him right instead of trying to be right on his own" (Romans 4:2, MSG).

When God created man, he didn't want us to sin. Grace was not a gift for us so that we could go about freely sinning. God knows our weaknesses. So before the beginning of time, he planned grace and knew that someday we would need grace if we were to have fellowship with him.

So, fellow standers, we are saved by God's grace and not by our works. It is a free gift from God to his beloved children who seek his forgiveness.

Standing firm until parted by death.

God's Grace

Marriage reconciliation is really about self-examination of my relationship with God, of where I have fallen short of his will for my life and my marriage relationship. Beginning to fathom the hurt I caused my wife, I realized how much more I had hurt my Heavenly Father in all the things I had done that were outside of his will. I am greatly troubled as I envision the scene at Calvary, of my God hanging on that cross, bleeding, suffering in agony, there because of me. Yes, me! Jesus Christ willingly went to the cross because of his great love for me. There he suffered, bled, and died for me that I might be covered with his blood, his righteousness. His love for me is so great that his only wish is that I might be able to come before my Heavenly Father, pure and clean, spotless in his eyes. This is true reconciliation with my Heavenly Father. Then and only then can true reconciliation begin to occur with my spouse, my wife.

> Come and listen, all you who fear God,
> and I will tell you what he did for me.
> For I cried out to him for help,
> praising him as I spoke.
> If I had not confessed the sin in my heart,
> the Lord would not have listened.
> But God did listen!
> He paid attention to my prayer.
> Praise God, who did not ignore my prayer
> or withdraw his unfailing love from me.

Psalm 66:16–20 (NLT)

Standing firm until parted by death.

Grace: A Gift From God

This devotional is based upon chapter 5 of Romans. I suggest you first read chapter 5 and then this devotional about grace, a gift from God, that he freely gives. In the passage below, note the number of times *gift* is mentioned.

> But God's free *gift* is not like Adam's sin. Many people died because of the sin of that one man. But the grace that people received from God was much greater. Many received God's *gift* of life by the grace of this other man, Jesus Christ. After Adam sinned once, he was judged guilty. But the *gift* of God is different. His free *gift* came after many sins, and it makes people right with him. One man sinned, and so death ruled all people because of that one man. But now some people accept God's full grace and

his great *gift* of being made right. Surely they will have true life and rule through the one man, Jesus Christ. So that one sin of Adam brought the punishment of death to all people. But in the same way, Christ did something so good that it makes all people right with God. And that brings them true life.

Romans 5:15–18 (ERV; italics added)

As Christians, you and I have been justified through faith in Jesus Christ as our Lord and Savior. It is through grace, a free gift from God, that we have been saved. From the above passage, we see that we receive a gift of God's grace, which came through the actions of one man, our Lord and Savior Jesus Christ. Did we deserve it? No! Scripture states, "For all have sinned and fall short of the glory of God" (Romans 3:23, NASB). What is this glory? It is what God intended for man to be, what mankind was before the fall. Yet we are now declared righteous (justified) through the grace of God's Son, Jesus Christ, when we accept him as our Lord and Savior. It is through the action of Jesus Christ that the gift of righteousness is given to mankind, a gift of God's grace freely given. It is through this justification that we receive the gift of eternal life. God's glory expressed in believers is the ultimate purpose for which God created mankind. We are God's beloved children. When the one man (Adam) fell and mankind was condemned, God sent His Son to redeem us from our sins and give us his gift of righteousness to rule in our hearts.

But God demonstrates his own love for us in this: While we were still sinners, Christ died for us.

Romans 5:8 (NIV 1984)

As we stand for our marriages, we know that each of us must first become reconciled to our Heavenly Father. Being sinful, we must profess our faith in God's only Son, Jesus Christ, and prayerfully seek forgiveness for our sins. He went to the cross, bearing our sins upon his body. Through this grace gift, we inherit righteousness and are now able to come before a Holy God, spotless and free of our sin.

> Since we have now been justified by his blood, how much more shall we be saved from God's wrath through him! For if, when we were God's enemies, we were reconciled to him through the death of his Son, how much more, having been reconciled, shall we be saved through his life! Not only is this so, but we also rejoice in God through our Lord Jesus Christ, through whom we have now received reconciliation.

> Romans 5:9–11 (NIV 1984)

In the above scripture, the last part reads, "Not only is this so, but we also rejoice in God through our Lord Jesus Christ, through whom we have now received reconciliation." The key word in this passage is *reconciliation*. Marriage reconciliation begins with the reconciliation of each one of us to God. Then and only then will God orchestrate the reconciliation process between each marriage partner. Thus, each stander must earnestly seek to become reconciled to God. God seeks a relationship with each of us, longing for his children to come home and live with him forever in eternity. Each of us were made sinners through the disobedience of one man (Adam), and it was through the obedience of one man (Jesus Christ) that the gift of grace was extended to mankind so that we might be made righteous.

> One man disobeyed God and many became sinners. But in the same way, one man obeyed God and many will be made right. The law was brought in so that more people would sin the way Adam did. But where sin increased, there was even more of God's grace. Sin once used death

to rule us. But God gave us more of his grace so that grace could rule by making us right with him. And this brings us eternal life through Jesus Christ our Lord.

Romans 5:19–21 (ERV)

Yes, God loved the world so much that he gave.

John 3:16a (ERV)

Yes, our Heavenly Father gave, gave from his own heart because he loved us then and he loves us now. God's grace, a gift freely given to believers, should spur all of us on to seek to mirror Jesus's life each day. To repeat in plain language, *grace cannot be earned; it is a free gift from God.* As standers and sinners saved by God's grace, we should praise God for his mercy and his loving-kindness. After being reconciled to God, we can then rebuild our marriages with Jesus Christ at the center of our relationships with our spouses. Remember, God's grace is there for all who seek and believe.

God makes people right through their faith in Jesus Christ. He does this for all who believe in Christ. Everyone is the same. All have sinned and are not good enough to share God's divine greatness. They are made right with God by his grace. This is a free gift. They are made right with God by being made free from sin through Jesus Christ.

Romans 3:22–24 (ERV)

Standing firm until parted by death.

God's Amazing Grace

Amazing grace! (how sweet the sound)
That sav'd a wretch like me!
I once was lost, but now am found,
Was blind, but now I see.

'Twas grace that taught my heart to fear,
And grace my fears reliev'd;
How precious did that grace appear
The hour I first believ'd!

Thro' many dangers, toils, and snares,
I have already come;
'Tis grace hath brought me safe thus far,
And grace will lead me home.

The Lord has promis'd good to me,
His word my hope secures;
He will my shield and portion be
As long as life endures.

Yes, when this flesh and heart shall fail,
And mortal life shall cease;
I shall possess, within the veil,
A life of joy and peace.

The earth shall soon dissolve like snow,
The sun forbear to shine;
But God, who call'd me here below,
Will be forever mine.

[When we've been there ten thousand years,
Bright shining as the sun,
We've no less days to sing God's praise
Than when we'd first begun.] *

*last stanza added in 1829, author unknown
John Newton (1725–1807)

John Newton wrote these words more than two hundred years ago when he accepted Jesus Christ and realized God's amazing grace had freed him from his sinful life. He wrote his own epitaph about his life:

JOHN NEWTON, Clerk
Once an infidel and libertine
A servant of slaves in Africa,
Was, by the rich mercy of our Lord and Saviour
JESUS CHRIST,
restored, pardoned, and appointed to preach
the Gospel which he had long laboured to destroy.
He ministered,
Near sixteen years in Olney, in Bucks,
And twenty-eight years in this Church.

As I look at my own walk with Jesus Christ, I realize that I am where I am today only by God's grace, his amazing grace! How many of us, as we stand with Jesus for the restoration of our marriages, can look back at our dysfunctional marriages and place ourselves into this classic old hymn? I know I can. I have been churched all my life, and I had considered myself a Christian, yet it was only when I began to experience the pain and despair of marital separation (and later divorce) that I was brought to my knees. It was then that I sought Jesus Christ and truly accepted him into my life as my Lord and Savior.

Read the words of this hymn. Put yourself in the story, and see for yourself where you are in your stand for your covenant marriage vows. If you have not yet accepted Jesus Christ into your life, now is the time to do so. Do it now! It is not too late. Marriage reconciliation can only begin with your being reconciled to God. That starts with you accepting Jesus Christ as your personal Lord and Savior. Take your sins to the foot of the cross, confess them to Jesus, and ask his forgiveness. Accept his forgiveness and his righteousness today as you take your first step in being reconciled to God. Be dead to the sin in your life and alive in Jesus Christ, and you will receive the indwelling of the Holy Spirit in your heart.

That saved a wretch like me! I was dead in my sins, and those sins helped destroy my marriage.

Was blind, but now I see. I look back at the many mistakes I made for I was blind and did not see. Accepting Jesus Christ into my life has freed me of my sins and mistakes. It is by God's grace and his love that I now see and I am free from the bondage of my sins.

'Twas grace that taught my heart to fear. It was through grace that I came to know God's love for me and how to praise and respect God as my Heavenly Father.

How precious did that grace appear the hour I first believed! I didn't have an earth-shaking conversion but one of gradual awareness that I was saved. What I do remember was the peace that came over me one Sunday afternoon after godly friends prayed over me. I knew from that moment that I was going survive this separation and that God had a plan for my life.

'Tis grace hath brought me safe thus far, and grace will lead me home. Here again, God's grace carries me each and every day for I know that although I am saved, I am flawed and I still sin. My sins are forgiven. It is through God's grace that I strive to be more like Jesus, looking toward my eternal home.

He will my Shield and Portion be, as long as life endures. God is with me, watching over me, guiding me, protecting me, helping me throughout my days until that time he calls me home.

How do you fit in this hymn? You should be able to see yourself in each phrase.[29]

> Did you forget that all of us became part of Christ Jesus when we were baptized? In our baptism, we shared in his death. So when we were baptized, we were buried with Christ and took part in his death. And just as Christ was raised from death by the wonderful power of the Father, so we can now live a new life…. If we died with Christ, we know that we will also live with him.
>
> Romans 6:3–4, 8 (ERV)

> But God is rich in mercy, and he loved us very much. We were spiritually dead because of all we had done against him. But he gave us new life together with Christ. (You have been saved by God's grace.)
>
> Ephesians 2:4–5 (ERV)

Standing firm until parted by death.

Grace: The Simple Truth Of God's Love

The Easter season with the Jewish Passover feast, the Last Supper, the cross, the burial, and Christ's Resurrection has long since come and gone for this calendar year. Yet as Christians, we see God's great love for us in his victory over sin and death and Satan. The cross is meaningless without the events of the resurrection. We remember those Holy Week events and the crucifixion of our Lord and Savior and his resurrection each time we share in the Holy Communion meal. Our Jewish brethren celebrate the Passover as a time in their history when God exhibited his great love for his people as he emancipated them from the Egyptians. God's love for his people, the pinnacle of his creation, is the central theme in both of these events in world history.

> For God so loved the world, that He gave His only begotten Son, that whoever believes in Him shall not perish, but have eternal life. For God did not send the Son into the world to judge the world, but that the world might be saved through Him.

> John 3:16–17 (NASB)

> But God demonstrates His own love toward us, in that while we were yet sinners, Christ died for us.

> Romans 5:8 (NASB)

> In this is love, not that we loved God, but that He loved us and sent His Son to be the propitiation for our sins.

> 1 John 4:10 (NASB)

From these verses, we see that in God's great, unfathomable love for you and me, he sent his Son to take the punishment that we so rightly deserved for our multitude of sins. It is through this act that we find the true meaning of grace, God's unmerited gift of love to mankind. Let us look at the Apostle Paul's writings to the Romans (read Romans 5:12–21 and 6:1–2 for completeness).

> One man sinned, and so death ruled all people because of that one man. But now some people accept God's full grace and his great gift of being made right. Surely they

will have true life and rule through the one man, Jesus Christ…. But where sin increased, there was even more of God's grace. Sin once used death to rule us. But God gave us more of his grace so that grace could rule by making us right with him. And this brings us eternal life through Jesus Christ our Lord.

Romans 5:17, 20b–21 (ERV)

Do you get it? Jesus Christ died for your personal sins. He would have gone to the cross even if you were the only sinner remaining in the world. Christ's love, God's love, for you is so great that he did not want to lose a single person, not even you, to the enemy. It was through God's grace that Jesus went to the cross for your personal sins. We all have been saved from eternal damnation by our faith in God's one and only Son, Jesus Christ. He died for you so that you might inherit his righteousness and be able to stand in the presence of Almighty God clean, pure, and righteous. Without Christ's gift, his unmerited gift of love and grace, you and I would have been doomed to hell for eternity.

I cry every time I hear or sing John Newton's powerful hymn "Amazing Grace." Study the words of this beautiful statement of redemption by a sinner. (Read the lyrics elsewhere in this book.) In it, I see myself. For once I was lost, but God found me, and through his grace, he rescued me from my sinful life. Jesus could have left me where I was, but his great love for me was such that he did not wish to lose me to the enemy. So Jesus willingly went to the cross, taking my richly deserved punishment for my sins upon his body so that I, through faith in him, might spend eternity in heaven. There I will be with my Heavenly Father (God), Jesus Christ, and the Holy Spirit. That is grace; that is God's love!

Are you saved? Ask God. Believe, for God is love. His grace is sufficient. He wishes for you to spend eternity with him. Believe. Place your sins at the foot of the cross. Ask for forgiveness. Believe. You can have peace in your life through our Lord Jesus

Christ. Just believe in God's one and only Son, Jesus Christ! Accept God's unmerited gift of grace. Believe.

> I am proud of the Good News, because it is the power God uses to save everyone who believes—to save the Jews first, and now to save those who are not Jews. The Good News shows how God makes people right with himself. God's way of making people right begins and ends with faith. As the Scriptures say, "The one who is right with God by faith will live forever."
>
> Romans 1:16–17 (ERV)

Standing firm until parted by death.

GOD'S LOVE

Agape Love, God's Love

Have you noticed that the word *love* translates into three different words in the Greek language, the principal language of the New Testament? One of those words is *agape*. It is rarely used in extrabiblical Greek. It is used by believers to denote the special unconditional love of God. It is also used interchangeably with the Greek word *phileo* to designate Father God's love for Jesus, his love for the individual believer, and for Christ's love for a disciple. *Phileo* also refers to tender affection and is often used in nonbiblical Greek. *Phileo* is never used in reference to a believer's love for God. The third word is *eros*, which is erotic or sexual love.

> For God so loved the world that he gave his one and only Son.
>
> John 3:16a (NIV 1984)

This is *agape* love. God so loved the world, his creation, that he gave. Agape love is not a feeling; that kind of love is *eros*. *Phileo* love is more of a brotherly love. Agape love is a decision, an action. Agape love comes from God to his children, a deliberate choice that reflects God's own nature. God will not let you go or desert you. He is bound to you as if you are chained together. You cannot win his love because you already have it. When you look at Christ's life two thousand years ago, agape love explains why he came to live among his people and how he endured all the events associated with the cross.

> Observe how Christ loved us. His love was not cautious but extravagant. He didn't love in order to get something from us but to give everything of himself to us.
>
> Ephesians 5:2b (MSG)

In our walk with Christ, we exhibit agape love, an enduring love that bears a semblance of God's love for us when we take care of a loved one through months and years of a debilitating illness. Agape love thinks of another's comfort before its own; it is sacrificial. Agape love is that love that lingers in the heart of the terminally ill who hang on for just a few more minutes or hours to allow friends and family to gather to say a final good-bye. Agape love gives and gives but never takes; it wants nothing in return. [30]

Fellow standers, examine your own relationships with God, with your spouse, with your family, and with your friends. Identify the type of love you exhibit with each of these. Where in your relationships can you show agape love, a love like Jesus expresses? Paul speaks of love:

> Love is patient and kind. Love is not jealous, it does not brag, and it is not proud. Love is not rude, it is not selfish, and it cannot be made angry easily. Love does not remember wrongs done against it. Love is never happy when others do wrong, but it is always happy with the truth. Love never gives up on people. It never stops trusting, never loses hope, and never quits. Love will never end.... So these three things continue: faith, hope, and love. And the greatest of these is love.
>
> 1 Corinthians 13:4–8a, 13 (ERV)

Max Lucado, in his new book *3:16*, says, "God loves you with an unearthly love. You can't win it by being winsome. You can't lose it by being a loser. But you can be blind enough to resist it. Don't. For heaven's sake, don't. For your sake, don't."[31]

Take in with all Christians the extravagant dimensions of Christ's love. Reach out and experience the breadth! Test its length! Plumb the depths! Rise to the heights! Live full lives, full in the fullness of God.

Ephesians 3:18b–19 (MSG)

Standing firm until parted by death.

In The Morning, God Is Still God!

This devotional is mainly scripture, scriptures of reassurance and hope. Read, meditate upon them, and feel the power of God's Word deep in your heart and soul. We start with two verses from Psalm 119, contrasting the wording of two different translations.

Remember your word to your servant, for you have given me hope. My comfort in my suffering is this: Your promise preserves my life.

Psalm 119:49–50 (NIV 1984)

Remember your promise to me; it is my only hope. Your promise revives me; it comforts me in all my troubles.

Psalms 119:49–50 (NLT)

Dearly beloved, God loves you! He loves you deeply with a love that is unconditional. You are his beloved child! Despite the turmoil in your marriage, the anger, the frustration, the uncertainty, etc., there is hope. You have probably heard the old cliché, "Things will look better in the morning." You say, "No way! You don't know my problems! No one understands, especially my husband [wife]!" You seek help from family, friends, and even from your pastor, yet you do not find the answers you seek. As a last resort, you cry out to God. This should be your first choice in seeking help, not your last, but we hesitate. Is it because we feel we are not hearing any answers from God? Know this: in the morning, God is still God, and he is still in charge. As David says in the scripture above, God's promises had given him hope, and despite all his suffering and troubles, he could depend upon God's promises. Our God is the God of hope, the God of marriage, the God of resurrection, and the God of healing. All these faces of God we can seek as we stand for our covenant marriage vows. We need only to be still, taking the time to listen for God's soft voice. David knew how to talk and listen for God to speak to him. Throughout his life, he had a unique intimacy with God. Believe it or not, you and I can have a similar intimacy with God. Isaiah states, "Then you will know that I am the LORD, and anyone who trusts in me will not be disappointed" (Isaiah 49:23b, MSG).

When we seek God's face and listen for His voice, we will never be disappointed. The answer may not always be what we want, but God is still God, and his answers are perfect both in timing and in content. You ask, "How do I hear God? How do I know it is God speaking and not Satan trying to trick me?" Listening requires your undivided attention. Hearing God speak to us is a gift from God. He often speaks to us through the scriptures we read as well as through thoughts that come into our minds. God can speak to us through our dreams. Even day-to-day events occurring in our lives contain messages from God if we just take time to seek out their meaning. If you are not sure if

God is speaking, sift the message through God's Word. He will never tell you to do anything evil or wrong. So take a few minutes and meditate on the scriptures below as you seek God's help with your problems.

Be still, and know that I am God.

Psalm 46:10a (NKJV)

Trust in the LORD and wait quietly for his help.

Psalm 37:7a (ERV)

Beloved, do not believe every spirit, but test the spirits, whether they are of God; because many false prophets have gone out into the world. By this you know the Spirit of God: Every spirit that confesses that Jesus Christ has come in the flesh is of God, and every spirit that does not confess that Jesus Christ has come in the flesh is not of God. And this is the *spirit* of the Antichrist, which you have heard was coming, and is now already in the world. You are of God, little children, and have overcome them, because He who is in you is greater than he who is in the world. They are of the world. Therefore they speak *as* of the world, and the world hears them. We are of God. He who knows God hears us; he who is not of God does not hear us. By this we know the spirit of truth and the spirit of error.

1 John 4:1–6 (NKJV)

And do not be conformed to this world, but be transformed by the renewing of your mind, that you may prove what *is* that good and acceptable and perfect will of God.

Romans 12:2 (NKJV)

We live in this world, but we don't fight our battles in the same way the world does. The weapons we use are not human ones. Our weapons have power from God and can destroy the enemy's strong places. We destroy people's arguments, and we tear down every proud idea that raises itself against the knowledge of God. We also capture every thought and make it give up and obey Christ.

2 Corinthians 10:3–5 (ERV)

So trust in the LORD and do good. Enjoy serving the LORD, and he will give you whatever you ask for. Depend on the LORD. Trust in him, and he will help you. He will make it as clear as day that you are right. Everyone will see that you are being fair.

Psalm 37: 3a, 4–6 (NASB)

And lest I should be exalted above measure by the abundance of the revelations, a thorn in the flesh was given to me, a messenger of Satan to buffet me, lest I be exalted above measure. Concerning this thing I pleaded with the Lord three times that it might depart from me. And He said to me, "My grace is sufficient for you, for My strength is made perfect in weakness." Therefore most gladly I will rather boast in my infirmities, that the power of Christ may rest upon me. Therefore I take pleasure in infirmities, in reproaches, in needs, in persecutions, in distresses, for Christ's sake. For when I am weak, then I am strong.

2 Corinthians 12:7–19 (NKJV)

My grace is sufficient for you for My strength is made perfect in weakness. What a powerful promise from God! Each of us can experience this grace if we will only ask God for his help. And how marvelous grace is once you experience it. With grace, faith grows, and those insurmountable problems become more and more manageable as we learn to trust and lean on God. God smiles down on each of us when we trust him and lean on him for our every need. After all, we are his children, and he wants only the best for each of us.

Dearly beloved, remember this: *in the morning, God is still God!* Don't ever forget that. He is there waiting for you. Take advantage of God's amazing love. He speaks if we are willing to listen.

Standing firm until parted by death.

Amazing Love!

And Can It Be That I Should Gain?
Charles Wesley, 1738

And can it be that I should gain
An interest in the Savior's blood?
Died He for me, who caused His pain—
For me, who Him to death pursued?
Amazing love! How can it be,
That Thou, my God, shouldst die for me?
Amazing love! How can it be,
That Thou, my God, shouldst die for me?

He left His Father's throne above
So free, so infinite His grace—
Emptied Himself of all but love,
And bled for Adam's helpless race:
'tis mercy all, immense and free,
For O my God, it found out me!
'tis mercy all, immense and free,
For O my God, it found out me!

Still the small inward voice I hear,
That whispers all my sins forgiven;
Still the atoning blood is near,
That quenched the wrath of hostile Heaven.
I feel the life His wounds impart;
I feel the Savior in my heart.
I feel the life His wounds impart;
I feel the Savior in my heart.

No condemnation now I dread;
Jesus, and all in Him, is mine;
Alive in Him, my living Head,
And clothed in righteousness divine,
Bold I approach th'eternal throne,
And claim the crown, through Christ my own.
Bold I approach th'eternal throne,
and claim the crown, through Christ my own[32]

Amazing love! How can it be, that Thou, my God, shouldst die for me? What's this? I asked God to die for me? How can it be? These words haunted me during worship today. I have selected four verses from this hymn by Charles Wesley. Charles and his older brother, John, started the Christian movement that eventually became the Methodist denomination. Charles wrote over six thousand hymns during his lifetime. The words above may be slightly different from those you know (modern versions have slightly different words and slightly different scoring), but the theme is the same, but for God's amazing love and grace, you and I would be condemned to eternal hell. I think back to the time when I thought I was a good Christian and compare it to my present walk with Christ. Wow! What happened? Where did I miss the boat? What did it take to bring me to my knees and see the wrong path I was on? What it took was a tumultuous marriage not centered on Christ, a separation, and the receipt of a petition for divorce. I woke up to the reality that I needed a Savior because I did not have a future in heaven as I thought, but I sure did in hell. Your own personal story may be similar. As I sought God's advice through prayer and reading his Word, he called me to be obedient to his will by standing for my covenant marriage vows. Our marital separation went on to a divorce. Yet as I look back on all those events, I now realize that it was the best thing that has ever happened to me in my life. I thank God that he has allowed me to experience these years as he extended his grace and love to me. I love my wife, and each and every day I pray for her and for our reconciliation to God and eventually to each other. As I pen these thoughts, I am reminded of Paul's words in 2 Corinthians.

> And He has said to me, "My grace is sufficient for you, for power is perfected in weakness." Most gladly, therefore, I will rather boast about my weaknesses, so that the power of Christ may dwell in me. Therefore I am well content with weaknesses, with insults, with distresses, with persecutions, with difficulties, for Christ's sake; for when I am weak, then I am strong.

> 2 Corinthians 12:9–10 (NASB)

God's power is made perfect and is manifested in our weakness. Yes, in my weakness, in my brokenness, and in my desperation about my marriage, God's grace was sufficient; and through his love and grace, I became strong.

Now let us look at the words of this hymn. How often do you think about the meaning of the words of the worship music you are singing? "Died He for me, who caused His pain." You and I and all humanity caused our God and our Savior such pain, the pain of our sins. But if we look at the words right before this—"And can it be that I should gain an interest in the Savior's blood?"—do you understand that it was your sins and my sins that sent Jesus Christ to his death on a cross, that the shedding of his blood was necessary for the atonement of those sins? The writer of Hebrews, looking back at Old Testament times, stated that all sacrifices for the atonement of sins required the shedding of blood.

> In fact, the law requires that nearly everything be cleansed with blood, and without the shedding of blood there is no forgiveness.
>
> Hebrews 9:22 (NIV 1984)

The first stanza concludes that it was Christ's amazing love for you and me that he would die for us. What an awesome gift from God!

The next verse talks about Jesus leaving his father's side, and through his infinite grace and love, he became a blood sacrifice when he *bled for Adam's helpless race* (you and me). The writer goes on to say that this gift, this mercy, was *immense and free.*

> For it was the *Father's* good pleasure for all the fullness to dwell in Him, and through Him to reconcile all things to Himself, having made peace through the blood of His cross; through Him, *I say*, whether things on earth or things in heaven.
>
> Colossians 1:19–20 (NASB)

Continuing on, the writer states that if we listen carefully, we can hear Christ whisper to us that our (yours and mine) sins are forgiven. Yet it is only through the shedding of blood that God's wrath for our sin is quenched. *Still the atoning blood is near, that quenched the wrath of hostile Heaven.* God abhors sin; sin cannot exist in his presence. We are his children, and he desires fellowship with each of us. So God sent his one and only Son, Jesus, to be a blood sacrifice for our sins. It is through the new covenant of Christ's blood sacrifice that mankind's sins were forgiven once and for all time. Never again will mankind need to shed blood for the atonement of his sins. It was done for us by Jesus Christ at the cross two thousand years ago.

In the final stanza, we see our victory song. *No condemnation now I dread; Jesus, and all in Him, is mine; Alive in Him, my living Head, And clothed in righteousness divine, Bold I approach th'eternal throne, And claim the crown, through Christ my own.* What greater gift can we ever receive? See the picture: we are clothed in Christ's righteousness, which he gave us as we traded in our baggage of sins. And now, you and I can boldly approach and stand before God's throne and claim our crown because of Christ sacrifice for us.

> Yet now he has reconciled you to himself through the death of Christ in his physical body. As a result, he has brought you into his own presence, and you are holy and blameless as you stand before him without a single fault.
>
> Colossians 1:22 (NLT)

Without a single fault! It truly is *amazing love.* Thank you, Lord Jesus, for your awesome gift of love. It is in your precious name that I pray. Amen.

So I ask each of you who are standing or are thinking about standing for your covenant marriage vows, are you reconciled to God? Have you accepted Jesus Christ as your Lord and Savior and asked for his forgiveness of your sins? If not, now is the time to take that step. Don't waste another minute. For until you do, any efforts at a lasting reconciliation with your spouse will surely fail. Marriage reconciliation begins with our own personal reconciliation to God and developing a personal relationship with him. A reconciled marriage is a God-centered marriage, and it is built upon the Solid Rock of Jesus Christ. All other avenues fail over time. *Amazing love!* It can be yours today.

Standing firm until parted by death.

For Love Is As Strong As Death

The Song of Solomon, also called Solomon's Song of Songs, is one of the most beautiful expressions of love between a man and woman written in the Bible. Yet it is also the most erotic book found in the Bible. It is a book containing the poetry of love, a celebration of love—erotic, sensuous, passionate. Solomon (the assumed author) tells of the relationship of a Shulammite woman and her love for her shepherd lover who has captured her heart and of Solomon's own pursuit of the maiden for his harem. Take time to read this short book of the Bible. It is spoken in a woman's voice, speaking profoundly about love. If you have never read it before, read it slowly and embrace the intense emotions and moments of separation, intimacy, anguish, ecstasy, and contentment expressed here in this ancient Middle Eastern love poem (song). Older analysis of the Song suggested it is an allegory of the love relationship of God and Israel, or perhaps the relationship between Christ and his church. Whatever the author's point of reference, it is an intense love poem from the past sharing feelings about love expressed by many cultures down through the ages. Listen to the Shulammite woman as she speaks of her love:

> Place me like a seal over your heart, like a seal on your arm. *For love is as strong as death*, its jealousy as enduring as the grave. Love flashes like fire, the brightest kind of flame. Many waters cannot quench love, nor can rivers drown it. If a man tried to buy love with all his wealth, his offer would be utterly scorned.
>
> Song of Songs 8:6–7 (NLT; emphasis added)

Love has many languages. I think this book of the Bible best describes those feelings each of us had when we got married. It is full of passion, pure and simple. The Greek word for this type of love is *eros,* the root word for *erotic.* Yet in the passage above, there are other aspects of love not found in the word *eros* that we all seek and want in our relationships with our spouses. This passage speaks to the permanence in our love relationships, a love that is as unyielding as death. This book is part of the biblical wisdom literature as it describes these relationships between a man and woman. It speaks of both wisdom and love as gifts from God, thus the reason for man to celebrate love. Years ago, early in my deceased wife's illness, she saw in her own life a need to express her love for me. She gave me a dog tag with this passage, highlighted above, inscribed on it: *for love is as strong as death.* She wished to express to me the depth and permanence of her love for me, a love that came from her heart and soul, a love that could not be quenched by death.

Each of us, when we got married, made promises to our spouses. Love, honor, cherish, etc. You know the phrases. Let us look at the most quoted passage on love in the Holy Bible as written by the Apostle Paul.

> Love is patient and kind. Love is not jealous, it does not brag, and it is not proud. Love is not rude, it is not selfish, and it cannot be made angry easily. Love does not remember wrongs done against it. Love is never happy when others do wrong, but it is always happy with the truth. Love never gives up on people. It never stops trusting, never loses hope, and never quits. Love will never end…. So these three things continue: faith, hope, and love. And the greatest of these is love.

> 1 Corinthians 13:4–8a, 13 (ERV)

Yet with all its poetry and honesty about God's love as well as human love, Paul's description of love's permanence does not match in my own mind this passage from the Song of Songs. Yes, Solomon's book is full of the passion of smitten lovers, but still, there is a statement of a never-ending love. Read the passage again and sense the strength of commitment. Oh, that our own marriages were that committed! But our marriages can have that commitment if we will just look to our Lord and Savior, Jesus Christ. When our marriages falter, he is there if we seek him, and he will redirect our paths to the road that leads to healing and permanence in your marriage and in mine.

Remember once again your marriage vows, those covenant marriage vows, and that they *only* end when you or your spouse dies. *For love is as strong as death.*[33]

Standing firm until parted by death.

Unrequited Love, Redeeming Love

Unrequited love is a term many of you may not know, but it is a situation that most of us who are experiencing marital discord will or have experienced as we stand for our marriage relationships. It involves loving someone with such a passion that it hurts, only to have that love not returned. It results in a very deep emotional hurt, an excruciating ache that can bring a strong person to their knees. Such is the pain experienced when we are rejected by our one-flesh mate, our marriage partner, our spouse. Yet even our Lord and Savior, Jesus Christ, experienced such feelings of rejection while living among us, being fully man with all our human emotions, yet fully God.

> All things were made through Him, and without Him nothing was made that was made.... He was in the world, and the world was made through Him, and the world did

not know Him. He came to His own, and His own did not receive Him.

John 1:3, 10–11 (NKJV)

Jesus experienced these feelings of rejection throughout his ministry, yet he continued to love his fellow man. So great was Jesus's love for each of us that he went to the cross to pay the penalty for our many sins, a penalty rightfully due each of us. The only request he ever made of us is that as we seek his forgiveness for our sins, that we return his love through belief (faith) in him as God's one and only Son. On the cross, he experienced rejection one last time.

And when they had come to the place called Calvary, there they crucified Him, and the criminals, one on the right hand and the other on the left. Then Jesus said, "Father, forgive them, for they do not know what they do." And they divided His garments and cast lots.

Luke 23:33–34 (NKJV)

There on the cross with his executioners casting lots for his clothing below him, Jesus cries out to his Father, "Father, forgive them." Jesus reveals his unconditional love for mankind that was only returned as scorn and brutal acts to elicit greater pain to him. Yet Christ's love (God's love) for each of us was displayed that day at Calvary. "Christ died for us when we were unable to help ourselves. We were living against God, but at just the right time Christ died for us…. But Christ died for us while we were still sinners, and by this God showed how much he loves us" (Romans 5:6, 8 ERV).

You and I are unworthy of such love, yet Jesus Christ's love for each of us motivated him to die for those who believe in him so he and the Father might have eternal fellowship with each of us. What a wonderful God we serve!

There is a romance novel called *Redeeming Love* by Francine Rivers. While some may think that this is just for the ladies, I read this book at the urging of some ladies standing for their respective marriage relationships. It is 479 pages long, and I could not put it down. And it brought me to tears in many parts. The story line follows the biblical story from the book of Hosea, of Hosea's love and faithfulness to his wayward wife, Gomer. The time frame of this novel takes place in the California Gold Rush days in the early 1850s. I highly recommend it to those who want to read a story about a man's unconditional love for his less-than-honorable wife. It reflects the kind of love that each of us need to be showing our spouse (and our family), a love that has no boundaries, a sacrificial love where we would be willing to lay down our very lives for the one we love.

Do you have unconditional love, a redeeming love for your spouse? If not, I hope that you will develop such a love as you seek Christ's guidance in rebuilding your marriage relationship.[34]

Standing firm until parted by death.

God's Timeless Love

Are there times when you feel unloved? Do you feel unworthy of your spouse's love? What about the love of your family? Does the world with all its problems (relationships, financial, job, health, war, etc.) make you feel insignificant? Has sin taken control of your very being? Take heart for God loves you more than you can even imagine!

> For God so loved the world, that He gave His only begotten Son, that whoever believes in Him shall not perish, but have eternal life. For God did not send the Son into the world to judge the world, but that the world might be saved through

Him. He who believes in Him is not judged; he who does not believe has been judged already, because he has not believed in the name of the only begotten Son of God. This is the judgment, that the Light has come into the world, and men loved the darkness rather than the Light, for their deeds were evil. For everyone who does evil hates the Light, and does not come to the Light for fear that his deeds will be exposed. But he who practices the truth comes to the Light, so that his deeds may be manifested as having been wrought in God.

John 3:16–21 (NASB)

John 3:16 is perhaps the single most quoted verse in the whole Bible. Yet I have come to believe that we shortchange Jesus's message when we don't include the next five verses. These six verses comprise the message of the Good News: *God is love!* God's love is in all and through all. His love encompasses our total being, our very existence, and our purpose in life.

For God so loved the world. His love is timeless for as you study the Word, you see that God had each of us in mind, in the palm of his hand, before the world was ever formed and before time began. He knew who your parents would be, the grades you would make in school, and the time you fell and broke your arm. He knew that you would cheat on your final exam in the ninth grade and would later be caught by the police for stealing a bike. God knew of your love of art and your future success as an artist, and he knew of your successes and failures as an adult. God knew that your first sexual experience would be with someone whom you knew only casually and that you would shun the faith of your parents. He knew that after many broken relationships, you would marry for all the wrong reasons. He foresaw the divorce that came and broke the hearts of your young children. He knew that you would continue to run from him until, exhausted, beaten down, and without hope, you would finally listen to that small voice inside: "Come to me." God knew all this about you and all the billions of other people who have lived, are living, and who will live because his love for mankind is timeless.

His love is so timeless that before the beginning of time, he covenanted with his Son, Jesus Christ, to come into this world as a man, fully man yet fully God, to be our Lord and Savior. God's timeless love set in motion the events for Jesus's journey to the cross some two thousand years ago. Yet those events were planned before the beginning of time. His love is timeless! Paul speaks of this timeless love in the first chapter of Ephesians.

> Blessed be the God and Father of our Lord Jesus Christ, who has blessed us with every spiritual blessing in the heavenly places in Christ, just as *He chose us* in Him before the foundation of the world, that we would be holy and blameless before Him. In love He *predestined us* to adoption as sons through Jesus Christ to Himself, according to the kind intention of His will, to the praise of the glory of His grace, which He freely bestowed on us in the Beloved. In Him we have redemption through His blood, the forgiveness of our trespasses, according to the riches of His grace which He lavished on us. In all wisdom and insight He made known to us the mystery of His will, according to His kind intention which He purposed in Him with a view to an administration suitable to the fullness of the times, that is, the summing up of all things in Christ, things in the heavens and things on the earth. In Him also we have obtained an inheritance, having been *predestined* according to His purpose who works all things after the counsel of His will, to the end that we who were the first to hope in Christ would be to the praise of His glory.

> Ephesians 1:3–12 (NASB; emphasis added)

God's timeless love for you and me is shown in his willingness to allow the death of his Son on Calvary for the atonement of our many sins. Yet all this was planned before time began. He loved you and me so much that he provided a way for each of us, his adopted children, to spend eternity with him in heaven. Yes, it was before time began! He *predestined* these events; *we were chosen*, you know when: before time began!

I say all of this to impart a message of hope for each of us who are struggling with our marriages. God knew this was in your life plan, yet he loves you unconditionally. God says because he planned your life before time began, it is of great value to him. You are not worthless; you are not insignificant. You are worthy of the salvation he planned for you because he loves you. And yes, your life choices may have left you wounded, but don't despair because Jesus Christ came to bring healing. He can bring healing to your marriage. You are worthy because of God's eternal love for you (planned before time began) and his abundant grace given to you (also planned before time began). Because you are worthy, living as you see fit is a losing battle because you are fighting against God's destiny for you. And yes, your destiny was planned...before time began.

You are holy in God's sight. So is your marriage. When you accept anything less than that, your faith is too small, too limited, and not worthy of our Father God who has had his eyes on you since...before time began. My message is this: God's love is timeless! So put your faith in Jesus Christ and believe in him for he is the Son of the Most High God. Ask his forgiveness for your sins so that God's plan for you can be complete—eternal life with God and his Son, Jesus.

God's love is timeless.

Standing firm until parted by death.

Fruit Of The Spirit: Love

But the fruit that the Spirit produces in a person's life is *love*, joy, peace, patience, kindness, goodness, faithfulness, gentleness, and self-control. There is no law against these kinds of things. Those who belong to Christ Jesus have crucified their sinful self. They have given up their old selfish feelings and the evil things they wanted to do. We get our new life from the Spirit, so we should follow the Spirit.

Galatians 5:22–25 (ERV; emphasis added)

The Apostle Paul speaks of the fruit of the Spirit in Galatians, and the first one is *love*. So let's take a look at love. *Love*...what can I say? While we may think of it as an emotion, a tingling, a fluttering of our heart, it is so much, much more. In the secular world, love is object-oriented. Paul was not talking here about erotic love (from the Greek word *eros*), that love one experiences in love at first sight or during moments of great passion (involving the flesh). He was speaking of a love that one sees in Christ's relationship with his bride, the church. Love is an action that, when present, transcends emotion and describes for us the essence of God. When we are fortunate enough to experience this type of love, we experience Jesus in our lives. Once again, Paul wrote about love in 1 Corinthians in what I feel is the greatest statement ever written about what love is.

Love is patient, *love* is kind. It [*love*] does not envy, it [*love*] does not boast, it [*love*] is not proud. It [*love*] is not rude, it [*love*] is not self-seeking, it [*love*] is not easily angered, it [*love*] keeps no record of wrongs. *Love* does not delight in evil but [*love*] rejoices with the truth. It [*love*] always protects, [*love*] always trusts, [*love*] always hopes, [*love*] always perseveres. *Love* never fails.... And now these three remain: faith, hope and *love*. But the greatest of these is *love*.

1 Corinthians 13:4–8a, 13 (NIV 1984; emphasis added)

Do you see Jesus Christ in this description of love? I hope you do. We talk and sing that God is love. What do we really mean? We are stating that the character of God is embodied in the concept of love. This kind of love is found in the Greek word *agapao* or *agape*, denoting unconditional love. God's love is also described using the Greek word *phileo* as in (1) his love and tender affection for his Son Jesus, (2) God the Father's love for the individual believer, and (3) Christ's love for his disciples. So when we speak of God's love, we see it manifested in Jesus Christ, God's ultimate example of love.

For God so *loved* the world, that He gave His only begotten Son, that whoever believes in Him shall not perish, but have eternal life. For God did not send the Son into the world to judge the world, but that the world might be saved through Him. He who believes in Him is not judged; he who does not believe has been judged already, because he has not believed in the name of the only begotten Son of God.

John 3:16–18 (NASB; emphasis added)

I go back to Paul's statement above about love as it denotes the character of Jesus. God is love; Jesus is love. Yet there are some differences. At times in the scriptures, God pours out his wrath upon mankind, seeking to chastise us, to correct us, as any loving father would his children. We see this repeated many times in the Old Testament as the Israelites strayed from God's Law. Such action by our Heavenly Father was done in love. Jesus, on the other hand, shows a more gentle side of love as he heals the sick, feeds the multitudes, comforts the lost, and teaches about loving God and loving your neighbor as yourself. Christ's message is this: *love God, love people.* Once during his ministry, Jesus was questioned by one of the teachers of the law, "Of all the commandments, which is the most important?" (Mark 12:28b, NIV 1984).

> Jesus answered, "The most important command is this: 'People of Israel, listen! The Lord our God is the only Lord. Love the Lord your God with all your heart, all your soul, all your mind, and all your strength.' The second most important command is this: 'Love your neighbor the same as you love yourself.' These two commands are the most important."
>
> Mark 12:29–31 (ERV)

In his prayer for the Ephesians (and for us today), Paul states what those rooted in the Christian faith can expect.

> I ask the Father with his great glory to give you the power to be strong in your spirits. He will give you that strength through his Spirit. I pray that Christ will live in your hearts because of your faith. I pray that your life will be strong in *love* and be built on *love*. And I pray that you and all God's holy people will have the power to understand the greatness of Christ's *love*—how wide, how long, how high, and how deep that *love* is. Christ's *love* is greater than anyone can ever know, but I pray that you will be able to know that *love*. Then you can be filled with everything God has for you.
>
> Ephesians 3:16–19 (ERV; emphasis added)

When you look at the human race, those that follow the ways of the world, they do not mirror Paul's description of Christ's love. They mirror Satan. Those who mirror Jesus are God's children. In the Gospel of John, the Apostle records for us Jesus's parable about the Good Shepherd (Jesus). The Good Shepherd knows his flock (hopefully that includes you and me) and guides and directs them to the safety of eternity with our Heavenly Father and his Son, Jesus. It speaks of Christ's love for his followers, his flock.

> I am the shepherd who cares for the sheep. I know my sheep just as the Father knows me. And my sheep know me just as I know the Father. I give my life for these sheep.... My sheep listen to my voice. I know them, and they follow me. I give my sheep eternal life. They will never die, and no one can take them out of my hand. My Father is the one who gave them to me, and he is greater than all. No one can steal my sheep out of his hand. The Father and I are one.
>
> John 10:14–15, 27–30 (ERV)

It is through God's unconditional love for mankind and his desire for eternal fellowship with his children that he sent his Son to die on Calvary's cross for our salvation. Again I say Christ's message is this: *love God, love people.* This is an *agape* type of love. This is what Christ was trying to teach us throughout his ministry. Some got it, others didn't. Will you?

> This is my commandment: Love each other in the same way I have loved you. There is no greater love than to lay down one's life for one's friends.
>
> John 15:12–13 (NLT)

Jesus Christ showed his love for each of us as he willingly went to the cross for you and me. This is unconditional, sacrificial love! Should you and I, could you and I, not do the same for our spouses, to be willing to literally lay down our own lives for our spouses? This is a love that the world just doesn't get. Yet you and I can demonstrate this *agape* type of love as we emulate Christ in our daily walk with him.

My hope is that you will examine your own life, your relationships, and your walk with Christ and that you will refocus your efforts to follow his example. *Agape* love is beautiful, it is fulfilling, and it brings great joy and happiness. Go for it! The first fruit of the Spirit is *love*.

Standing firm until parted by death.

THEOLOGY

Images

Have you ever given much thought to your image or appearance? Thoughts of who you look like or perhaps how you wish you looked? Well, I can hear a resounding yes! Our appearance, both outwardly and inwardly, is central to our very being. Due to humanity's vanity, we spend billions and billions of dollars (and other currencies) annually on clothing, plastic surgery, cosmetics, diets, exercise, etc., to change our outward physical appearance toward that which we believe will improve our feeling of self-worth. However, these changes amount to nothing when we look at the big picture of who we are in Jesus Christ. Moreover, our vanity counts for nothing positive when it comes to who will spend eternity with God. All our striving toward outward physical perfection can only bring us momentary pleasures (if any). It is our heart's image that is important, whether the Holy Spirit resides in our hearts. It is through faith in Jesus Christ that our temporal viewpoint of our physical appearance changes to the appearance of what God expects to see in our heart.

Looking at our outer physical image (and also our heart image), we look first to Genesis and the creation story. "Then God said, 'Now let's make humans who will be like us....' So God created humans in his own image. He created them to be like himself. He created them male and female" (Genesis 1:26a, 27; ERV).

Yes, we are created in the *perfect* image of God. This is from creation, and it was perfection. Today, when we look into the face of an infant, we see mirrored back an image of God. In the Gospel of John, Jesus was talking to his disciples, and Philip put forth a question in response.

> "If you really knew me, you would know my Father too. But now you know the Father. You have seen him." Philip said to him, "Lord, show us the Father. That is all we need." Jesus answered, "Philip, I have been with you for a long time. So you should know me. Anyone who has seen me has seen the Father too. So why do you say, 'Show us the Father'? Don't you believe that I am in the Father and the Father is in me?"
>
> John 14:7–10a (ERV)

My point is that at birth, each of us, even with all our physical imperfections, mirror our creator, our perfect Heavenly Father (and his Son Jesus and the Holy Spirit). What an inheritance we have received by being born! Yes, we have inherited the characteristics of our parents, our grandparents, and all our ancestors because they likewise mirrored the Creator. So at birth, we mirror our Creator in both our image (we are created in his image) and in our heart.

Then sin entered the picture and changed our image before God. Now, while outwardly we appear okay, our heart is covered with the scars of sin in our lives. With this sin condition, God hides his face from us, and we cannot come into the presence of a Holy God, our Heavenly Father. Thus, to you and me, our physical appearance may not look so bad, but to God, it is our sinful heart that he looks at "for God *sees* not as man sees, for man looks at the outward appearance, but the LORD looks at the heart" (1 Samuel 16:7b, NASB).

But God, our Creator, wishing to have fellowship with his children in eternity, had a plan. He sent his one and only Son, Jesus, to live among us as sinless man, and at his death on Calvary, Jesus took upon his body our sins and gave us his righteousness to cover our nakedness. For it is written, "Christ had no sin, but God made him become sin so that in Christ we could be right with God" (2 Corinthians 5:21, ERV).

Jesus Christ, by becoming sin for us, our image before our Heavenly Father became the perfection of a sinless person, pure and spotless in every way. We, through our redemption, have been remade in the image of God's one and only Son, Jesus Christ. We are now children of the New Covenant through our faith in Jesus Christ. We now mirror the image of Jesus Christ.

> The Lord is the Spirit, and where the Spirit of the Lord is, there is freedom. And our faces are not covered. We all show the Lord's glory, and we are being changed to be like him. This change in us brings more and more glory, which comes from the Lord, who is the Spirit.
>
> 2 Corinthians 3:17–18 (ERV)

As we seek to heal our troubled marriages, we must first seek to know our Heavenly Father and his Son, Jesus Christ. When we seek Christ's forgiveness for our sins, we receive redemption, and our image becomes the most beautiful and perfect image of our Lord and Savior, Jesus Christ. It is through redemption that Jesus Christ and the Holy Spirit come into our hearts. So go right now and look in the mirror. Who do you see? Is it your sinful self, or is it Jesus? I hope you see Jesus. (If not, get down on your knees right now and confess your sins to Jesus, asking for his forgiveness. Accept him as your Lord and Savior today.) If you see Jesus, go and live out the reflection of him you saw in the mirror and know that the resurrection and restoration of your marriage may be just around the corner. Our prodigal spouses will find it hard to resist a spouse (one who is standing for their marriage relationship) who reflects the image of Jesus.

So my final request of you is this: may you reflect Jesus to all those you come in contact with today, tomorrow, and forever.

Standing firm until parted by death.

God's Armor

> Finally, my brethren, be strong in the Lord and in the power of His might. Put on the whole armor of God, that you may be able to stand against the wiles of the devil. For we do not wrestle against flesh and blood, but against principalities, against powers, against the rulers of the darkness of this age, against spiritual *hosts* of wickedness in the heavenly *places*. Therefore take up the whole armor of God, that you may be able to withstand in the evil day, and having done all, to stand. Stand therefore, having girded your waist with truth, having put on the breastplate of righteousness, and having shod your feet with the preparation of the gospel of peace; above all, taking the shield of faith with which you will be able to quench all the fiery darts of the wicked one. And take the helmet of salvation, and the sword of the Spirit, which is the word of God; praying always with all prayer and supplication in the Spirit, being watchful to this end with all perseverance and supplication for all the saints.

> Ephesians 6:10–18 (NKJV)

The Apostle Paul in this scripture is entreating us to examine our situation and prepare for battle. Is he talking about Iraq or Afghanistan or some other conflict around the globe? No, he is talking about the spiritual battle with the evil forces that are around us every day. For you and me, these are the forces that are tearing our marriages and families apart. If you haven't realized by now, this battle is bigger than our own actions or even our spouse's actions. We need some support greater than ourselves. This is where you and I must turn to God and seek his help. This battle belongs to God! Our God is an awesome God, a very powerful God. Just look in the Bible, both the Old Testament and the New Testament, and you can see the power of our God. Still this battle is also ours. God is in partnership with us as we seek to heal our broken marriages and families. So like any good soldier, we need to equip ourselves for battle.

First we must get dressed in our basic clothing. These items are on us whether we are in battle or resting before or after the battle. Note that we are to prepare for an offensive battle, not a defensive battle. We are fighting for the heart and soul of our marriages and families, and we must be the aggressors, be on the offensive. Note also that it is our front and not our backs that are covered for battle. We are on the offensive! There is no need to cover our back side.

We first put on the belt of truth about our waist to hold our tunic firmly in place. This truth is that God honors a Christ-filled marriage, and he hates divorce. Next, we place over the front of our chest the breastplate of righteousness. This righteousness comes from our submission to Jesus Christ as our Lord and Savior as we lay our sinful lives at the foot of the Cross and seek his forgiveness. Our final basic preparation is footwear for battles are won and lost on the adequacy of a soldier's footwear. Our feet are fitted with the footwear that allows us to be swift in battle (readiness), and this readiness comes from our mission statement. Our mission statement is the Gospel of peace, the peace and love that exists in a God-filled marriage. These are the basic items of clothing (armor) that prepare us for the next step in this battle.

Now the enemy is in sight. He is taunting us. Affairs, gossip, financial ruin, separation, divorce, custody of the children, you name it. These are the actions, the weapons, the items that our enemy is putting forth as he sees the approach of God's army. He is in a defensive mode because God is not on his side. The evil one, Satan, is more powerful than you or me. However, with God fighting alongside us, we have the upper hand for the battle belongs to the Lord. We are on the offensive! So let's get suited up with our weapons.

Prepare for battle! The enemy is on our doorstep! Pick up your weapons! We pick up the shield of faith in the power of God's Word and his desire for a healed marriage. This shield protects us from the verbal-attack arrows and the arrows of physical abuse and/or neglect. This also shields us from the onslaught of arrows of legal actions that are coming our way. We put on the helmet of salvation that comes from our faith in our Lord and Savior, Jesus Christ. Finally, we pick up our offensive weapon, the sword of the Spirit, which is the Word of God. We go forth into battle knowing that our cause (the healing of our marriages and families) is just, and it is based firmly on God's Word. We are armed with our knowledge of the truth that comes from the Bible, God's inerrant Word and message to a sinful world. Our sword is also prayer as we pray in the Spirit with all kinds of requests, including the healing of our marriages and families, and the defeat of the evil one, Satan.

> Finally, be strong in the Lord and in His mighty power. Put on the full armor of God so that you can take your stand against the devil's schemes.
>
> Ephesians 6:10–11 (NIV 1984)

Standing firm until parted by death.

Not My Will But Thine

As the Easter season begins to fade into history for yet another year, it is appropriate to think back to that time in our Lord's life when he was praying in the Garden of Gethsemane on the Mount of Olives. He knew the events that were about to unfold, events that would change the face of the world and humanity forever. The events of that evening and subsequent days some two thousand years ago have shaped our lives and continue to shape our lives and the lives of our loved ones, even our prodigal spouses. As Jesus prayed in the garden, he was in so much torment and anguish that "his sweat was like drops of blood falling to the ground" (Luke 22:44, NIV 1984). His prayer was "Yet not my will, but yours be done" (Luke 22:42b, NIV 1984). So often in my stand for my marriage, I have cried out to my Heavenly Father for relief from my torment, my loneliness, my heartache. I have cried out for the speedy return of my wife to our covenant marriage relationship. I have cried out for peace. But then I remember my Lord Jesus's plea to his Father as he was facing the horrors, the pain, and the separation from his Heavenly Father that was to occur in the events surrounding the Crucifixion. And then in my own personal anguish, remembering my Lord Jesus, I cry out, "Not my will but thine."

> Jesus Prays Alone. Jesus left the city and went to the Mount of Olives. His followers went with him. (He went there often.) He said to his followers, "Pray for strength against temptation." Then Jesus went about 50 steps away from them. He knelt down and prayed, "Father, if you are willing, please don't make me drink from this cup. But do what you want, not what I want." Then an angel from heaven came to help him. Jesus was full of pain; he struggled hard in prayer. Sweat dripped from his face like drops of blood falling to the ground. When he finished praying, he went to his followers. He found them asleep,

worn out from their grieving. Jesus said to them, "Why are you sleeping? Get up and pray for strength against temptation."

Luke 22:39–46 (ERV)

This and two other accounts of Christ's pleading before his Father (Matthew 26:36–45 and Mark 14:32–41) give us the full force of Christ's humanity, of his wish to bypass the events that were about to unfold in his life. Yet he chose, willfully chose, to go past his own human desires of comfort and safety to follow his Father's will. Isn't this what our Heavenly Father calls us to do? How often do we seek a bypass? How often have you and I been tempted by the enemy to just chuck it all and move on with our lives? I know I have. Some of my family have told me to do this. Some of my good Christian friends and, sadly, even some of the ministers in my own church have suggested I move on. But then I remember, as you should remember, Christ's obedience to his Father's will. This is Christ, who was and is fully man, who chose to follow his Father's will. This is Christ, who was and is fully God, who could have walked away from the cross; it was in his power. Yet he chose, in his humanity and in obedience to his Heavenly Father, to go willingly to the cross! This was his Father's will. This was his destiny.

In a similar way, we each have our own crosses to bear. Is it the cross of anger? Is it the cross of unforgiveness? Is it the cross of indifference or the cross of selfishness? Is it the cross of disbelief? There are so many areas of our lives in our relationship with our spouse where we stumble, and we fall away from our Father's will. But there is hope and peace if we will just turn to our Heavenly Father and cry out, "Not my will but thine." It is so freeing when we realize that our burdens, our anguish, and our crosses can be carried by our all-sufficient God. He loves us so much that he is willing to let us suffer long enough to realize that we cannot handle our troubled, dying, or dead marriages ourselves, and we turn to him.

> I've told you all this so that trusting me, you will be unshakable and assured, deeply at peace. In this godless world you will continue to experience difficulties. But take heart! I've conquered the world.
>
> John 16:33 (MSG)

Early in my stand, while I was unsure of my direction in my heart even though my mind told me to stand, my Heavenly Father spoke to me. He told me to stand firm for that was and is his will for me. He showed me that he expected obedience to his will and that if I would follow his will for my life, my deepest longings for restoration and reconciliation of my marriage with my covenant wife would become a reality. He told me that I needed only to be patient, putting my full trust in him, and he would orchestrate the rest. It is my hope that each of you will listen and know our Father's will for your lives. Then it is up to each of you to obey his will, no matter how uncomfortable it becomes. Know that the rewards and the riches of our Father's will for each of us are beyond our wildest dreams.

So I leave you with this message from the Lord: "Not my will but Thine" (Luke 22:42b, NIV 1984). God bless each of you in your stand.

Standing firm until parted by death.

We Are More Than Conquerors!

Before starting this devotional, read Romans 8:28–39 in whatever version you have. Below are selected verses I wish to emphasize and discuss.

And we know that in all things God works for the good of those who love him, who have been called according to his purpose.

Romans 8:28 (NIV 1984)

If God is for us, who can be against us.

Romans 8:31b (NIV 1984)

No, in all things we are more than conquerors through him who loved us.... [Nothing] will be able to separate us from the love of God that is in Christ Jesus our Lord.

Romans 8:37, 39b (NIV 1984)

These familiar writings of Paul affirm core Christian truths that each of us must come to affirm as we stand for our covenant marriage vows taken with our spouse before the Lord. If you were like me when I first started standing for my marriage, I wanted to get my marriage *fixed*, thinking that all that was required was fixing the horizontal relationship between myself and my wife. However, as I began attending a marriage reconciliation support ministry at my church, it was pointed out to me that this horizontal relationship with my wife was not the issue, and besides, I could not fix it. Only God could do that. What I needed to work on was a vertical relationship, my own personal relationship with God and his Son, Jesus Christ. I realized that my marriage was in shambles because my relationship with Jesus Christ was in shambles, and no amount of secular horizontal fixing of my marriage would be effective, period! My walk with Jesus was where I needed to start. Now as I stand for my covenant marriage vows, Jesus Christ is standing here with me, walking alongside me, feeling my pain but also my joy each moment of the day. He is here to lift me up when I stumble, support me when my walk with him becomes unsteady, and comfort me when my heart is troubled. He offers this to each of us if we will just surrender our lives to him (Jesus Christ), confess our sins to him, ask for his forgiveness, and accept him as our Lord and Savior. What peace can be ours if we will only trust him!

Another hard lesson that I learned was that I could not fix my wife, that only God could do that. I needed to turn her totally over to him, release her to him, and not try to interfere or help him out. Only the Lord can orchestrate the changes needed in our spouse for healing.

Renewing my relationship with Jesus, I realized how little I knew about him. This is when I realized that the troubles with my marriage were a wake-up call from the Lord, that he was calling me to be the person that I was meant to be. Romans states that "God works for the good of those who love him, who have been called according to his purpose" (Romans 8:28, NIV 1984). While we don't wish our marriages to fall apart, God can take that tragedy and turn it into good as he reconciles us (me) to him. To paraphrase Genesis 50:20 (NIV 1984), "[What was] intended [by Satan] to harm me, God intended it for good to accomplish what is now being done [my new walk with Jesus]." Now I have a peace in my soul and in my heart that I have never had in all my life. That is because God loves me unconditionally as I turn my life over to him. This is available to each one of us as we humble ourselves before our awesome God.

As God began to reconcile me to himself, I began to develop new values, values of substance, values with eternal worth. The greatest help in my stand has been the knowledge that Jesus is walking with me, standing with me, feeling my joys and my pain, and being my spouse (I am the bride of Christ) in the absence of my earthly spouse. So I look to verse 31b where it says, "If God is for us [me], who can be against us [me]?" Oh, these are such comforting words coming from God's Holy Word! Jesus is right here beside me, closer than any earthly friend, as he lives within my heart. He is my personal Lord and Savior, a personal Friend, someone I can count on, and you can too! What a wonderful comfort, a wonderful peace that we can have in our times of trouble in our marriages. All we have to do is put our hope and faith in Jesus Christ, the Son of the Living God.

One of my favorite scriptures is found in Jeremiah. This I meditate on almost every day in recent weeks as it reinforces my peace when Satan tries to derail my stand. "'For I know the plans I have for you.' declares the Lord, 'plans to prosper you and not to harm you, plans to give you hope and a future. Then you will call upon me and come and pray to me, and I will listen to you. You will seek me and find me when you seek me with all your heart. I will be found by you,' declares the Lord" (Jeremiah 29:11–14a, NIV 1984). I like also how the Message words this last part: "Yes, when you get serious about finding me and want it more than anything else, I'll make sure you won't be disappointed" (Jeremiah 29:13b, MSG). Oh, that we will allow the Lord to penetrate our hearts and nourish our souls. Our fondest desires of a restored marriage built on the Solid Rock of Jesus Christ will be reality and not just a dream.

Jesus and his Father are still in the miracle business, restoring dead and dying marriages. Our Lord is the God of resurrection, and if we believe in Easter, then we know that he can resurrect our dead marriages. This is what is spoken about in Jeremiah when the Lord talks about "plans to prosper you and not to harm you, plans to give you hope and a future" (Jeremiah 29:11, NIV 1984). Our future is a restored marriage and a living ministry and legacy to our families, our church family, and our friends that divorce is not the answer for troubled marriages. The answer is in Jesus Christ, our Lord and Savior, and making him number 1 in our lives and in our marriage.

Standing for our covenant marriage vows, we realize that despite all the trials of this world, we are truly conquerors! Paul writes in Romans, "We are more than conquerors through him who loved us" (Romans 8:37, NIV 1984). Who loved us? Jesus Christ! It is through Christ's example of his love for a fallen world that we can find the peace and hope that only come with a personal relationship with him. Once we get our relationship with Jesus Christ in order, he will orchestrate, in his perfect timing, the return home of our spouse to our marriage. Remember, as mentioned earlier, the only relationship that we can work on is the one between ourselves and the Lord. The Lord will take care of our spouse. Our spouse is not our problem. Our spouse is the Lord's problem. The only thing we can do for our spouse is pray for them while they are in the far country and petition the Lord on their behalf. To repeat, we are *more than conquerors* in our situations (our stand) because "[nothing] will be able to separate us from the love of God that is in Christ Jesus our Lord" (Romans 8:39b, NIV 1984). Satan has been defeated by the power of the blood of Jesus Christ shed at Calvary, leaving us as conquerors over Satan.

May God bless each and every one of you and keep you true to his Word as you stand for your marriage and the covenant vows you and your spouse took before God and each other. You and I are a *chosen people*, chosen by God to walk this special Christian walk, that of standing for our marriage until parted by death. Most of our fellow Christians are confused by our stand, so educate them as you proclaim your faith and your walk. Remember that each restored dead marriage is a modern-day miracle orchestrated by our Lord Jesus Christ. We are living proof to a fallen world that putting our faith in Jesus Christ is what is important in this life and the life to come.

Standing firm until parted by death.

Our God Answers To No One!

Have you ever had this thought? Our God, our Heavenly Father, answers to no one! That's right, no one! God existed before the beginning of time. No one preexisted him. He is both omnipotent and omniscient. God is sovereign, and he is holy. So try to wrap your mind around the following amazing truths about our God and our relationship with God.

1.   Before time, there was God:

In the beginning God.

Genesis 1:1a (NIV 1984)

No, we speak of God's secret wisdom, a wisdom that has been hidden and that God destined for our glory before time began.

1 Corinthians 2:7 (NIV 1984)

In the beginning was the Word, and the Word was with God, and the Word was God. He was with God in the beginning. Through him all things were made; without him nothing was made that has been made.

John 1:1–3 (NIV 1984)

2.   We are created in his image:

So God created man in his own image, in the image of God he created him; male and female he created them.

Genesis 1:27 (NIV 1984)

3. God desires a relationship with each of us, not as a ruler over us, but as our Heavenly Father, *our Daddy*. We are his adopted sons and daughters:

> For he chose us in him before the creation of the world to be holy and blameless in his sight. In love he predestined us to be adopted as his sons through Jesus Christ, in accordance with his pleasure and will—to the praise of his glorious grace, which he has freely given us in the One he loves.
>
> Ephesians 1:4–6 (NIV 1984)

4. God loves us with such a deep abiding love, an agape love, that he sent his one and only Son to die on a cross for us so that we might spend eternity with him:

> For God so loved the world that he gave his one and only Son, that whoever believes in him shall not perish but have eternal life. For God did not send his Son into the world to condemn the world, but to save the world through him.
>
> John 3:16–17 (NIV 1984)

5. When we accept God's Son as our Lord and Savior through confession of our sins and we truly seek repentance, we receive the gift of the Holy Spirit, who dwells in our heart forever:

> Because you are sons, God sent the Spirit of his Son into our hearts, the Spirit who calls out, "Abba, Father."
>
> Galatians 4:6 (NIV 1984)

Do you not know that your body is a temple of the Holy Spirit, who is in you, whom you have received from God?

1 Corinthians 6:19a (NIV 1984)

God is still God. All-powerful, all-knowing, Supreme Ruler, Holy—*he answers to no one!* Yet he is relational. His fondest desire is to spend eternity with each of us. He is my (our) personal God, my (our) personal Friend, my (our) ever-present help in my (our) troubled marriage(s) or in life's many other troubles. To have such a Friend is beyond description. He is my (our) God. He is my (our) Father. He is my (our) Friend!

Standing firm until parted by death.

Through The Valley

I started this manuscript with a poem written shortly after my wife of thirty-nine years passed away. It is called *Through The Valley*. This devotional, by the same title, takes another look at the twenty-third psalm in depth. I hope that you will read and reread this key scripture of comfort and of hope.

The LORD is my shepherd; I shall not want. He makes me to lie down in green pastures; He leads me beside the still waters. He restores my soul; He leads me in the paths of righteousness For His name's sake. Yea, though I walk through the valley of the shadow of death, I will fear no evil; For You are with me; Your rod and Your staff, they comfort me. You prepare a table before me in the presence of my enemies; You anoint my head with oil; My cup runs over. Surely goodness and mercy shall follow me All the days of my life; And I will dwell in the house of the LORD Forever.

Psalm 23 (NKJV)

This familiar scripture is one of the most quoted Bible passages, with the exception of John 3:16 (God's love for mankind) and 1 Corinthians 13:4–8a (Paul's description of love). It is a scripture many of us memorized early in life and one we see quoted most often at Christian funerals. It is a scripture expressing great faith in our God, a scripture that speaks of his watch care over us. At the time of the death of a loved one, there is much comfort in these words. I know this from personal experience, following the death of my first wife of thirty-nine years. My wife's death biblically ended my first marriage. So many of us have faced or are facing the death of our current marriages. Divorce or the looming threat of divorce spells death to our marriage relationship, a secular death to our marriage. In secular death of a marriage, I am speaking of a judge's decision to grant a divorce. In God's eyes, a marriage ends only when one of the partners of that marriage dies. That is the biblical end of a marriage.

But do not be discouraged for there is *hope!* That *hope* is in our relationship with our Lord and Savior, Jesus Christ. Jesus Christ, fully God and fully man, died on Calvary, taking your sins and my sins upon his body, and in exchange, he gives us his righteousness. This allows each of us to come before a Holy God and to spend eternity with him. Our Father God, using the same powers that he used in raising his Son from the grave on Easter morning, can resurrect our dead or dying marriages if we will truly seek his will and way for our lives. God ordained marriage with Adam and Eve, and despite the world's effort to distort his Word and his purpose of marriage, he still honors marriage. He sees the marriage relationship of a man and woman like the relationship between Jesus Christ and his church, the Body of Christ. Marriage reconciliation works best and is most permanent when both spouses work to rebuild their resurrected marriage upon the Solid Rock of Jesus Christ. With God at the center of a resurrected marriage, he will help each spouse through the difficult times that exist in any marriage, and with a rock-solid faith, those marriages just don't fail.

So let us look at David's psalm. So many places in the Bible, especially in the New Testament, Jesus (God) is spoken of as a *shepherd*.

> I am the good shepherd. The good shepherd lays down his life for the sheep.... I am the good shepherd; I know my sheep and my sheep know me—just as the Father knows me and I know the Father—and I lay down my life for the sheep.
>
> John 10:11, 14–15 (NIV 1984)

Jesus is our Protector, our Comforter. He is there for us to lean on as we stand for our covenant marriage vows, as we walk into the divorce court, and when we face a hostile spouse. Just remember, our spouse is not the enemy; they are being held *captive* by Satan. Satan is the enemy.

> I am the gate. Whoever enters through me will be saved. They will be able to come in and go out. They will find everything they need. A thief comes to steal, kill, and destroy. But I came to give life—life that is full and good.
>
> John 10:9–10 (ERV)

Jesus is our Shepherd, our Deliverer, our Savior. If we put our trust in Jesus, he will lead us through the minefields of our troubled marriage relationships and lead us to a place of calm and peace, Christ's abiding love. I like how the Message puts it: "True to your word, you let me catch my breath and send me in the right direction" (Psalm 23:3, MSG).

As we face separation, a hostile spouse, and/or the divorce court, we are truly walking *through the valley of the shadow of death*. Having experienced both the death biblically of my first marriage and now the secular death of my second marriage, the pain, the hurt, the anger, the confusion, the disbelief, and the grief are very real and very similar. This verse states that our God is there with us even in our darkest moments. What comfort there is in knowing we are not facing this time in our lives alone!

Further along, it states that God is our Provider, even when the wolves (hostile spouses and/or the divorce courts) are on our doorsteps. So many separated or divorced couples suffer financial difficulties. Both the standing spouse and the prodigal spouse do not escape this reality. But our God is merciful, and he will provide our needs. Seek his face in prayer and petition. Know his will and way for your life, and you will never be disappointed. And when you receive his blessings, be sure to give him the praise and the glory.

Finally, our God invites us home, home to spend eternity with him. The final statement speaks of this. I like the way the Message puts it: "Your beauty and love chase after me every day of my life. I'm back home in the house of God for the rest of my life" (Psalm 23:6, MSG).

How comforting David makes it sound: *back home.* Home to me is a place of rest, a place of comfort, a place of peace, a place to be with those I love (my God, my spouse, and my family). It is a place where God is on the throne, and my resurrected marriage can flourish. It is a *real place* if you and I keep our focus on Jesus.

Standing firm until parted by death.

Is Jesus Really God?

I am going to divert here and teach a little bit of theology. I am not formally trained in the Word like at a university or seminary. However, I read, and I have *sat at the feet* of some very knowledgeable Bible teachers and listened. Thus, I wish to share with you what I have learned and what many of you probably know in part but have never backed it up with the Word.

For those of us who have been involved in marriage reconciliation ministry for a while, we know the answer to the question, is Jesus really God? It is a resounding and emphatic *yes*! However, for those who are just beginning to seek some sort of marriage reconciliation for their troubled marriages, the answer is perhaps a weak *yes, I'm not sure, I don't know*, or even *no way*. For many, the idea that God would leave heaven and become a man and then die a horrible death on a Roman cross at the hands of those he came to minister to seems just too far-fetched. But for Christians around the world, the answer is simple: when God's own Son, Jesus Christ, came to live among us some two thousand years ago, he was both fully God and fully man. It was part of God's eternal plan. But first, we need to question and explore the Word of God. Jesus is speaking, and here is where we will start our journey through the Word.

> Ask, and it will be given to you; seek, and you will find; knock, and it will be opened to you. For everyone who asks receives, and he who seeks finds, and to him who knocks it will be opened.
>
> Matthew 7:7–8 (NKJV)

> Yes, God loved the world so much that he gave his only Son, so that everyone who believes in him would not be lost but have eternal life. God sent his Son into the world. He did not send him to judge the world guilty, but to save the world through him.
>
> John 3:16–17 (ERV)

We see from these scriptures that God had a master plan for eternal fellowship with mankind. When Adam sinned in the garden, he set the wheels in motion for a plan, a covenant, to be fulfilled through God's one and only Son, Jesus. God knew mankind needed a Savior, a Messiah. In Isaiah 7:14, the prophet foretells of the coming Messiah. Matthew quotes Isaiah as he begins his story of the birth of Jesus.

> So all this was done that it might be fulfilled which was spoken by the Lord through the prophet, saying: "Behold, the virgin shall be with child, and bear a Son, and they shall call His name Immanuel," which is translated, "God with us."
>
> Matthew 1:22–23 (NKJV)

Immanuel translates "God with us." Here then from Isaiah is one of the first biblical references stating that Jesus and God are one. Later in Isaiah, the prophet continues his prophesy in those so familiar words we have heard in Handel's *Messiah*.

> For unto us a Child is born,
> Unto us a Son is given;
> And the government will be upon His shoulder.
> And His name will be called
> Wonderful, Counselor, Mighty God,
> Everlasting Father, Prince of Peace.
>
> Isaiah 9:6 (NKJV)

Here Isaiah calls the Messiah as Mighty God. As we look further in the birth accounts of Jesus, we look to Luke, who was writing to a Gentile audience. In the first chapter, Luke speaks of the annunciation, when Jesus's mother Mary learned that she was to be a mother.

> During Elizabeth's sixth month of pregnancy, God sent the angel Gabriel to a virgin girl who lived in Nazareth, a town in Galilee. She was engaged to marry a man named

Joseph from the family of David. Her name was Mary. The angel came to her and said, "Greetings! The Lord is with you; you are very special to him." But Mary was very confused about what the angel said. She wondered, "What does this mean?" The angel said to her, "Don't be afraid, Mary, because God is very pleased with you. Listen! You will become pregnant and have a baby boy. You will name him Jesus. He will be great. People will call him the Son of the Most High God, and the Lord God will make him king like his ancestor David. He will rule over the people of Jacob forever; his kingdom will never end." Mary said to the angel, "How will this happen? I am still a virgin." The angel said to Mary, "The Holy Spirit will come to you, and the power of the Most High God will cover you. The baby will be holy and will be called the Son of God.

Luke 1:26–35 (ERV)

Jesus will be called the Son of the Most High God. This title translates as the divine Son of God and the Messiah. The term *Most High* is used in both the Old Testament and New Testament to refer to God. Gabriel went on to say that Mary's child, a human child, would be called the Son of God. Next, from the story of the angels announcing the birth to the shepherds, Luke records the following.

That night, some shepherds were out in the fields near Bethlehem watching their sheep. An angel of the Lord appeared to them, and the glory of the Lord was shining around them. The shepherds were very afraid. The angel said to them, "Don't be afraid. I have some very good news for you—news that will make everyone happy. Today your Savior was born in David's town. He is the Messiah, the Lord.

Luke 2:8–11 (ERV)

> For there is born to you this day in the city of David a Savior, who is Christ the Lord.

> Luke 2:11 (NKJV)

The names *Messiah* from the Hebrew and *Christ* from the Greek both translate "the anointed one." Luke goes on to relate in the last verse that Jesus is our *Savior* and that he is *Christ the Lord.* The term *Lord* is a designation originally reserved for God but later on was applied to the name *Messiah.* So we see in these verses that Jesus is the Messiah (Christ in the Greek), and he is Lord who is also God. Now let us look at further proof that exists in the Gospel of Luke in the story of Simeon.

> In Jerusalem at the time, there was a man, Simeon by name, a good man, a man who lived in the prayerful expectancy of help for Israel. And the Holy Spirit was on him. The Holy Spirit had shown him that he would see the Messiah of God before he died. Led by the Spirit, he entered the Temple. As the parents of the child Jesus brought him in to carry out the rituals of the Law, Simeon took him into his arms and blessed God: God, you can now release your servant; release me in peace as you promised. With my own eyes I've seen your salvation; it's now out in the open for everyone to see: A God-revealing light to the non-Jewish nations, and of glory for your people Israel.

> Luke 2:25–32 (MSG)

Here Luke relates yet another affirmation that Jesus is the Messiah of God. Simeon acknowledges that the salvation that comes through Jesus Christ will be for the Gentiles as well as Israel. Luke also tells the story of the twelve-year-old Jesus in the temple in Jerusalem:

After three days they found him in the temple courts, sitting among the teachers, listening to them and asking them questions. Everyone who heard him was amazed at his understanding and his answers. When his parents saw him, they were astonished. His mother said to him, "Son, why have you treated us like this? Your father and I have been anxiously searching for you." "Why were you searching for me?" he asked. "Didn't you know I had to be in my Father's house?"

Luke 2:46–49 (NIV 1984)

Here Jesus himself acknowledges that he is the Son of God, stating that he was in "my Father's house." Further on, Luke relates the baptism of Jesus by John the Baptist, and Jesus is acknowledged by God (a voice from heaven) as his Son.

After all the people were baptized, Jesus was baptized. As he was praying, the sky opened up and the Holy Spirit, like a dove descending, came down on him. And along with the Spirit, a voice: "You are my Son, chosen and marked by my love, pride of my life."

Luke 3:21–22 (MSG)

Later in Christ's ministry, Jesus tests his disciples and asks them who they think he is.

Now when Jesus came into the district of Caesarea Philippi, He was asking His disciples, "Who do people say that the Son of Man is?" And they said, "Some *say* John the Baptist; and others, Elijah; but still others, Jeremiah, or one of the prophets." He said to them, "But who do you say that I am?" Simon Peter answered, "You are the Christ, the Son of the living God."

Matthew 16:13–16 (NASB)

So we see that Jesus is the Christ, the Messiah, the Son of Man, and also the Son of the living God. Now let us look at Jesus as God.

> In the beginning was the Word, and the Word was with God, and the Word was God. He was in the beginning with God. All things were made through Him, and without Him nothing was made that was made…. And the Word became flesh and dwelt among us, and we beheld His glory, the glory as of the only begotten of the Father, full of grace and truth.
>
> John 1:1–3, 14 (NKJV)

This a very powerful and all-inclusive statement that introduces the Gospel of John. Jesus is the *Word*. John uses that name as synonymous with Jesus. We also see that the Word was present at the beginning of time, was with God, and *the Word was God*. Through him (the Word), all things on earth were made. He is the Creator. In verse 14 (the last verse), John states that the Word put on human flesh, becoming fully God and fully man. Thus, John acknowledges that Jesus is God. Further on, John relates the following as Jesus comforts His disciples.

> Jesus answered, "I am the way, the truth, and the life. The only way to the Father is through me. If you really knew me, you would know my Father too. But now you know the Father. You have seen him." Philip said to him, "Lord, show us the Father. That is all we need." Jesus answered, "Philip, I have been with you for a long time. So you should know me. Anyone who has seen me has seen the Father too. So why do you say, 'Show us the Father'? Don't you believe that I am in the Father and the Father is in me? The things I have told you don't come from me. The Father lives in me, and he is doing his own work. Believe me when I say that I am in the Father and the Father is in me.
>
> John 14:6–11a (ERV)

In this passage, Jesus is teaching his disciples that he is truly God who is living among them. In speaking with the Jewish crowds following him who had doubts, Jesus stated, "I and the Father are one" (John 10:30, NIV 1984). Both of these scriptures state emphatically that Jesus is God and God is Jesus. Having seen and being with Jesus is to see and be with God.

As we look at the Crucifixion, Mark records the following comment of the Roman centurion in charge of the crucifixion.

> And Jesus uttered a loud cry, and breathed His last. And the veil of the temple was torn in two from top to bottom. When the centurion, who was standing right in front of Him, saw the way He breathed His last, he said, "Truly this man was the Son of God!"
>
> Mark 15:37–39 (NASB)

The Apostle Paul makes the following statement, noting once again that Jesus was both fully God and fully man: "Have this attitude in yourselves which was also in Christ Jesus, who, although He existed in the form of God, did not regard equality with God a thing to be grasped, but emptied Himself, taking the form of a bond-servant, *and* being made in the likeness of men" (Philippians 2:5–7 NASB).

That statement of being "in the form of God" and shortly thereafter stating "made in the likeness of men" should make the case for Jesus, the human, being God. In Colossians, Paul offers further proof when he writes, "I say this because all of God lives in Christ fully, even in his life on earth" (Colossians 2:9, ERV).

I think by now that you can see from these accounts in the Holy Bible, God's inerrant revelation to mankind, that Jesus is God and God is Jesus. My final note comes from Paul's writings to the Colossians concerning Jesus Christ, stating that the Son of God is the same as God.

No one can see God, but the Son is exactly like God. He rules over everything that has been made. Through his power all things were made: things in heaven and on earth, seen and not seen—all spiritual rulers, lords, powers, and authorities. Everything was made through him and for him. The Son was there before anything was made. And all things continue because of him. He is the head of the body, which is the church. He is the beginning of everything else. And he is the first among all who will be raised from death. So in everything he is most important. God was pleased for all of himself to live in the Son. And through him, God was happy to bring all things back to himself again—things on earth and things in heaven. God made peace by using the blood sacrifice of his Son on the cross. At one time you were separated from God. You were his enemies in your minds, because the evil you did was against him. But now he has made you his friends again. He did this by the death Christ suffered while he was in his body. He did it so that he could present you to himself as people who are holy, blameless, and without anything that would make you guilty before him. And that is what will happen if you continue to believe in the Good News you heard. You must remain strong and sure in your faith. You must not let anything cause you to give up the hope that became yours when you heard the Good News.

Colossians 1:15–23a (ERV)

Paul admonishes us to stand firm in our faith that Jesus Christ is God and that he is our hope of salvation. He speaks of reconciliation to God, which is the first step in any marriage reconciliation. May each of you stand firm in your faith and stand firm in your covenant marriage vows. May God pour out his blessings upon you during this season of your life as you become reconciled to God, then reconciled to self, and ultimately reconciled to your spouse.

Standing firm until parted by death.

We Are God's Children

But some people did accept him. They believed in him, and he gave them the right to become children of God. They became God's children, but not in the way babies are usually born. It was not because of any human desire or plan. They were born from God himself.

—John 1:12–13 (erv)

In Galatians, the Apostle Paul tell us, "You were all baptized into Christ, and so you were all clothed with Christ. This shows that you are all children of God through faith in Christ Jesus" (Galatians 3:26, erv).

What an awesome thing. You and I are God's own children! One may ask, "How can this be?" We realize that each of us was born of a woman, our human mother, who bore us through union with our earthly human father. Yet when we come to know Jesus Christ as our Lord and Savior, we are *born again*. It is through our confession and faith in Jesus Christ that God, our Creator, adopts us as his children, and we gain membership in God's family. What greater or more awesome event could happen than to be included in the family of God? From this relationship, we have the spiritual benefit of knowing God as our Father. No one—not Satan, not the world, not even our spouse—can take our membership in his family away or call it into question.

Praise be to the God and Father of our Lord Jesus Christ. In Christ, God has given us every spiritual blessing in heaven. In Christ, he chose us before the world was made. He chose us in love to be his holy people—people who could stand before him without any fault. And before the world was made, God decided to make us his own children through Jesus Christ. This was what God wanted, and it pleased him to do it.

Ephesians 1:3–5 (ERV)

The above scripture sets the stage for our right to be called the children of God and our right to call God our Father. Following acceptance of Jesus Christ as our Lord and Savior, it is through the act of adoption that our family ties with God are established. In adoption, we are not biologically related to our adoptive parent, but that family relationship is established by the willful choice of God becoming an adoptive parent so that we may become his children. Adoption is just as binding and permanent as being biologically related to our parent. Yet willfully and in accordance with his pleasure, God adopted each and every one of us in love through Jesus Christ as his adopted sons (and daughters). As God's adopted sons and daughters, we receive full rights of a child born of God. The following scriptures speak of this.

> But when the right time came, God sent his Son, who was born from a woman and lived under the law. God did this so that he could buy the freedom of those who were under the law. God's purpose was to make us his children.... You are God's children, and you will receive everything he promised his children.
>
> Galatians 4:4–5, 7b (ERV)

> But you received the Spirit of adoption by whom we cry out, "Abba, Father." The Spirit Himself bears witness with our spirit that we are children of God, and if children, then heirs—heirs of God and joint heirs with Christ, if indeed we suffer with *Him*, that we may also be glorified together.
>
> Romans 8:15b–17 (NKJV)

From these two scriptures, we see our family tree delineated. Jesus Christ, the Son of God, is our brother. As he is our brother, we are coheirs with Christ in his sufferings as well as his glory. It is through this family relationship as God's children and with Jesus as our brother that we can come before a Holy God, Our Heavenly Father, and cry out, "Abba, Father."

Next, looking in Matthew's Gospel, we find Jesus is in the Garden, and he is praying to his Father just prior to his arrest. "And He went a little beyond *them*, and fell on His face and prayed, saying, 'My Father, if it is possible, let this cup pass from Me; yet not as I will, but as You will'" (Matthew 26:39, NASB).

As you and I stand for our covenant marriage vows, each of us must follow our brother's example in the Garden. There, Jesus emphasized the importance of obedience to God, his Father and our Father, when he prayed, "Yet not as I will, but as you will." We, like our brother Jesus, must ultimately trust our Heavenly Father that his will is proper and just and that it will be done in our lives and in our marriages. In Jesus's prayer, his human will obediently submitted to his Father's divine will. As God's adopted children, our human will should (must) submit in obedience to God's divine will. Looking at our troubled marriages, that *will* is to stand firm for our covenant marriage vows.

The story of the Garden of Gethsemane teaches us a great lesson as God's children. That lesson is the power of prayer when temptation from the world pulls at us to abandon our stand. Jesus knew the power of temptation because he himself was fully human. Yet he knew the source of resistance to that temptation: *prayer*. Yes, prayer to his Father God and to our Father God. Through prayer, Jesus garnered the strength to face what lay ahead for him. It is through prayer that you and I can garner strength to stand off the attacks of Satan in our stand. Jesus, our brother, gave us a model to follow: a perfect model of human trust in our Father, our Heavenly Father.

May each of us as God's children have renewed trust in our Heavenly Father as we remember and celebrate the birth of our brother, Jesus. Some two thousand years may have passed since that Christmas event, the birth of God's one and only Son, yet the world has been turned upside down and continues to react to the Good News that Jesus Christ is Lord and Savior. He is our brother, and we as his brothers and sisters are God's children. Stand firm in your faith and in your stand for your covenant marriage vows throughout this season of your life.

Standing firm until parted by death.

A Chosen People

In my reading today, I was once again reminded of the story of Moses and his confrontation with Pharaoh, the ruler of the most powerful nation of that day. Moses was getting resistance about letting the Israelites go, not only from Pharaoh, but also from the Israelites themselves. As Moses made demands on Pharaoh, Pharaoh put increasing demands upon the Israelites. Moses, a man of eighty years, feeling the pressure from both Pharaoh and his own people, cries out to God for further instructions.

> Therefore, say to the Israelites: "I am the LORD, and I will bring you out from under the yoke of the Egyptians. I will free you from being slaves to them, and I will redeem you with an outstretched arm and with mighty acts of judgment. I will take you as my own people, and I will be your God. Then you will know that I am the LORD your God, who brought you out from under the yoke of the Egyptians."
>
> Exodus 6:6–7 (NIV 1984)

"I will take you as my own people, and I will be your God." What a wonderful promise from God! Not just that "I will look after you," but there is to be a special bond, a unique relationship that sets you apart from all other peoples on earth. God goes on to say, "Know *that I am the* LORD *your God*" (Exodus 6:7b, NIV 1984; emphasis added). I am not just your God, "I am *the* LORD *your God*." What an honor God bestowed upon his chosen people, the Israelites, the unique people of God (out of all the different groups of people in the world at that time).

God's message to the Israelites is far-reaching. It is one of a special relationship that is closely linked to the establishment of God's covenant with Abraham, Isaac, and Jacob and the redemption that God brings through that covenant.

> Now then, if you will indeed obey My voice and keep My covenant, then you shall be My own possession among all the peoples, for all the earth is Mine; and you shall be to Me a kingdom of priests and a holy nation. These are the words that you shall speak to the sons of Israel.
>
> Exodus 19:5–6 (NASB)

It is through that covenant that God requires obedience from his people. They were to be *a kingdom of priests and a holy nation.* While these scriptures speak to the Israelites of that day, they also apply to us today as Christians, heirs in Christ's kingdom. Peter speaks of this.

> But you *are* a chosen generation, a royal priesthood, a holy nation, His own special people, that you may proclaim the praises of Him who called you out of darkness into His marvelous light.
>
> 1 Peter 2:9 (NKJV)

A *chosen generation*...a *special people.* Have you ever felt that you were a chosen or special person? We all have had that experience when we were chosen by our spouse to be their lifelong companion, partner, and friend in a marriage relationship. Yet something happened along the way. The dreams that existed on our wedding day faded, and troubles arose. Now we find ourselves separated from our spouse, possibly divorced in the secular courts of the land. But each of us has heard a calling deep down inside of us, a calling from God that this is not right. This is not what God had in mind when he brought you together with your spouse and made you one flesh. Whether you were aware of it or not, God was present as you took your marriage vows and became a partner and a witness to them. A three-way covenant was formed. Now, through marital discord, your spouse has chosen to break covenant and leave. Yet that covenant still exists between you and God and between you and your spouse. It is your spouse who has broken covenant. Now, as standers, we are standing with God for the resurrection and rebuilding of our marriages.

We are a chosen people. We are not here in this stand by accident but were chosen, singled out, to bring light into a fallen world of darkness, a world of darkness of marital separation and/or divorce. You are in a special priesthood of believers chosen by God to be a beacon of hope to those in troubled marriages. And you are a beacon of light and of hope to your spouse as you stand with God for the rebuilding of your marriage. God promised to the Israelites a plan of deliverance in the time of Moses, and he has a plan and a promise of deliverance today for your marriage. That deliverance is a restored marriage built upon the Solid Rock of Jesus Christ. His requirement for deliverance is simple: be obedient to his will. His will is this: put your trust in God, be obedient to your marriage vows, and God will see you through this dark valley of your life. This experience will be a time of spiritual awakening and growth in your life. And despite the pain of the experience, you will thank God that he took you through this time of darkness and fire into the light of a Christ-centered marriage.

You are a chosen people! God's chosen people! Trust and obey! He will see you through!

Standing firm until parted by death.

Psalm 118

To start the day off correctly, read Psalm 118 in its entirety in whatever version you have. I am quoting out of the Easy-to-Read Version of the Bible.

> Praise the Lord because he is good! His faithful love will last forever!
>
> Psalm 118:1 (ERV)

As I read through this psalm this morning, I couldn't help but notice that this psalm speaks so well to the plight and joy that each of us experience as we struggle in our marriage and family relationships. This is a psalm of thanksgiving, a hymn of praise for deliverance from the psalmist's enemies. The speaker may be King David or perhaps one of the Levitical (priest) leaders of the Israelites as they look back at their past experiences since their deliverance from bondage in Egypt. In much the same way, each of us can look at our own marriage and family relationships and do as the psalmist says. "Praise the Lord because he is good! His faithful love will last forever!" (Psalm 118:1, ERV).

In all things, we need to keep foremost in our hearts and minds that God's love for each of us does endure forever. Verses 1 and 29 form bookends enclosing a powerful statement of praise and thanksgiving that each of us can experience as we deal with our marriage and family relationships.

> I was in trouble, so I called to the Lord for help. The Lord answered and made me free. The Lord is with me, so I will not be afraid. No one on earth can do anything to harm me.
>
> Psalm 118:5–6 (ERV)

We all have cried out to the *Lord* as our lives appeared to be falling apart, and through his love, he set us free from the bondage of our sins and despair. He is our Rock, our Refuge in our struggle with what man (the world) throws at us. Look again at our scripture: "The Lord is my helper…. It is better to trust in the Lord than to trust in people" (Psalm 118:7a, 8; ERV).

All too often, we find ourselves looking for relationship help in all the wrong places. The psalmist states plainly that our hope is found in the *Lord*. No one else can comfort us like he can, no one else can shield us from danger as he does, and no one else can direct us in the correct path to take. Lean on him at these times (and always) for strength and guidance.

> The Lord is my strength and my reason for singing. He saved me! You can hear the victory celebration in the homes of those who live right. The Lord has shown his great power again!
>
> Psalm 118:14–15 (ERV)

All of us who struggle with our marriages understand the many sins we have committed. Yet our God is a God of love and grace. Yes, he points out our sins and chastens us, sometimes severely. But don't be discouraged for he wants only the best for each of us. Healing is found in the *Lord*.

> I will live and not die, and I will tell what the Lord has done. The Lord punished me, but he did not let me die. Gates of goodness, open for me, and I will come in and worship the Lord.
>
> Psalm 118:17–19 (ERV)

In all our anguish and sorrow over the problems we are dealing with in our relationships, there is hope. Hope in a God who cares about his people. Hope of a new beginning and of a bright future found in the rebuilding of our relationships upon the Solid Rock of our *Lord* and Savior, Jesus Christ. He truly is our salvation.

> Lord, I thank you for answering my prayer. I thank you for saving me. The stone that the builders rejected became the cornerstone…. This is the day the LORD has made. Let us rejoice and be happy today!
>
> Psalm 118:21–22, 24 (ERV)

It is when we face the adversity of unstable relationships that we can turn our eyes and hearts to the one true God who can give us answers to our prayers of supplication. Jesus Christ (our Rock) is the Stone rejected by the world, yet he has become our capstone, the cornerstone of our faith. Then like the psalmist, we can sing, "LORD, you are my God, and I thank you. My God, I praise you! Praise the LORD because he is good. His faithful love will last forever" (Psalm 118:28–29, ERV).

Standing firm until parted by death.

Jesus Christ: Man? Or God?

For two thousand years, mankind has wrestled with this question. Just who is Jesus Christ? Man? Or God? This question when answered is an essential tenet of our Christian faith. I (we) believe that Jesus Christ *was* fully man *and* fully God. Not part-man and part-God, but fully man and fully God. When Jesus was born in Bethlehem, he took on our humanity without losing his deity! We may never fully understand this concept until we meet Jesus face-to-face in eternity, but this basic Christian tenet must be accepted through faith in him. The Apostle Paul writes about God's plan for us through his son, Jesus Christ.

But share with me in the sufferings for the gospel according to the power of God, who has saved us and called *us* with a holy calling, not according to our works, but according to His own purpose and grace which was given to us in Christ Jesus before time began, but has now been revealed by the appearing of our Savior Jesus Christ, *who* has abolished death and brought life and immortality to light through the gospel.

2 Timothy 1:8b–10 (NKJV)

For this is the Good News that Jesus Christ, a sinless human, defeated death when he died on a Roman cross for our sins. Jesus bore his Father's wrath for our sinful nature so that we might stand before a Holy God, blameless and clothed (covered) in Christ's righteousness. Colossians states, "But now he has made you his friends again. He did this by the death Christ suffered while he was in his body. He did it so that he could present you to himself as people who are holy, blameless, and without anything that would make you guilty before him" (Colossians 1:22, ERV).

I want to look at several scriptures that address the nature of Jesus Christ. I think we first need to ponder the fact that if Jesus had not been fully human, we would then say that he could not sin because he is God and not subject to falling into sin as humans do. But Jesus was human. He experienced temptations like you and I but remained sinless. Despite Satan's numerous attempts, Jesus never lived outside the will of his Father. We find the following selections from Hebrews.

Therefore, since we have a great high priest who has passed through the heavens, Jesus the Son of God, let us hold fast our confession. For we do not have a high priest who cannot sympathize with our weaknesses, but One who has been tempted in all things as *we are, yet* without sin.

Therefore let us draw near with confidence to the throne of grace, so that we may receive mercy and find grace to help in time of need.

Hebrews 4:14–16 (NASB)

For the law, having a shadow of the good things to come, *and* not the very image of the things, can never with these same sacrifices, which they offer continually year by year, make those who approach perfect. For then would they not have ceased to be offered? For the worshipers, once purified, would have had no more consciousness of sins. But in those *sacrifices there is* a reminder of sins every year. For *it is* not possible that the blood of bulls and goats could take away sins. Therefore, when He came into the world, He said: "Sacrifice and offering You did not desire, But a body You have prepared for Me. In burnt offerings and *sacrifices* for sin You had no pleasure. Then I said, 'Behold, I have come—In the volume of the book it is written of Me—To do Your will, O God....'" By that will we have been sanctified through the offering of the body of Jesus Christ once *for all....* But this Man, after He had offered one sacrifice for sins forever, sat down at the right hand of God.

Hebrews 10:1–7, 10, 12 (NKJV)

This is the *Good News!* Jesus Christ, being fully human, could understand our weaknesses because he was tempted like us. Yet he did not succumb to his temptations. Jesus Christ is both *Lord and Savior.* Notice the last sentence: "But this Man...offered one sacrifice for sins...sat down at the right hand of God." This man was Jesus, and he sits at the right hand of God. Now let us look at the Gospel of John.

> In the beginning the Word already existed. The Word was with God, and the Word was God. He existed in the beginning with God. God created everything through him, and nothing was created except through him. The Word gave life to everything that was created, and his life brought light to everyone. The light shines in the darkness, and the darkness can never extinguish it.
>
> John 1:1–5 (NLT)

The Word, another name for Jesus Christ, *existed* before the beginning of time. He was with God and was God. John states that Jesus Christ and God are one. This mystery as explained by John is a key tenet of the Christian faith. John also states that through Christ, everything that exists (you and I, plants, animals, the earth and sky, the universe, etc.) was created.

> So the Word became human and made his home among us. He was full of unfailing love and faithfulness. And we have seen his glory, the glory of the Father's one and only Son.
>
> John 1:14 (NLT)

Thus, we see that Jesus is proclaimed as human (The Word became flesh... [John 1:14a, NIV 1984]), and he came and lived among a sinful people, the world. Let us now look at a passage from Hebrews.

> Long ago God spoke many times and in many ways to our ancestors through the prophets. And now in these final days, he has spoken to us through his Son. God promised everything to the Son as an inheritance, and through the Son he created the universe. The Son radiates God's own glory and expresses the very character of God, and he

sustains everything by the mighty power of his command. When he had cleansed us from our sins, he sat down in the place of honor at the right hand of the majestic God in heaven.

Hebrews 1:1–3 (NLT)

As in John's Gospel, Hebrews says that everything in the universe was created through Jesus. In like manner, Jesus reflects God's own glory and character and holds everything together by his mighty power (command). Jesus is God! From multiple verses in the Gospel of John, Jesus acknowledges his unity with the Father and his deity.

Jesus answered: "Don't you know me, Philip, even after I have been among you such a long time? Anyone who has seen me has seen the Father. How can you say, 'Show us the Father'? Don't you believe that I am in the Father, and that the Father is in me?"

John 14:9–10a (NIV 1984)

I and My Father are one.

John 10:30 (NKJV)

No one has ever seen God. But the unique One, who is himself God, is near to the Father's heart. He has revealed God to us.

John 1:18 (NLT)

The Apostle Paul states in Colossians that Jesus Christ is God. "Christ is the visible image of the invisible God" (Colossians 1:15a, NLT). Finally, we look at the Apostle Paul's Epistle to the Philippians for confirmation as to who Jesus Christ is. Is he man or God or both?

He was like God in every way, but he did not think that his being equal with God was something to use for his own benefit. Instead, he gave up everything, even his place with God. He accepted the role of a servant, appearing in human form. During his life as a man, he humbled himself by being fully obedient to God, even when that caused his death—death on a cross. So God raised him up to the most important place and gave him the name that is greater than any other name. God did this so that every person will bow down to honor the name of Jesus. Everyone in heaven, on earth, and under the earth will bow. They will all confess, "Jesus Christ is Lord," and this will bring glory to God the Father.

Philippians 2:6–11 (ERV)

Paul confirms it. Jesus Christ *was like God in every way* and *appearing in human form,* was fully human (man) and fully God. What an awesome God we serve!

May God bless your stand for your marriage covenant and your walk with Jesus Christ throughout the coming year and the years to come. It is through our reconciliation to God as mentioned above and by placing God number 1 in our personal lives that our dysfunctional marriages can begin to heal. [35]

Standing firm until parted by death.

The Torn Curtain

There are many events in the Crucifixion story that stand out as significant in our Christian faith. The *torn curtain* is one such event. In the temple in Jerusalem, there was an area known as the Holy of Holies or Most Holy Place. In this area resided the Ark of the Covenant and the Mercy Seat. It was where God resided as he sat on the Mercy Seat to judge the Israelites. Once a year, the chief priest could enter the Holy of Holies behind a thick cloud of incense, seeking atonement for the sins of the Israelites. So fearsome was this event that a rope was tied around the ankle of the priest so if he was struck dead in the Holy of Holies, his body could be retrieved by pulling him out using the rope. Such were the events that occurred on the Day of Atonement, also called Yom Kippur.

The Holy of Holies was separated from the Holy Place by two overlapping thick curtains from floor to ceiling. At the time of the Crucifixion, the moment Jesus gave up his Spirit, there was a great earthquake, and these curtains were torn from top to bottom. With Jesus's death, a new era of access to God was ushered in. Now all believers could approach God directly for the veil of separation had been removed. Mankind now had direct access into the holy realm of God. Of significance was that the curtains were torn from *top* to *bottom*, showing that this was God's action, not man's. Symbolically, the torn curtain also represents Jesus Christ's torn (broken) body by which he gives his followers direct access to his Father.

> But Jesus, again crying out loudly, breathed his last. At that moment, the Temple curtain was ripped in two, top to bottom. There was an earthquake, and rocks were split in pieces.
>
> Matthew 27:50–51 (msg)

The torn curtain, probably next to the event of the resurrection and the empty tomb, is what I feel is the second most important event in the Crucifixion story. For with the torn curtain, an action initiated by God himself, mankind acquired direct access to God. No longer was there necessity for mankind to be ritually cleansed by a priest by a blood sacrifice on a yearly basis and then have his petitions presented to God. With Jesus Christ's death upon the cross, he became our Great High Priest, our perfect, unblemished sacrifice presented once and for all time to God for the atonement of mankind's sins. No longer did we need to have the blood of lambs or goats to atone for our sins. Jesus Christ's death on the cross ushered in the New Covenant between God and mankind, allowing believers direct access to our Heavenly Father. Now clothed in Christ's righteousness, you and I can come before a Holy God and sit at his feet and worship him, presenting our petitions directly to him. The curtain that kept mankind separated from the throne room of our Heavenly Father was destroyed by God himself. God welcomes you and me as believers to come into his presence, clothed in Christ's righteousness; we are no longer covered in sin, but we are forgiven sons and daughters of the King. How awesome is this! Direct access to our Heavenly Father!

> We have a great high priest who has gone to live with God in heaven. He is Jesus the Son of God. So let us continue to express our faith in him. Jesus, our high priest, is able to understand our weaknesses. When Jesus lived on earth, he was tempted in every way. He was tempted in the same ways we are tempted, but he never sinned. With Jesus as our high priest, we can feel free to come before God's throne where there is grace. There we receive mercy and kindness to help us when we need it.
>
> Hebrews 4:14–16 (ERV)

> But Christ came *as* High Priest of the good things to come, with the greater and more perfect tabernacle not made with hands, that is, not of this creation. Not with the blood of goats and calves, but with His own blood He entered the Most Holy Place once for all, having obtained eternal redemption. For if the blood of bulls and goats and the ashes of a heifer, sprinkling the unclean, sanctifies for the purifying of the flesh, how much more shall the blood of Christ, who through the eternal Spirit offered

Himself without spot to God, cleanse your conscience from dead works to serve the living God? And for this reason He is the Mediator of the new covenant, by means of death, for the redemption of the transgressions under the first covenant, that those who are called may receive the promise of the eternal inheritance.

Hebrews 9:11–15 (NKJV)

At this Easter season, let us remember that we serve a risen Lord who is Jesus Christ. He is the sinless Son of God. Remember God's action of tearing the temple curtain from top to bottom. God's action gives us direct access to sit and worship at the foot of our Heavenly Father. The temple curtain under the Old Covenant separated mankind from God. However, as believers in Jesus Christ and the work he did for us on the cross, our Great High Priest under the New Covenant has opened up our Heavenly Father's throne room to you and me.

Praise be to God that we now have direct access to our Heavenly Father to be able to petition him with all our needs, especially those dealing with our marriage and family problems.

Standing firm until parted by death.

CHRISTIAN LIVING

Living Beyond The Moment

When the boys grew up, Esau became a skillful hunter, a man of the field, but Jacob was a peaceful man, living in tents. Now Isaac loved Esau, because he had a taste for game, but Rebekah loved Jacob. When Jacob had cooked stew, Esau came in from the field and he was famished; and Esau said to Jacob, "Please let me have a swallow of that red stuff there, for I am famished." Therefore his name was called Edom. But Jacob said, "First sell me your birthright." Esau said, "Behold, I am about to die; so of what *use* then is the birthright to me?" And Jacob said, "First swear to me"; so he swore to him, and sold his birthright to Jacob. Then Jacob gave Esau bread and lentil stew; and he ate and drank, and rose and went on his way. Thus Esau despised his birthright.

—Genesis 25:27–34 (NASB)

The story of Jacob and Esau is probably familiar to many of us. What we often remember is the story of Isaac's blessing going to Jacob rather than to Esau. However, in the story recorded above, there is another lesson to be learned. It is the lesson of patience. In the hustle and bustle of this modern world, patience runs thin for most of us. We are a people bent on instant gratification. We want it now, not later. Why wait until tomorrow when we can have it today for just a few easy payments, as the salesman states. And so the debts mount up. Or on another note, we find romance on the first date, fall in love, and decide to get married, only to find out that there is little or no commitment involved in this marriage. However, in this last example, a covenant vow has been made before the Lord and our spouse. In our desire for instant gratification, we seek a divorce rather than solutions, and we proceed to discard our starter marriage! Instant gratification has claimed yet another set of victims. This couple sold out for what felt good in the moment. In the deeper lesson, they sold out their birthright of a lasting covenant marriage for lack of commitment, a moment of instant gratification. They did not have a vision of marriage lasting for a lifetime. They were not thinking long-term. They were merely living in the moment.

In the above story from Genesis, Esau sold his birthright for a bowl of soup and some bread rather than exhibit patience and fix himself some food. His desire for instant gratification completely clouded his vision. And the results were forever, eternal. Each of us may face crossroads in our own lives and in our own marriages where, if we fall under the influence of Satan and the world, foolish choices are made and the scars left behind are eternal. Yes, healing can occur, but still scars remain to remind us of our prior poor choices. When we live in the moment, our choices invariably have life-altering consequences. When a marriage goes sour, many think their only choice is divorce. Here each partner suffers far beyond the time of the divorce decree, and the children involved are scarred for a lifetime. Yet when faced with a dysfunctional marriage, there is a third option besides (1) living together but leading separate lives or (2) seeking a divorce. That third option is...*try God!*

Marriage reconciliation is centered on our own reconciliation with God. When we follow Esau's example and seek the easy road, we do not have the end in mind. We are living in the moment. Sustainable marriages with a track record of forty-five, fifty, or even sixty years of history have one thing in common: they are a work in progress until the death of one of the partners. Each partner sees beyond the moment of discord in the marriage; they see beyond themselves and seek godly solutions to problems rather than take the easy way out, that of living in the moment. Learn to live beyond the moment. So as we seek reconciliation in our marriages, we need to keep our focus upon Jesus.

> Therefore, since we have so great a cloud of witnesses surrounding us, let us also lay aside every encumbrance and the sin which so easily entangles us, and let us run with endurance the race that is set before us, fixing our eyes on Jesus, the author and perfecter of faith, who for the joy set before Him endured the cross, despising the shame, and has sat down at the right hand of the throne of God. For consider Him who has endured such hostility by sinners against Himself, so that you will not grow weary and lose heart.

> Hebrews 12:1–3 (NASB)

Standing firm until parted by death.

The Lord Is On Our Team

Earlier this evening, I watched a movie that I would recommend to anyone who is in a situation where it looks like the odds are stacked against them. You have all heard about this wonderful movie. It is the story of a small-town high school football team with a history of six losing seasons. Now in their seventh season with the same head coach, they find themselves in the state championship finals, and despite unusual odds, they beat the three-time state champion team that everyone thought was unbeatable. The movie is *Facing the Giants*. It is a movie of encouragement for anyone who is facing overwhelming odds to life's ever-changing situations. It is a story of a head coach who discovered hidden strengths within himself and in his players when they put their faith and trust in God. He discovered that by allowing God to turn each of his players into a living testimony of God's power in each of their own lives, the football team became unbeatable as God was on their side. Their philosophy was this: whether they won or lost, they would praise God. In the hearts of the team members, the Lord became a member of their team, and he wore jersey number 1. The following scripture became their rallying call.

> Jesus looked at them and said, "With man this is impossible, but with God all things are possible."
>
> Matthew 19:26 (NIV 1984)[36]

Do you believe this scripture? If not, meditate on it. When you come to accept this simple truth about God, it will change your life forever.

As we stand for our marriage vows, a covenant we made before God and our spouse, we look around and realize that our Lord Jesus Christ is there with us; he is on the team. However, I see this in yet another profound way. The Lord is on *our* team. And just what do I mean by *our* team? *Our* team refers to our spouses and you and me! Yes, I said *our spouses*. Our Lord Jesus Christ is on *our* team, *our* marriage team, and *our* team is facing a formidable foe. Without the Lord on *our* team, we are fighting a losing battle, the battle for the survival of our marriages. And who is that foe? It is Satan. Our enemy in this battle for our marriages is not our spouses; it is Satan. Our Lord Jesus is on the team with you and your spouse, and *you* together (the Lord, your spouse, and you) are fighting the enemy. For we know that when a marriage is restored and reconciled, our Lord is there as our coach. A restored marriage only has lasting power if it is rebuilt on the Solid Rock of Jesus Christ.

While a stand for a troubled marriage starts with one of the marriage partners, it really involves both partners. As God starts working in the heart of the standing partner, he is also working behind the scenes in the heart of the prodigal spouse. After all, God loves marriage. Didn't he ordain it in the Garden with Adam and Eve?

> And the LORD God said, "*It is* not good that man should be alone; I will make him a helper comparable to him...." But for Adam there was not found a helper comparable to him. And the LORD God caused a deep sleep to fall on Adam, and he slept; and He took one of his ribs, and closed up the flesh in its place. Then the rib which the LORD God had taken from man He made into a woman, and He brought her to the man. And Adam said: "This *is* now bone of my bones And flesh of my flesh; She shall be called Woman, Because she was taken out of Man." Therefore a man shall leave his father and mother and be joined to his wife, and they shall become one flesh.
>
> Genesis 2:18, 20b–24 (NKJV)

God ordained the union of a man and a woman in marriage not only so man would have a helpmate, but that they would be fruitful and multiply and have children and subdue the earth.

> Adam lay with his wife Eve, and she became pregnant and gave birth to Cain. She said, "With the help of the LORD I have brought forth a man." Later she gave birth to his brother Abel.
>
> Genesis 4:1–2a (NIV 1984)

Then God blessed Noah and his sons, saying to them, "Be fruitful and increase in number and fill the earth.

Genesis 9:1 (NIV 1984)

God wants husbands and wives to become one body and one spirit. Why? So that they would have holy children and protect that spiritual unity.

Malachi 2:15a (ERV)

Is Christ on your team? Is he there fighting alongside you for your marriage as you stand? The choice is yours. Let us look at what Paul says about reconciliation.

Therefore, if anyone *is* in Christ, *he is* a new creation; old things have passed away; behold, all things have become new. Now all things *are* of God, who has reconciled us to Himself through Jesus Christ, and has given us the ministry of reconciliation, that is, that God was in Christ reconciling the world to Himself, not imputing their trespasses to them, and has committed to us the word of reconciliation. Now then, we are ambassadors for Christ, as though God were pleading through us: we implore *you* on Christ's behalf, be reconciled to God. For He made Him who knew no sin *to be* sin for us, that we might become the righteousness of God in Him.

2 Corinthians 5:17–21 (NKJV)

Isn't this such a great promise from our Father God! Our Lord Jesus Christ is on *our* team, and we are now reconciled to God. Accept the fact that "with God, all things are possible" (Matthew 19:26, NIV 1984). True reconciliation with our prodigal spouse can only come when we standers are first reconciled to God.

So what should we say about this? If God is for us, no one can stand against us. And God is with us.

Romans 8:31 (ERV)

Hurray for our team! Stand firm with Christ! Standing firm until parted by death.

Press On

I gave up all that inferior stuff so I could know Christ personally, experience his resurrection power, be a partner in his suffering, and go all the way with him to death itself. If there was any way to get in on the resurrection from the dead, I wanted to do it. Focused on the Goal. I'm not saying that I have this all together, that I have it made. But I am well on my way, reaching out for Christ, who has so wondrously reached out for me. Friends, don't get me wrong: By no means do I count myself an expert in all of this, but I've got my eye on the goal, where God is beckoning us onward—to Jesus. I'm off and running, and I'm not turning back.

—Philippians 3:10–14 (MSG)

In this powerful text, the Apostle Paul is seeking to instruct the first-century Christians of Philippi what they needed to do to obtain Christ's righteousness by using the example of his own personal story. All too often, as we stand for the healing of our failing or failed marriages, we get discouraged and want to pull back to the *safety* of doing nothing. Paul, who was in prison at that time, wanted to spur these new Christians on by showing them that their (our) own personal circumstances should not detract them (or us) from pressing on toward the eternal goals to which Christ Jesus had called them (or us). So let us look at some of the messages of this text.

First, Paul addresses the desire that he *could know Christ personally, experience his resurrection power.* Isn't that what we are called to do as we first seek reconciliation with God? It is by knowing (studying) who Jesus is, what he taught, and what he did that we can begin to really know *who* Jesus Christ is. We will never *truly know* Jesus until that day we meet him face-to-face in heaven. Yet on this earth and at this time, we can strive to understand the essence of Christ.

Paul mentions he desires to *be a partner in his suffering.* No one needs to say much here because we are all going through various degrees of suffering with our marriages. Yet Christ also suffered, and in his humanity, he understands our sufferings. What comfort to know that our Christ, our personal God, understands us and knows the pain of our sufferings. He can relate to each of us because he is fully man, and he can comfort us because he is fully God.

Paul goes on to say that he has not been made perfect but that "I am well on my way, reaching out for Christ, who has so wondrously reached out for me." Paul realizes that he is far from perfect, that he has not got it all together, or that he has made it. However, he had his eye on the goals that Jesus Christ had put before him. As for you and me, Jesus Christ has set goals, each different yet each similar. We are to keep our focus on Jesus—not our spouse, not our situation, not our family, nor the world— just on Jesus. Notice that as Paul reached out to God, God was reaching out to Paul. This precious relationship was a two-way street! It can be the same for you and me.

Next, Paul speaks to what we so frequently hear in today's world: *your past is the past; you need to look to the future.* Paul says it this way: "I've got my eye on the goal, where God is beckoning us onward—to Jesus. I'm off and running, and I'm not turning back." What solid wisdom from two thousand years ago! The hope for the healing of our marriages can be found only in our relationship with Jesus Christ—not in our spouse, not in our family, not in our friends, nor the world. Our hope is found in Christ Jesus. The author of Hebrews sums up these thoughts as follows.

> We have all these great people around us as examples. Their lives tell us what faith means. So we, too, should run the race that is before us and never quit. We should remove from our lives anything that would slow us down and the sin that so often makes us fall. We must never stop looking to Jesus. He is the leader of our faith, and he is the one who makes our faith complete. He suffered death on a cross. But he accepted the shame of the cross as if it were nothing because of the joy he could see waiting for him. And now he is sitting at the right side of God's throne.
>
> Hebrews 12:1–2 (ERV)

Finally, Paul sums up his life of leaving his past behind, of pressing on, of persevering in running the race that has been set before him. As he pressed on, he was letting go of everything that was slowing him down and pulling him in a different way. Paul's message to you and me is this: When the world pulls one way, we are to keep our focus on Jesus. He is our leader who has spelled out what our faith is about and how it differs from the ways of the world. Jesus Christ urges us to *press on*. Finally, nearing the end of his life and ministry, Paul sums up his life in perhaps one of the most powerful statements ever of an ambassador for Christ in his letter to Timothy, his brother in Christ.

> I have fought the good fight, I have finished the race, I have kept the faith. Now there is in store for me the crown of righteousness, which the Lord, the righteous Judge, will award to me on that day—and not only to me, but also to all who have longed for his appearing.
>
> 2 Timothy 4:7–8 (NIV 1984)

Standing firm until parted by death.

Pathways

Most of us as parents will sooner or later experience one of those *aha* moments in the rearing of our children: that how they turn out as adults depends upon the example lived before them by us, their parents. We know that they are also greatly influenced by their peers, their teachers, the TV shows and movies they watch, and the many other people that come into their sphere of influence. Looking back to when God created marriage, he desired godly children from that union. Today, the raising of godly children has become extremely difficult. It is greatly compromised when the family unit is under attack from Satan. Marital discord frequently leads to verbal and/or physical violence, the absence of love displayed in the family, affairs by one or both parents, separation, abandonment, and even divorce. In the face of these and other sinful family dynamics, our young people can suffer many psychological injuries, leaving them with scars that last a lifetime. As badly as I have painted this picture, there is hope. That hope comes in a personal relationship that our children (and each of us) can have with Jesus Christ, our Lord and Savior.

Recently, at a men's prayer breakfast, I heard Brad McCoy speak. This Christian father of Colt McCoy (University of Texas quarterback) and high school coach spoke about the choices in this world that constantly pull us and our teenagers toward the world and away from our Christian values. He gave us a catchphrase to remember as we raise our children: *Prepare our children for the path, not the path for our children!*

As I thought about this statement, one verse in the Bible jumped out at me: "Teach children in a way that fits their needs, and even when they are old, they will not leave the right path" (Proverbs 22:6, ERV).

This writer (probably King Solomon) knew the value of setting the proper example for a child. When we think back, how easy it has been at times to go ahead of our children and prepare their path, removing the potholes and obstacles to make their journey easy. What we thought was a loving gesture was in reality a recipe for problems down the road. This becomes more critical when the family unit breaks up through separation and/or divorce, leaving the rearing of the children essentially on the shoulders of one hurting parent.

Our children are a precious treasure that God has placed in our care for but a short time as they grow and mature in Christ. We teach them the difference between right and wrong, how to make correct choices, thus preparing them for that time when we are no longer with them. In like manner, we are all God's children, adopted by him, and thus we have a special place in his heart. We are his masterpiece, created in his image and born on purpose for a purpose.

> You formed the way I think and feel. You put me together in my mother's womb. I praise you because you made me in such a wonderful way.
>
> Psalm 139:13–14a (ERV)

> You should know that your body is a temple for the Holy Spirit that you received from God and that lives in you. You don't own yourselves. God paid a very high price to make you his. So honor God with your body.
>
> 1 Corinthians 6:19–20 (ERV)

Parents have the unique task of rearing children as temples of God. When we get overprotective, we do them harm. We need to instill in them that they are a temple of God through our nurturing, our love, and giving them the needed tools to navigate life's path. Then they know who they are in Christ, that they are no accident, and that God knew them before they were born. "The LORD called me before I was born. He called my name while I was still in my mother's womb" (Isaiah 49:1b, ERV). Then God went a step further: "But God had special plans for me even before I was born. So he chose me through his grace" (Galatians 1:15, ERV).

When a family unit breaks up, it falls to the custodial parent to prepare their children for the path. Frequently, that parent tends to pad the path, thinking they are shielding them from life, when in essence, they are doing them great harm. Separation and/or divorce necessitate extra effort in preparing our children for the path. Biblical instruction early in a child's life is essential. They should hear that they are loved by God and have value in his eyes. All this begins with one or both parents and is augmented by Bible class teachings at a good Bible church that also has a strong youth ministry. All families should seek such a church.

So I leave you with this charge: *prepare your child for the path, not the path for your child!*

Standing firm until parted by death.

I Am Second!

In recent weeks, we have seen testimony after testimony of various people, both great and small, declaring their faith in Jesus Christ as their Lord and Savior. They have openly and proudly declared that he is number 1 in their lives and that their role in this life comes second, following God's will for their lives. Christ taught this throughout his ministry. Nowhere in Christ's time among us is this more clear than in the garden of Gethsemane shortly before his arrest when Jesus cried out to his Father, "Father, if it is Your will, take this cup away from Me; nevertheless not My will, but Yours, be done" (Luke 22:42, NKJV).

Christ, being both fully God and fully man, states plainly here that he is yielding to or showing obedience to his Father's will about the path to the cross. Have you ever thought about what our own destiny would have been if Christ had followed his own will and took a path away from the cross? Yet Christ humbled himself, choosing to be second to (yielded to) his Father's will and sticking to the plan for our salvation that had existed since before the beginning of time.

> Do nothing out of selfish ambition or vain conceit, but in humility consider others better than yourselves. Each of you should look not only to your own interests, but also to the interests of others. Your attitude should be the same as that of Christ Jesus: Who, being in very nature God, did not consider equality with God something to be grasped, but made himself nothing, taking the very nature of a servant, being made in human likeness. And being found in appearance as a man, he humbled himself and became obedient to death—even death on a cross!
>
> Philippians 2:3–8 (NIV 1984)

Many times throughout the Gospels, Jesus, being fully God and fully man, took a lesser role than being number 1, demonstrating what true humility is: "You have heard Me say to you, 'I am going away and coming *back* to you.' If you loved Me, you would rejoice because I said, 'I am going to the Father,' for My Father is greater than I" (John 14:28, NKJV).

Jesus states, "For My Father is greater than I." Jesus modeled his life in such a way as to show us how we should live. His life was full of love and humility. Have you ever thought where each of us would be if we had recognized our role in our families and placed Christ first in our lives rather than placing our jobs, our spouse, our money, or our position in the number 1 spot on the pedestal of our lives and marriages? We would not be facing family breakdown with separation and/or divorce. So many marriages would have survived the family stresses that are so common these days. Families (a father and a mother) would be raising their children with Christian values rather than a single parent juggling to keep a job while parenting their children without the daily help of the other parent. How many of you have said, "I am second to Christ"? While some of us may have taken a lesser role than number 1 in our personal lives, who or what held the number 1 spot? In many cases, it may have been your spouse, your position, your money (possessions), or your job. None of these choices live up to Christ's standards, and they have but one result in the long run—failure. Your spouse cannot measure up to being God, and your job has only limited satisfaction over time. Your position (station) in this life is fleeting as are the possessions we acquire. The long and the short of it is that without Christ on the throne of our lives, nothing else in this world matters. Family relationships crumble, and marriages end up in divorce court.

Was not Christ's message for mankind a message of humility in everything we do? The following scriptures speak of this.

> Young people, I have something to say to you too. You should accept the authority of the elders. You should all have a humble attitude in dealing with each other. "God is against the proud, but he is kind to the humble." So be humble under God's powerful hand. Then he will lift you up when the right time comes.
>
> 1 Peter 5:5–6 (ERV)

> So, as a prisoner for the Lord, I beg you to live the way God's people should live, because he chose you to be his. Always be humble and gentle. Be patient and accept each other with love.
>
> Ephesians 4:1–2 (ERV)

This is My commandment, that you love one another as I have loved you. Greater love has no one than this, than to lay down one's life for his friends.

John 15:12–13 (NKJV)

Be Christ-like! Be humble. Be willing to give up your life for your spouse as Christ did for you at Calvary. Shout out that you are second so that Jesus Christ (God) can take number 1 billing in your life. When you do, healing of your marriage relationship will occur, and your family life will be restored as your spouse sees and understands that Jesus Christ is *number 1* in your life and in the family.

Remember this: *I am second*!

Standing firm until parted by death.

Passing The Baton

Through the years, many of us have either watched track meets or have been involved in them as a participant or the family of a participant. One of the exciting moments during these events centers around a team effort, usually involving four members of the team. Each runs a portion of the race carrying a stick or baton, and when that member finishes his portion of the race, he (she) hands off the baton to the next member of the team to do their part to complete the team effort. Races are often won or lost in how well the baton is passed. Life is much the same way when we look at the impact our marriages and/or our divorces have upon our families. How we pass our baton (our family's culture, our faith, our values) on to the next generation(s) of our families is our legacy. The Holy Bible is full of stories of great men of faith and their walks with God. Our greatest example, of course, is Jesus Christ and how he showed us a picture of the Living

God. I will single out just one mortal man, the Apostle Paul, who left a legacy of Christ's love for all mankind. In one of Paul's last writings, he summarizes his life and speaks of what lies ahead for those who choose to follow Jesus Christ.

> I have fought the good fight, I have finished the race, I have kept the faith. Now there is in store for me the crown of righteousness, which the Lord, the righteous Judge, will award to me on that day—and not only to me, but also to all who have longed for his appearing.

> 2 Timothy 4:7–8 (NIV 1984)

The phrase "also to all who have longed" speaks of legacy, the passing of the baton. What greater gift can we give (leave) to our family and friends than to model Christ's love and his gift of salvation for all mankind? This is a true legacy, a baton passed on from generation to generation in our families.

For those who are in stable marriages, your marriage relationship reflects Christ's relationship with his bride, the church. What you model to your family and friends tells them about the love of Jesus Christ and our Heavenly Father. Your actions, words, and deeds reflect that Christ's love lives in your heart. In showing forth the love of Jesus Christ, you are passing your baton on.

For those of us who are in troubled marriages or who are divorced, our actions, words, and deeds likewise reflect to our families and the world who we are. For some, there is bitterness, unforgiveness, and hatred. They are reflecting a person with a hardened heart, caught up in the sins of the world. Is that what you wish to pass on? Or do you reflect the love of Jesus Christ? God has called all of us to be ministers of reconciliation (ministers of healing), and even if we have been wounded through broken fellowships and relationships, it is how we respond that profoundly affects current and future generations. It is how we pass on the baton, or perhaps how we drop it.

When anyone is in Christ, it is a whole new world. The old things are gone; suddenly, everything is new! All this is from God. Through Christ, God made peace between himself and us. And God gave us the work of bringing people into peace with him. I mean that God was in Christ, making peace between the world and himself. In Christ, God did not hold people guilty for their sins. And he gave us this message of peace to tell people. So we have been sent to speak for Christ.

2 Corinthians 5:17–20a (ERV)

It is this spirit of peace (reconciliation) that is so important as we pass the baton on to our families and friends. There is also the baton of forgiveness we need to pass on. Just as Christ forgives those who come to him at the foot of the cross, we also need to be forgiving. Thus, you can see that our personal legacy needs forgiveness, which leads to reconciliation (peace), the gift (baton) we pass on. Paul goes on to charge us to speak for Christ as his ambassadors.

So my charge to you is this. Take an inventory of your successes and failures. What difference has your life made in those you love and with whom you are associated? What value have you added to (or taken from) the lives of your family as you pass on (or drop) the baton you are carrying? Hopefully, you will hear Jesus saying to you, "Well *done*, good and faithful servant; you were faithful over a few things, I will make you ruler over many things. Enter into the joy of your lord" (Matthew 25:21, NKJV).

The following are some legacies worth leaving behind as one passes on his (her) baton. There is the legacy of love and service, or perhaps the legacy of sacrifice, or perhaps the legacy of integrity. What about the legacy of character or patience? All these are things found in a marriage built upon the Solid Rock of Jesus Christ. When it comes to our covenant marriage vows, we see legacies of commitment and perseverance. But greater than any of these is the legacy of our Christian faith, our faith in our Lord and Savior, Jesus Christ, that we pass on to others.

What will your baton contain when you pass it on?

Standing firm until parted by death.

The Gift Of Life

In my reading several days ago, I came across a blog by Dr. Richard Tate, founder of Tate Publishing and Enterprises, LLC, in Mustang, Oklahoma. He was talking about the wonderful blessing that God gives each of us, what I have labeled a gift of life. We are told that our lives, that time span between birth and death, have been planned by our Creator for three score and ten years (seventy years). For some it is more, and for others it is less. Any way you look at your life span, your time on this side of eternity is a *gift of life* from our Creator. Thus, each hour, each minute, even each second is a precious *gift of life*, not only to each of us, but also to our Creator. Only God knows when our *candle* will be snuffed and he calls us home. In the quiet of the evening or at some special time during your day, get in touch with your body and your heartbeats, realizing that each beat of your heart signals to you *a-gift, a-gift, a-gift,* and on and on. Those heartbeats are truly a *gift of life* from God. What you do with these gifts (and they may number in the millions and billions) is ultimately how you choose to honor (or dishonor) your Creator, Jesus Christ.[37]

> Before the world began, the Word was there. The Word was with God, and the Word was God. He was there with God in the beginning. Everything was made through him, and nothing was made without him. In him there was

life, and that life was a light for the people of the world. The light shines in the darkness, and the darkness has not defeated it.

John 1:1–5 (ERV)

Jesus Christ is our Creator. Scripture states that in him there is life. Jesus Christ is the source of our *gifts of life*. It is him whom we honor when we choose to live in the light. Today, sit quietly and feel your pulse (your heartbeat) at your wrist. Then contemplate this, that each one of those beats is a precious gift from God. And with each *a-gift* heartbeat, thank him. Only he knows how many more you or I will have before he calls us home. So what are in your plans for today, tomorrow, or next week? Are you going to waste these gifts, or use them wisely for Christ's Kingdom?

Those of us who find ourselves in dysfunctional marriages that don't honor our Creator have an important choice to make. While we may be suffering through our current situation, each moment offers us a chance to change and to use our *gifts of life* to bring glory and honor to Jesus Christ. How we face our marriage situations have eternal consequences. This is where our commitment to Jesus Christ and our faith come together. In the confusion of the days, weeks, months, or possibly years that may pass by before we experience a healing and reconciliation of our marriages, our faith in Jesus Christ and the hope he gives is of paramount importance. This is our stand with Jesus Christ. It is during this time that those millions of *a-gift* beats mean so much to each of us and to our families and also to God.

Faith is the confidence that what we hope for will actually happen; it gives us assurance about things we cannot see.

Hebrews 11:1 (NLT)

How are you choosing to use your *gifts of life* that your Creator has given you? Each moment, each minute, each hour, etc., is so important, and they are just wasting away. Are you getting in the Word? What about your prayer life? What about your Christian fellowship and service? How are you living your life before those you love and care about? Is Jesus Christ the model you follow, or is it the world? All these things have eternal consequences as you use each one of your *gifts of life* that your Creator has given you.

We have choices, so many lifestyle choices, yet only a few are appropriate at this time in our lives, in our marriages, and in our families. God created each of us in his image, and he created marriage and families from the beginning of mankind's time in the Garden. He desires that each marriage and family reflect his values through godly living. Yet when we get out of sorts with our spouses, our families, our friends, and our neighbors, we sadden our Creator. We are misusing and wasting those precious *gifts of life*, those *a-gift* heartbeats he has given to each of us. The Apostle Paul writes to the Colossians:

> And we pray this in order that you may live a life worthy of the Lord and may please him in every way: bearing fruit in every good work, growing in the knowledge of God, being strengthened with all power according to his glorious might so that you may have great endurance and patience, and joyfully giving thanks to the Father, who has qualified you to share in the inheritance of the saints in the kingdom of light.
>
> Colossians 1:10–12 (NIV 1984)

With our *gifts of life*, God expects us to bear fruit through good works. He gives each of us power, endurance, patience, and as well as his knowledge to live a life before our spouses and families worthy of his great gifts. So as God reconciles our spouses and families to himself in preparation for the rebuilding of our marriages and families, let each of us use our *gifts of life* wisely to bring honor and glory to our Creator and live lives worthy of the Lord.

May your life be worthy of your *gifts of life*, those *a-gift* heartbeats given to each of us by our Creator.

Standing firm until parted by death.

On A Hill Far Away

On a hill far away stood an old rugged cross,
the emblem of suffering and shame;
and I love that old cross where the dearest and best
for a world of lost sinners was slain.

Chorus:
So I'll cherish the old rugged cross,
till my trophies at last I lay down;
I will cling to the old rugged cross,
and exchange it some day for a crown.

O that old rugged cross, so despised by the world,
has a wondrous attraction for me;
for the dear Lamb of God left his glory above
to bear it to dark Calvary.

(Chorus)

In that old rugged cross, stained with blood so divine,
a wondrous beauty I see,
for 'twas on that old cross Jesus suffered and died,
to pardon and sanctify me.

(Chorus)

To that old rugged cross I will ever be true,
its shame and reproach gladly bear;
then he'll call me some day to my home far away,
where his glory forever I'll share.

(Chorus) [38]

This familiar old hymn, written in 1912 by Reverend George Bennard (1873–1958), brings us to the central theme of our Christian faith: the death, burial, and resurrection of our Lord and Savior, Jesus Christ. On that cross, Jesus took upon his body the weight of humanity's sins (yours and mine) so that we, through faith in him as the Son of God, might inherit his righteousness and be welcomed to approach the throne of Almighty God. Jesus knew that the wrath of God for the punishment of our sins was more than we could bear, and through his love for us, he bore our punishment upon his body. On that cross, one of the greatest events in history took place: the *great exchange*, my sins and my rightful punishment for Christ's righteousness. As we stand in the shadow of the cross, let us realize what a marvelous gift of salvation has been given us through his grace.

He made Him who knew no sin *to be* sin on our behalf, so that we might become the righteousness of God in Him.

2 Corinthians 5:21 (NASB)

As each of us struggle with our troubled marriages, our separations, and unfortunately for some our divorces, we realize what an awesome team (Father, Son, and Holy Spirit) we have on our side as we stand in the gap for our marriages. In this season of our lives, we need to look to the fundamentals of our faith and to examine who we are, where we have been, and where we are headed. For many of us, we realize that our marriage problems began because of a weak or nonexistent relationship with our Lord and Savior, Jesus Christ. It is Jesus, the bedrock of a Christian marriage, that was missing in our marriage. Isn't it time you invited Jesus to live in you and through you?

> For it is by grace you have been saved, through faith—and this not from yourselves, it is the gift of God—not by works, so that no one can boast.
>
> Ephesians 2:8–9 (NIV 1984)

Soon we realize that if each marriage partner is living for Jesus in their daily lives, it is almost impossible for that marriage to fail. In the meantime, it is Jesus we need to lean on as we rebuild our marriages and as we become reconciled with our spouses. But first, each of us must become reconciled to God. Remember, as stated in the scripture above, we have been saved by grace!

> Therefore if anyone is in Christ, *he is* a new creature; the old things passed away; behold, new things have come. Now all *these* things are from God, who reconciled us to Himself through Christ and gave us the ministry of reconciliation, namely, that God was in Christ reconciling the world to Himself, not counting their trespasses against them, and He has committed to us the word of reconciliation. Therefore, we are ambassadors for Christ, as though God were making an appeal through us; we beg you on behalf of Christ, be reconciled to God.
>
> 2 Corinthians 5:17–20 (NASB)

Our personal reconciliation to God must occur first; this relationship is at the core of marriage reconciliation. So let us look again to the cross and its lessons. It is at the cross that we come face-to-face with our sinful lives. It is at the cross that we receive salvation. It is at the cross that our lives find their true meaning. It is at the cross that we meet God in all his majesty and righteousness. It is at the cross we face our eternity. It is at the cross that we witness Christ's spiritual suffering for our sins. And it is on the cross that Christ was stripped bare of his righteousness before his Father as he took on the weight of our sins, crying out, "Eloi, Eloi, lama sabachthani?" which means, "My God, my God, why have you forsaken me?" (Matthew 27:46b, NIV 1984).

Oh, the pain that our Lord and Savior suffered as he realized that he was separated from his Father. He was experiencing the torments of hell for you and me. As Jesus hung there on that cross, he forsook all his power as God that could have set him free of all that suffering. Yet he bore that suffering because of his great love for all mankind. He bore our sins, the sins of our prodigal spouses, and the sins of all mankind on that cross. As Christ did this for us, our sins were stripped away, and he gave us his robe of righteousness to cover our nakedness before a Holy God. Through grace, we witness the awesome, incredible, *great exchange.* When he died bearing our sins, we became reconciled to God, clothed only in Christ's righteousness. With Christ's death, the huge curtain that separated the Holy of Holies from the common people in the temple was ripped from top to bottom. No longer was a priest needed to offer yearly sacrifices to atone for the sins of the people. The barrier between God and all mankind no longer existed. Jesus Christ was the ultimate sacrifice, once and for all time. He is our Great High Priest, our Advocate before our Father God. Now we can freely enter into the presence of God for we are clothed in the righteousness of Christ.

> Jesus, our high priest, is able to understand our weaknesses. When Jesus lived on earth, he was tempted in every way. He was tempted in the same ways we are tempted, but he never sinned. With Jesus as our high priest, we can feel free to come before God's throne where there is grace. There we receive mercy and kindness to help us when we need it.
>
> Hebrews 4:15–16 (ERV)

Then on the third day, the day we call Easter, Jesus arose from the grave for he had defeated death; he arose victorious over death (sin). God's resurrection power demonstrated! He is our Living God!

> The day after the Sabbath day was the first day of the week. That day at dawn Mary Magdalene and the other woman named Mary went to look at the tomb. Suddenly an angel of the Lord came from the sky, and there was a huge earthquake. The angel went to the tomb and rolled the stone away from the entrance. Then he sat on top of the stone. The angel was shining as bright as lightning. His clothes were as white as snow. The soldiers guarding the tomb were very afraid of the angel. They shook with fear and then became like dead men. The angel said to the women, "Don't be afraid. I know you are looking for Jesus, the one who was killed on the cross. But he is not here. He has risen from death, as he said he would. Come and see the place where his body was. And go quickly and tell his followers, 'Jesus has risen from death. He is going into Galilee and will be there before you. You will see him there.'" Then the angel said, "Now I have told you." So the women left the tomb quickly. They were afraid, but they were also very happy. They ran to tell his followers what happened. Suddenly, Jesus was there in front of them. He said, "Hello!" The women went to him and, holding on to his feet, worshiped him. Then Jesus said to them, "Don't be afraid. Go tell my followers to go to Galilee. They will see me there."

Matthew 28:1–10 (ERV)

Embrace the truth and the power of the resurrection! It is by that same power that God will use to resurrect your marriage and my marriage from the junk pile of marriages that Satan has created. Do you believe in Easter and the resurrection of Jesus? If you do, then you can believe that your marriage can be resurrected and put back on the path to recovery. Remember that our God is in the resurrection business, and he has his eye on you, his faithful servant and child. He wants to resurrect your dead or dying marriage. So remember Jesus's statement: "With man this is impossible, but with God all things are possible." (Matthew 19:26b, ERV).

May you meet God the Father, God the Son, and God the Holy Spirit at the cross throughout the year as you stand, praying for the healing of your marriage. May God bless each of you in your personal stand.

Standing firm until parted by death.

The Lord's Prayer

Holy Week is upon us. This is the time of year that we remember and celebrate the events that occurred at the Passover season in Jerusalem some two thousand years ago. There was the triumphal entry of Jesus into Jerusalem (Palm Sunday) followed by his continued teaching of his disciples, including the prediction of his death. Then there was the washing of his disciples' feet followed by the Passover feast (the Last Supper) and the betrayal of Judas. At the Garden of Gethsemane, Jesus prays for himself, his disciples, and all believers. Finally, Jesus's arrest and his trial, then Peter's denial, the Crucifixion, and the Resurrection on that first Easter morning. Holy Week marks the culmination of Christ's ministry! But besides all the miracles and all his teachings, etc., one item stands out in Jesus's earthly ministry: prayer. Throughout his ministry, Jesus's prayer life was center stage. On one occasion, his disciples asked him to teach them how to pray. Let us look at his answer. "One day he was praying in a certain place. When he finished, one of his disciples said, 'Master, teach us to pray just as John taught his disciples'" (Luke 11:1, MSG).

And when you pray, you shall not be like the hypocrites. For they love to pray standing in the synagogues and on the corners of the streets, that they may be seen by men. Assuredly, I say to you, they have their reward. But you, when you pray, go into your room, and when you have shut your door, pray to your Father who *is* in the secret *place;* and your Father who sees in secret will reward you openly. And when you pray, do not use vain repetitions as the heathen *do.* For they think that they will be heard for their many words. Therefore do not be like them. For your Father knows the things you have need of before you ask Him…. Our Father in heaven, Hallowed be Your name. Your kingdom come. Your will be done On earth as *it is* in heaven. Give us this day our daily bread. And forgive us our debts, As we forgive our debtors. And do not lead us into temptation, But deliver us from the evil one. For Yours is the kingdom and the power and the glory forever. Amen.

Matthew 6:5–8, 9b–13 (NKJV)

We who are seeking the healing of our marriages understand the importance of prayer. Consistent prayer is essential as we stand for our covenant marriage vows.

The Lord's Prayer. Some have called this the Disciples' Prayer or Believers' Prayer for this is the prayer that Jesus gave us to be a model of how we should pray. I am going to dissect this prayer as I understand it and invite you to do likewise. Like me, so many of you grew up in churches or are currently members of a church where the Lord's Prayer is recited weekly as part of the order of service. Throughout my youth and much of my adult life, this prayer was repeated from memory, by rote, a mechanical repetition that stirred up little if any spiritual connection with my Heavenly Father. However, when we take time to understand and study this great model prayer, we can learn how to apply this model to our own prayer life, making our praise and petitions to God become meaningful, spiritual, and effective.

Our Father. This is where we start a prayer. We address the person (God) to whom we are praying. God is our Father, not our biological father, but our spiritual Father.

Which art in heaven. Here we are acknowledging that the Father we are praying to resides not in this world as does our biological father, but in heaven, a place that serves as a home for God and his heavenly creatures. It is commonly believed that at creation, heaven was created above the earth. Needless to say, heaven is a realm, a dimension different from that which we perceive. To recap, we are praying to our spiritual Father who resides in heaven. Simple yet far-reaching and complex.

Hallowed be your name. Here is where we need to put special emphasis in our prayers. This is the part where we give our praise and render our homage to our spiritual Father, our God. Hallowed means "holy." Holy is God's name! God is our Creator, he is our Sustainer, he is Sovereign, he is the Alpha and Omega. For us in marriage reconciliation, God is the Great Physician, the Healer of our marriages. He is the God of Resurrection, not only of his Son, Jesus, but also the God of resurrection of our dead marriages. Remember, our God, our spiritual Father, loves praise and loves to be recognized for who he is. Throughout human history, our God has been worshiped. So in our prayers to our spiritual Father, always acknowledge God for who he is, bringing glory to his name and personage.

Your kingdom come. Your will be done on earth as it is in heaven. These two sentences contain three important acknowledgments. First, we are acknowledging that Christ's Kingdom, his Lordship, as planned before the beginning of time, is coming. This second statement is profound. Remember when Jesus was praying in the Garden of Gethsemane, he prayed, "Father, if you are willing, take this cup from me; yet not my will, but yours be done" (Luke 22:42, NIV 1984). Finally, we are stating that we acknowledge that God's will supersedes our own, that God's will and his plans for Christ's Kingdom should come into being here on earth and mirror what exists in heaven.

Give us this day our daily bread. Here we are acknowledging that everything we have comes from God. Much as the Israelites were sustained in the desert for forty years on manna from heaven, all we have—our food, our clothing, our shelter, our health, our material wealth—all comes from God. We acknowledge that and ask for our daily portion.

And forgive us our debts as we forgive our debtors. This statement is a big one! Here we are seeking God's forgiveness for our sins (debts) and acknowledging that we forgave those who sin (do wrong or evil) against us. This is far-reaching; we want forgiveness, but too often we are reluctant to forgive others. Look at what Christ says in explanation: "For if you forgive men when they sin against you, your heavenly Father will also forgive you. But if you do not forgive men their sins, your Father will not forgive your sins" (Matthew 6:14–15, NIV 1984). We are to forgive as we have been forgiven! Far-reaching, isn't it! Does this hit home as we seek to reconcile our troubled marriages? Have you forgiven your spouse? If not, it is time to do it!

And do not lead us into temptation, but deliver us from the evil one. Here we are seeking God's protection from Satan and all the evils of this world. Temptation is all around us. Questionable TV shows, movies, magazines, drugs, alcohol—the sins of the flesh are everywhere. Here we ask for help. The Apostle Paul says it well as follows.

> Finally, my brethren, be strong in the Lord and in the power of His might. Put on the whole armor of God, that you may be able to stand against the wiles of the devil. For we do not wrestle against flesh and blood, but against principalities, against powers, against the rulers of the darkness of this age, against spiritual *hosts* of wickedness in the heavenly *places.* Therefore take up the whole armor

of God, that you may be able to withstand in the evil day, and having done all, to stand.

Ephesians 6:10–13 (NKJV)

We cannot fight this battle alone; we need the help of God. In the Lord's Prayer, we are seeking the Lord's help. But as seen in Paul's letter to the Ephesians, we have an essential part in this battle: we must put on the full armor of God.

For yours is the kingdom, and the power, and the glory forever. Amen. In some translations, this last part is not included. However, from the New King James Version, it is listed as the second half of verse 14 and a part of the prayer. This is the way most of us learned this prayer. Here we see that we end our prayer with praise to God, reiterating and acknowledging that it is his Kingdom and he has all the power and all the glory and that God's Kingdom will reign forever. *Amen.* From the Hebrews in the Old Testament, it is sometimes translated as "so be it." Jesus, in the New Testament, used it to affirm the truth of his own statements. From Revelation 3:14, Jesus is called the Amen, meaning that he himself is the reliable and true witness of God.

I hope by now that you begin to appreciate the depth of this simple yet concise prayer, which can be used as a model for our own prayers to our Heavenly Father. This is not an in-depth study of the Lord's Prayer. If such is desired, do your own research at your church, at the library, on the Internet, or through questions directed to your pastor. May God bless your stand for your covenant marriage vows and bless your prayer life as you seek God's healing of your marriage.

Standing firm until parted by death.

In Christ Alone

The Christmas season is upon us. For many, this is a joyous season filled with worship of God's one and only Son, Jesus Christ. Many people will enjoy a special time of being with family, many of whom have come great distances to celebrate with family and all the wonderful fellowship connected with the holiday season. For others, it will bring much anguish, heartache, and sorrow, not because of whose birth we celebrate, but because of our fractured families. Yes, fractured families torn apart by such things as harsh words, anger, violence, and violated trust. These things often have led to marital separation or even divorce. So instead of the warmth of family and the sounds of joyful laughter and singing, there is emptiness and sadness because of an empty chair. Yet not all is lost, even at this season, because we have Christ in our corner. For in Christ, we have the fullness of the Gospel message. For *in Christ alone* we can find the joy sought after at this time of year.

The beautiful song lyrics printed below summarizes where our thoughts should center during this Christmas season as well as all year long. Our hope and our future are truly found *in Christ alone* when we choose to surrender our future to his sovereign will. Written by Keith Getty and Stuart Townend, its words are convicting for they state in simple words the core tenets of our Christian faith.

In Christ Alone

In Christ alone my hope is found;
He is my light, my strength, my song;
This cornerstone, this solid ground,
Firm through the fiercest drought and storm.
What heights of love, what depths of peace,
When fears are stilled, when strivings cease!
My comforter, my all in all—
Here in the love of Christ I stand.

In Christ alone, Who took on flesh,
Fullness of God in helpless babe!
This gift of love and righteousness,
Scorned by the ones He came to save.
Till on that cross as Jesus died,
The wrath of God was satisfied;
For ev'ry sin on Him was laid—
Here in the death of Christ I live.

There in the ground His body lay,
Light of the world by darkness slain;
Then bursting forth in glorious day,
Up from the grave He rose again!
And as He stands in victory,
Sin's curse has lost its grip on me;
For I am His and He is mine—
Bought with the precious blood of Christ.

No guilt in life, no fear in death—
This is the pow'r of Christ in me;
From life's first cry to final breath,
Jesus commands my destiny.
No pow'r of hell, no scheme of man,
Can ever pluck me from His hand;
Till He returns or calls me home—
Here in the pow'r of Christ I'll stand.[39]

The words say it all. As we stand in the power of Christ for the healing of our marriages, we turn our spouses over to the capable hands of Almighty God. It is only through our personal reconciliation to God and his reconciliation of our spouses to himself that the healing of our marriages can begin. So in this season of the year, we look to Bethlehem and to the birth of the Christ Child. Yet more importantly, it is in Christ's death on a

Roman cross and subsequent resurrection that our destiny lies. The above lyrics are a statement of our faith for our hope lies where we stand, in the love and power of Christ. Read again and meditate on the last stanza for it is at the core of Christianity.

> For God so loved the world that He gave His only begotten Son, that whoever believes in Him should not perish but have everlasting life. For God did not send His Son into the world to condemn the world, but that the world through Him might be saved.

> John 3:16–17 (NKJV)

> By this we know love, because He laid down His life for us. And we also ought to lay down *our* lives for the brethren.

> 1 John 3:16 (NKJV)

As the Christmas season approaches, let us leave Christ in Christmas. When we consider all the gifts we wish to receive, let us consider God's greatest gift to mankind—our Lord and Savior, Jesus Christ. For our hope of eternal life in heaven and our hope for the healing of our marriages can only be found *in Christ alone.*

May God bless each of you this Christmas season with Christ's healing of your marriage as we each declare, "In the pow'r of Christ I'll stand."

Standing firm until parted by death.

We Stand Forgiven At The Cross

Once again, Christmas is just around the corner. The seasons are changing, and as I write this devotional, a cold wintery blast is coming out of the north with temperatures dropping below freezing tonight. Christmas decorations are going up everywhere, and Christmas programs at neighborhood churches have commenced. We come into this season to celebrate the birth of the Christ Child, God's one and only Son, born to a Jewish virgin from Nazareth in Galilee some two thousand years ago. This baby, born of a human mother but fathered by God, was both fully man and fully God. This baby grew into a man, a simple man by many standards of his day, yet with wisdom previously unknown to mankind. In the three years of his ministry, he started a revolution in the hearts and minds of men that continues to ripple down through the ages. Yet the impact on humanity of the ministry of this sinless man is minuscule compared to the impact of his death and his subsequent resurrection by his Father from the death to life. From before the beginning of time, Jesus Christ was destined to come and live among us, but it is in his death on a Roman cross and subsequent resurrection to life at the human age of thirty-three that is the focal point of Christianity. It is the cross that beckons us to redemption and life eternal with God.

> In the beginning was the Word, and the Word was with God, and the Word was God. He was in the beginning with God. All things were made through Him, and without Him nothing was made that was made. In Him was life, and the life was the light of men. And the light shines in the darkness, and the darkness did not comprehend it.

John 1:1–5 (NKJV)

John speaks to the fact that Jesus Christ (the Word) was with God in the beginning and that he is God. Jesus is Light, but the world ruled by Satan lives in darkness that does not understand the Light. Satan and the world refuse to understand God's message of redemption and his message of grace. Here Jesus states for what purpose he came:

For God so loved the world that He gave His only begotten Son, that whoever believes in Him should not perish but have everlasting life. For God did not send His Son into the world to condemn the world, but that the world through Him might be saved. "He who believes in Him is not condemned; but he who does not believe is condemned already, because he has not believed in the name of the only begotten Son of God. And this is the condemnation, that the light has come into the world, and men loved darkness rather than light, because their deeds were evil. For everyone practicing evil hates the light and does not come to the light, lest his deeds should be exposed. But he who does the truth comes to the light, that his deeds may be clearly seen, that they have been done in God."

John 3:16–21 (NKJV)

Jesus Christ came to live among us for one purpose: that we might believe in him as our Lord and Savior and that through him, our sins would be forgiven. It is not his birth that saves us, but it is in his death on a Roman cross and the resurrection to life from that death. For it is by his shed blood that our sins are forgiven and washed away as we live in victory over Satan, death, and the world. Isaiah prophesied Christ's journey to that Roman cross centuries before he was born.

Who has believed our message and to whom has the arm of the LORD been revealed? He grew up before him like a tender shoot, and like a root out of dry ground. He had no beauty or majesty to attract us to him, nothing in his appearance that we should desire him. He was despised and rejected by men, a man of sorrows, and familiar with suffering. Like one from whom men hide their faces he was despised, and we esteemed him not. Surely he took up our infirmities and carried our sorrows, yet we considered him stricken by God, smitten by him, and afflicted. But he was pierced for our transgressions, he was crushed for our iniquities; the punishment that brought us peace was upon him, and by his wounds we are healed.

Isaiah 53:1–5 (NIV 1984)

So I challenge you not to get too tied up in the beauty and majesty of the events of the birth of the Christ Child. For redemption is not in his birth but in his death and resurrection. The power of the cross is where we are forgiven. Keith Getty wrote along with songwriter Stuart Townend the following beautiful praise hymn.

The Power of the Cross

Oh, to see the dawn
Of the darkest day:
Christ on the road to Calvary.
Tried by sinful men,
Torn and beaten, then
Nailed to a cross of wood.

Chorus:
This, the pow'r of the cross:
Christ became sin for us;
Took the blame, bore the wrath—
We stand forgiven at the cross.

Oh, to see the pain
Written on Your face,
Bearing the awesome weight of sin.
Ev'ry bitter thought,
Ev'ry evil deed
Crowning Your bloodstained brow.

Now the daylight flees;
Now the ground beneath
Quakes as its Maker bows His head.
Curtain torn in two,
Dead are raised to life;
"Finished!" the vict'ry cry.

Oh, to see my name
Written in the wounds,
For through Your suffering I am free.
Death is crushed to death;
Life is mine to live,
Won through Your selfless love.

Final chorus:
This, the pow'r of the cross:
Son of God—slain for us.
What a love! What a cost!
We stand forgiven at the cross.[40]

Truly, Christ became sin for us. He took his Father's wrath for our personal sins upon his human body, and it is through his shed blood that we are forgiven, that our sins are washed away. In doing so, he transferred his righteousness (in the *great exchange*) to us so that we could come before a Holy God, pure and sinless, covered only in Christ's righteousness. Thus, we now can have eternal fellowship with our Creator, God the Father, God the Son, and God the Holy Spirit.

> Therefore, having been justified by faith, we have peace with God through our Lord Jesus Christ, through whom also we have access by faith into this grace in which we stand, and rejoice in hope of the glory of God.

Romans 5:1–2 (NKJV)

May God bless each of you as you stand for God's healing of your marriages. Merry Christmas, but don't forget *the power of the cross.*

Standing firm until parted by death.

No More Sorrow, No More Pain

As is the case in the genesis of many of my devotional writings, a song we sang in service at my church last Sunday spoke volumes to me. That song is "I Will Rise." In the chorus, there is the phrase "no more sorrow, no more pain." It brought to mind where I now stand in my walk with Jesus Christ and in my stand for his healing of my marriage relationship.

In looking for a scripture to tie in with these thoughts, I found the following passage of hope and comfort toward the end of the book of Revelation in the New Living Translation.

> I heard a loud shout from the throne, saying, "Look, God's home is now among his people! He will live with them, and they will be his people. God himself will be with them. He will wipe every tear from their eyes, and there will be no more death or sorrow or crying or pain. All these things are gone forever." And the one sitting on the throne said, "Look, I am making everything new!"
>
> Revelation 21:3–5a (NLT)

For those who are reading this meditation, this scripture should be an answer to your prayers. Read it over and over again and see what God is promising each of us. We all have suffered a huge emotional (and possibly a physical) blow that has put each of us literally on the floor! But there is hope, and there is salvation. That hope is in the healing powers that come through our Lord and Savior, Jesus Christ! For those who have not yet accepted him as your personal Lord and Savior, you need to do it now. Don't wait. Time is running out. Get with a friend who is a Christian to discuss your personal salvation that can be found only in Jesus Christ. Then get down on your knees and ask Jesus Christ for forgiveness for your personal sins and accept him into your life as your personal Lord and Savior.

Look at God's message to his people in this scripture. God is declaring that his home is with each of us for we are his people. He will live with us, a promise of his presence with us and comfort to all who suffer the pain and sorrow of marital problems. The scripture uses the words *God himself* to show that he is not delegating this duty to anyone else. It is a promise you can stake your life and your eternity on.

God promises that he will wipe the tears of sorrow from our eyes that have come from our marital problems. He will heal the death of your marriage relationship with your spouse if you will only turn over your problems to him. He also promises that all that crying and pain you are suffering now will be gone...gone forever. Yes, forever!

It sounds simple, and it is truly simple. All it requires is faith in Jesus Christ as your Lord and Savior and in God's resurrection powers to heal (resurrect) your marriage relationship. It requires surrender of self to his will for your life and for your marriage.

Look again at the last verse. It is a promise you can take to the bank! "Look, I am making everything new!" (Revelation 21:5a, NLT). God promises that just as you are a new person in Christ, your spouse will also be a new person in Christ, and your resurrected marriage relationship also will be new as it is rebuilt upon the Solid Rock of Jesus Christ.

> That anyone who belongs to Christ has become a new person. The old life is gone; a new life has begun! And all of this is a gift from God, who brought us back to himself through Christ. And God has given us this task of reconciling people to him. For God was in Christ, reconciling the world to himself, no longer counting

people's sins against them. And he gave us this wonderful message of reconciliation.

2 Corinthians 5:17–18 (NLT)

You are a new person in Christ. Your spouse is a new person in Christ. Your resurrected marriage is a new marriage relationship in Christ. Praise be to God for his grace to each of us. Think on this: *no more sorrow, no more pain!*

Standing firm until parted by death.

Lord, I Cannot Do This Alone

Last evening during my quiet time before climbing into bed, I began to reflect that without God, I am nothing. Yet more than that, it hit me once again that without God, standing for the healing of my marriage relationship is futile. As humans, we have finite abilities to accomplish what is required to live moment to moment, hour to hour, day to day, etc. All works well when we are dealing with the mundane things of life. However, you and I have taken on a new and very difficult task: that of dealing with Satan and the world. God has called each of us to stand in the gap for our marriage relationships and our relationships with others who are close to us. Yet Satan is determined to tear us away from God and his precepts. It is then in the quietness of my prayer closet or my empty bedroom and house that I realize that I am lost without my Lord and Savior, Jesus Christ.

In the Great Commission, Jesus Christ tells us, "And lo, I am with you always, *even* to the end of the age. Amen" (Matthew 28:20b, NKJV). That is all fine and good, but I don't know what to do today, right now. I feel overwhelmed; am I doing all that I can (my part) in this thing called standing? My family, my friends, my peers, my associates at work, and even my church friends and leaders think I am confused, not sure of my future, or even downright crazy. To whom do I look? My faith and my religious convictions tell me to cry out to God. As I search the Scriptures, the Apostle Paul's letter to the Corinthian church offers me some hope.

> Blessed *be* the God and Father of our Lord Jesus Christ, the Father of mercies and God of all comfort, who comforts us in all our affliction so that we will be able to comfort those who are in any affliction with the comfort with which we ourselves are comforted by God. For just as the sufferings of Christ are ours in abundance, so also our comfort is abundant through Christ. But if we are afflicted, it is for your comfort and salvation; or if we are comforted, it is for your comfort, which is effective in the patient enduring of the same sufferings which we also suffer; and our hope for you is firmly grounded, knowing that as you are sharers of our sufferings, so also you are *sharers* of our comfort.

> 2 Corinthians 1:3–7 (NASB)

The key word here is *comfort*. As I cry out to God, his comfort flows through to me, lifting me up and giving me new direction. It is our God's comfort that carries you and me through these difficult times. In like manner, as our fellow standers experience difficulties, we can pass on the comfort we have received from God to help those going through similar tough times. It is here that the Body of Christ, the church family, becomes so important. Hopefully those who surround us are of like mind and beliefs about the sanctity of our marriage covenant. Paul relates further in his letter to the Corinthian church how God's comfort ministers through the Body of Christ.

> But God, who comforts the depressed, comforted us by the coming of Titus; and not only by his coming, but also by the comfort with which he was comforted in you, as he

reported to us your longing, your mourning, your zeal for me; so that I rejoiced even more.

2 Corinthians 7:6–7 (NASB)

Paul speaks of the church's role in strengthening Titus, which helped strengthen Paul in his own personal troubles. It is God ministering directly in each of our lives that comforts us, yet he works through fellow standers who can guide, direct, and comfort other standers.

So when those moments of despair occur, hit your knees and cry out to Jesus, our Savior and Lord. Get with a prayer partner who has an understanding of marriage covenant and marriage reconciliation. Allow God to work through a fellow stander and believer to give you the comfort you need at that moment to get you over the hump. Standing is not easy. It is strange to our Christian community, which is very unfortunate. But when we see divorce rates of greater than 50 percent among the evangelical church, you can see why we need to seek like-minded Christians as prayer partners.

Jesus Christ is the God of all comfort. He will carry you through the difficult times. Seek his face and his comfort. He will never fail you. For he has said, "and lo, I am with you always, *even* to the end of the age. Amen" (Matthew 28:20b, NKJV).

Standing firm until parted by death.

Faultless Before His Throne

One day, each one of us will stand before the throne of God to plead our case before a Holy God, our Heavenly Father. Each one of us, great or small, will have our lives laid bare before God as he looks for our name in the Lamb's Book of Life. Those of us who have been redeemed by Jesus's blood will find Jesus Christ standing there beside us as our advocate, our attorney, pleading our case before his Father. "Father, this brother [sister] of mine is faultless for he [she] has been cleansed by my blood at Calvary. He [she] has no sin as he [she] is clothed in my righteousness, which I gave him [her] at Calvary. He [she] stands faultless before your throne and, as such, deserves to spend eternity in heaven with us." This scenario is affirmed in the scriptures below:

> For we must all appear before the judgment seat of Christ, that each one may receive what is due him for the things done while in the body, whether good or bad.
>
> 2 Corinthians 5:10 (NIV 1984)

> He who overcomes will, like them, be dressed in white. I will never blot out his name from the book of life, but will acknowledge his name before my Father and his angels.
>
> Revelations 3:5 (NIV 1984)

> If anyone's name was not found written in the book of life, he was thrown into the lake of fire.
>
> Revelations 20:15 (NIV 1984)

> My dear children, I write this to you so that you will not sin. But if anybody does sin, we have one who speaks to the Father in our defense—Jesus Christ, the Righteous One. He is the atoning sacrifice for our sins, and not only for ours but also for the sins of the whole world.
>
> 1 John 2:1–2 (NIV 1984)

But I tell you that men will have to give account on the day of judgment for every careless word they have spoken. For by your words you will be acquitted, and by your words you will be condemned.

Matthew 12:36–37 (NIV 1984)

All that the Father gives me will come to me, and whoever comes to me I will never drive away. For I have come down from heaven not to do my will but to do the will of him who sent me. And this is the will of him who sent me, that I shall lose none of all that he has given me, but raise them up at the last day. For my Father's will is that everyone who looks to the Son and believes in him shall have eternal life, and I will raise him up at the last day.

John 6:37–40 (NIV 1984)

If we confess our sins, he is faithful and just and will forgive us our sins and purify us from all unrighteousness.

1 John 1:9 (NIV 1984)

Behold, I am coming soon! My reward is with me, and I will give to everyone according to what he has done.

Revelations 22: 12 (NIV 1984)

All these words of our hope of eternity with our Creator can be summed up in the following song:

The Solid Rock

My hope is built on nothing less
Than Jesus's blood and righteousness.
I dare not trust the sweetest frame,
But wholly trust in Jesus's Name.

Refrain:
On Christ the solid Rock I stand,
All other ground is sinking sand;
All other ground is sinking sand.

When darkness seems to hide His face,
I rest on His unchanging grace.
In every high and stormy gale,
My anchor holds within the veil.

(Refrain)

His oath, His covenant, His blood,
Support me in the whelming flood.
When all around my soul gives way,
He then is all my Hope and Stay.

(Refrain)

When He shall come with trumpet sound,
Oh may I then in Him be found.
Dressed in His righteousness alone,
Faultless to stand before the throne.

(Refrain)[41]

Yes, may each of us, through reconciliation with our Heavenly Father, have our hope resting on the Solid Rock of Jesus Christ, our Lord and Savior. For when we look at ourselves, we wonder how we could ever be saved; yet when we look at Jesus, we realize how lost we were and how much we needed him!

> Therefore God exalted him to the highest place and gave him the name that is above every name, that at the name of Jesus every knee should bow, in heaven and on earth and under the earth, and every tongue confess that Jesus Christ is Lord, to the glory of God the Father.

> Philippians 2:9–11 (NIV 1984)

It is through Christ's blood and his righteousness that you and I can finally sing with a voice loud and clear: *"When He shall come with trumpet sound, Oh, may I then in Him be found. Dressed in His righteousness alone, faultless to stand before the throne."*
Standing firm until parted by death.

ENDNOTES

1   D. Mark Parks, Comments on Faith, *Holman Illustrated Bible Dictionary* (Nashville: Holman Bible Publishers, 2003), pp 547-551.

2   Max Lucado, *Facing Your Giants* (Nashville: W Publishing Group, a Division of Thomas Nelson, Inc., 2006).

3   Charlotte Elliott, 1835, *Just As I Am*, Public Domain.

4   Rick Atchley, *We Be Free, sermon series title* (The Hills Church of Christ, Fort Worth, TX, 1995).

5   Tim Coody, *Meaningless Words and Broken Covenants: How Our Words and the Agreements Built on Them are Becoming Increasingly Meaningless* (Mustang, OK: Tate Publishing, LLC, 2006).

6   Rejoice Marriage Ministries and Charlyne Cares, www.rejoiceministries.org (Pompano Beach, FL.)

7   Parts of the comments are from the devotional for July 19, 2008, *Today in the Word* (a ministry of Moody Bible Institute of Chicago, 2008).

8   Theme statement, Jim Dornan, CEO, Network Twentyone, Suwanee, GA.

9   Thoughts on *radical faith* and *radical Savior* reviewed here are discussed by David Platt, Radical (Colorado, CO: Multnomah Books, 2010).

10 Robert Frost, 1916, *The Road Not Taken, Public Domain.*

11   Rick Atchley, some thoughts from sermon message *Alien Nation* (The Hills Church of Christ, Fort Worth, TX, 22 June 2008).

12   Theme title and some thoughts are from blog site JimDornansJournal.com, Praise Update, dated 1 March 2012.

13   Andy Stanley, *White Flag, Part 1:Resistance is Futile* (North Point Community Church, Alpharetta, GA, 28 February 2010).

14   Max Lucado, *Facing Your Giants ibid,* Chapter 14.

15   Steven B. Cowan. *Comments on Covenant, Holman Illustrated Bible Dictionary* (Nashville: Holman Bible Publishers, 2003), pp 355-359.

16   Parts of the comments are from the devotional for 19 June 2008, Today in the Word (a ministry of Moody Bible Institute of Chicago, 2008).

17   Tim Coody, *ibid.*

18   Sections on Marriage, Betrothal, and Covenant, Holman Illustrated Bible Dictionary (Nashville: Holman Bible Publishers, 2003).

19   Tim Coody, *ibid.*

20   Rev. Martin Luther King, I Have a Dream speech, Public Domain.

21   Corrie ten Boom, *The Hiding Place* (Uhrichsville, OH: Barbour Publishing, Inc., 2000).

22   Corrie ten Boom, *ibid.*

23   Max Lucado, *A Love Worth Living: Living in the Overflow of God's Love* (Nashville: W Publishing Group, 2002).

24   Pastor Ryan Williams, *Seven Last Words of Jesus* (Grace Baptist Church, Fort Worth, TX, 6 April 2007).

25   The story about Ronald and Jennifer was told on *This I Believe*, National Public Radio, Thursday, 5 March 2009.

26 Jimmy A. Millikin, Comments on Grace, *Holman Illustrated Bible Dictionary* (Nashville: Holman Bible Publishers, 2003), pp 678-680.

27 Max Lucado, *In the Grip of Grace* (Dallas: Word Publishing, 1996).

28 Max Lucado, *In the Grip of Grace ibid.*

29 John Newton, *Amazing Grace,* ca. 1760-1770, Public Domain.

30 Section on Love, Holman Illustrated Bible Dictionary, ibid.

31 Max Lucado, *3:16: The Numbers of Hope* (Nashville: Thomas Nelson, 2007).

32 Charles Wesley, *And Can It Be That I Should Gain?*, 1738, Public Domain.

33 Information on the Song of Songs was obtained from the introduction notes and the study footnotes on the book, The NIV Study Bible (Grand Rapids, MI: Zondervan Publishing House, 1995).

34 Francine Rivers, *Redeeming Love* (Colorado Springs, CO: Multnomah Books, 1997, 2007).

35 Rick Atchley, some thoughts from sermon message *All I Want for Christmas Is Forgiveness* (The Hills Church of Christ, Fort Worth, TX, 21 December 2008).

36 *Facing the Giants* (movie by Sherwood Baptist Church of Albany, GA, Inc., 2006).

37 Dr. Richard Tate, Executive Staff Blogs (Tate Publishing & Enterprises, LLC, 26 June 2011).

38 George Bennard, *Old Rugged Cross*, 1912. Public Domain.

39 Words and music by Keith Getty and Stuart Townend. Copyright © 2001 Kingsway Thankyou Music.

40 Lyrics by Keith Getty. Copyright © 2005 Thankyou Music.

41 Edward Mote, *The Solid Rock,* (circa 1834). Public Domain.

GLOSSARY

These are terms used in these devotionals that may need some clarification:

covenant vows. Refers to those marriage vows we say in the presence of witnesses, the most important witness being God.

evil one. Satan or the devil.

far country. This refers to the place that a spouse *runs to* when they leave a marriage or family unit. (Reference: Luke 15:11–32, the story of the prodigal son.)

prodigal. This refers to the person who leaves, as in the parable of the prodigal son.

stander, standing. Refers to the person or action of the one standing with God for the healing of the marriage relationship and/or the family unit.

Triune God or Trinity. God the Father, God the Son (Jesus Christ), and God the Holy Spirit.

Subject Matter Index

Note to the Reader: This Subject Matter Index is not meant to be exhaustive. Each devotional covers several subjects. This index is meant to help you get started in your study.

About the Author

Ben N. Benson, M.D., a longtime resident of Fort Worth, Texas, was born and raised in Knoxville, Tennessee. He holds both a B.S. degree and an M.D. degree from the University of Tennessee. Raised in a Christian home and active in church all his life, Ben's Christian walk was weak, with one foot in the church and one in the world. He married Linda June Miller, his college sweetheart, in December 1962. Linda, a strong Christian wife, planted many seeds of faith in Ben but few matured during her lifetime. Following her death in 2001, Ben was not sure he would see her in eternity because of his flawed Christian walk. Ben remarried in 2003. His second wife (name withheld for privacy) watered and nurtured the seeds planted by Linda and planted some new seeds of her own. However, it took the turmoil in their marriage to bring Ben to his knees and to accept Jesus Christ as his personal Lord and Savior; he was baptized by immersion on November 10, 2004. On February 12, 2006, shortly after receiving the divorce petition from his second wife, his life changed forever. A broken man, a small group of believers rallied around him, and laying on hands, they prayed over him. Shortly thereafter, he experienced an indescribable sense of peace enter his heart and mind, the peace of the Holy Spirit. That peace has never left him. Through the guidance of the Holy Spirit, he wrote the meditations contained herein. It is the ever-present Holy Spirit that strengthens him to *stand firm* for his second marriage and for the promised healing by God of that fellowship and relationship in God's own timing.

He retired in 1997 after thirty-four years of medical practice as an anesthesiologist, including eight years in the US Air Force. Following a short marriage to his second wife that ended in divorce in 2006, the Holy Spirit prompted Ben to start writing devotionals and statements of faith.

Ben is active in both Christian medical and ministry short-term mission trips to southeast Asia and east Africa. He has been a facilitator in a marriage reconciliation support group and is a volunteer at the Rapha unit of Healing Hands International, a humanitarian aid organization. He is active in Covenant Keepers Inc., an international marriage reconciliation ministry.

Ben remains firm in his stand with God for the healing of his second marriage. Called by God in March 2006 to stand, he signs each of his devotionals "Standing firm until parted by death." He remains a firm believer in the covenant marriage vows that we make before God and our spouse, including the one so many ignore: "until parted by death."

Blessings.

Standing firm until parted by death.